John Zinkin, Chris Bennett
Criminality and Business Strategy

John Zinkin, Chris Bennett

Criminality and Business Strategy

Similarities and Differences

DE GRUYTER

ISBN 978-3-11-071189-9
e-ISBN (PDF) 978-3-11-071215-5
e-ISBN (EPUB) 978-3-11-071216-2

Library of Congress Control Number: 2022940548

Bibliographic information published by the Deutsche Nationalbibliothek
The Deutsche Nationalbibliothek lists this publication in the Deutsche Nationalbibliografie;
detailed bibliographic data are available on the internet at http://dnb.dnb.de.

© 2022 Walter de Gruyter GmbH, Berlin/Boston
Cover image: People Images/E+/Getty Images
Typesetting: Integra Software Services Pvt. Ltd.
Printing and binding: CPI books GmbH, Leck

www.degruyter.com

Advance Praise for *Criminality and Business Strategy: Similarities and Differences*

"All great works come in trilogies. The first makes the name, the second consolidates it, and the third either takes it to greater heights or disappoints. Having made their name in *The Principles and Practice of Effective Leadership*, corporate governance experts John Zinkin and Chris Bennett have embarked on two sequels, *Criminality and Business Strategy: Similarities and Differences*, to be followed by *The Challenge of Leading an Ethical and Successful Organization* (to be published).

Criminality and Business Strategy: Similarities and Differences is a subject most people would prefer to sweep under the carpet. But the issue of criminality, by states, firms and individuals, lies at the heart of good leadership. Just as ethical individuals find it hard to survive in criminal firms, so do firms find it hard to operate in criminal states, or at least very corrupt ones.

This book reviews cases of state criminality, organized crimes from Mafia and Triads to Yakuza, and draws insights that are invaluable to the practicing corporate leader. No leader can be naïve as to the challenges of operating in corrupting environments and this book provides good advice on how to diagnose and think through criminality in context and detail. The best businesses survive and prosper because of strong ethics and professional teamwork. To build that team with values is the hallmark of all good leaders. That is why the third book in this trilogy is keenly awaited."

–Andrew Sheng, former Central Banker and Chairman,
Securities and Futures Commission, Hong Kong

"The authors of this book are excellent debaters – they examine arguments from all angles to ensure that they are completely watertight. Here, they have taken a step back and discuss the behaviors and characteristics of recognized governments, comparing them with the behaviors of organized crime groups. Taking this very different perspective generates very surprising insights into the functioning of government, the 'monopoly of violence' which governments claim, and the similarities between the operational strategies of governments and crime organizations. It brings the reader, mentally, into a space which few have explored, but once there, allows a surprising set of new insights to emerge while reading the book.

In a world which is increasingly dominated by autocratic 'big men', and democracy appears to be struggling to function effectively, these insights are particularly important, an essential underpinning of thought for policy makers, politicians and societal reformers. The reader will have assumptions challenged, the accepted overturned, and the unacceptable contrasted with the acceptable. Reading this book, I was challenged and surprised – but was not able to reject the arguments made. At

https://doi.org/10.1515/9783110712155-202

the same time, the book is practical, down to earth and the lessons can be applied to improve the ethics of both business and government organizations.

–Edward Clayton, Partner, Capital Projects and Infrastructure Leader,
PwC, Malaysia and Vietnam

"In *Criminality and Business Strategy: Similarities and Differences*, and in particular in its concluding chapter, John Zinkin and Chris Bennett make it abundantly clear that if a legitimate business is only committed to making profits with little or no regard to ESG goals, there will be little to distinguish it from organized crime and it thus may run the risk of forfeiting its social 'license to operate'."

–Dato Dr R. Thillainathan, Director of Genting Berhad,
Public Investment Bank Berhad, IDEAS Policy Research Berhad

"*Criminality and Business Strategy* made me question my behavior in ways I was not expecting, and come to uncomfortable conclusions as a result. I consider myself an honest businessman. However, this book demonstrates to me that I exist on a spectrum. My transgressions are arguably harmless, but I, like everyone in business, have concluded that there are some rules that are ok for me to ignore. Or, to put it another way, that I am *entitled* to ignore. I realise that there is a correlation between my *entitlement* and my level of influence and financial capacity. The more one has, the more rules one may ignore, and the less one has, the more constrained one is by the rules. Hardly a level playing field, but shocking when considered in context of where we sit on a spectrum of criminality and by extension therefore, the more wealthy or influential one becomes, the increased likelihood of also being more criminal. This book challenges me to decide whether this is the society I want to participate in, or indeed to pass on to my children for them to be part of."

–Tony Heneberry, Founder of CEO Solutions

Acknowledgments

We were helped by many people in developing our thoughts, refining our arguments, and structuring the case. We would like to thank Dr Gary Dirks and Professor Sander Van Der Leeuw for their early comments on the potential for criminality in the political process. We would like to thank Professor Anna Sergi for her work and insights into organized crime in Italy, and in particular for her work on the 'Ndrangheta which we have used in the book. We would also like to thank the following for the time they invested in reading our drafts to ensure that the case we make is correct, clear, and, relevant; based on their respective experiences as academics, company director of long standing; senior management consulting partner; entrepreneur; central banker and capital markets regulator; and lawyer: Professor John Rudd, John Colvin, Dato Dr R. Thillainathan, Edward Clayton, Tony Heneberry, Tan Sri Andrew Sheng, and Sujata Shekar Naik. If we have misunderstood or misrepresented their views, the fault is entirely ours.

We would like to thank Stefan Giesen, our excellent editor, for challenging our assumptions robustly and constructively, including simplifying the structure of the book. We are grateful to Mary Sudul, our copy editor, whose meticulous attention to detail and care in improving the text makes the book all the better. We would like to thank Jaya Dalal for her excellent coordination of production, as usual; and Matthias Wand for final production.

John Zinkin and Chris Bennett
Kuala Lumpur, Malaysia

https://doi.org/10.1515/9783110712155-203

Contents

Introduction

When we were commissioned to write *The Principles and Practice of Effective Leadership*, we agreed to write a sequel about the lessons legitimate businesses could learn from organized crime (OC). Our research led us to some unexpected conclusions that changed our approach. We realized we had to write two books, instead of one: this book and *The Challenge of Leading an Ethical and Successful Organization* about overcoming ethical challenges faced by leaders in their search for success.

To our surprise we found that defining a "crime" is a contested issue. Criminality forms a spectrum reflecting the types of crime, the range of harms caused, and the variety of punishments involved; and the similarities between OC and legitimate businesses were greater than the differences.

Instead of leaving our readers with this depressing realization, we concluded we should write two books instead of one. This book would focus only on the lessons to be learned from OC, whereas *The Challenge of Leading an Ethical and Successful Organization*, as its title makes clear, would focus on how to confront the ethical challenges decision-makers face when leading successful organizations. Both books have been written as independent standalone books, but they work better as companion volumes to give readers an integrated perspective of the ethical issues faced by business leaders making decisions.

Crimes committed by non-state actors divide into those undertaken by OC, which share certain defining characteristics, but "one size does not fit all," as illustrated by the differences in modus operandi between Mafias, Triads, and Yakuzas. There are two other categories of crime that we have defined as "crime that is organized," and "opportunistic disorganized crime," usually undertaken by individuals.

The types of crime committed by state actors range from states as criminal enterprises to state-organized crime. The state defines what constitutes a "crime," at least from a strictly legalistic point of view. Consequently, the state is able to decide which actions undertaken by non-state actors are classified as crimes, but are not, when undertaken by the state. To complicate definitional matters further, what is seen as a crime in one culture may not be seen as a crime in another.

The seriousness of crimes is defined by the harms they are perceived to cause. These include external and internal harms, existential threats to the state, a breakdown in law and order, economic damage caused by wars and civil wars, financial crime, and criminal economic harm. Additionally, social harms are created by OC and the shadow economy.

Punitive sanctions applied by governments and their effectiveness depends on willingness, and ability to enforce them, and on their societal legitimacy. How punitive sanctions or approvals are applied reflects social mores and assumptions based on culture, religion, and ideology, and how sanctions are reported by the media.

When it comes to strategy, the overwhelming similarities between OC and legitimate business are the result of both types of organizations seeking to extract profit

https://doi.org/10.1515/9783110712155-205

from their environments. Dealing with external environments requires both OC and legitimate businesses to consider how they deal with political, economic, social, technical, legislative, and ecological (PESTLE) contexts within which they operate. *Consequently, we show that differences in criminality between organized crime and legitimate businesses are ones of degree and not ones of kind.*

When dealing with internal environments, both types of organization define and adhere to their declared missions, visions, and values and assess how well the organizations are aligned with them in terms of their "purpose," "principles," "power," "people," and "processes" that form the "Five P" performance framework.

Organized crime has three advantages over legitimate business: it does not have to reconcile the different requirements of as many stakeholders as legitimate businesses, making it easier to make decisions and stay focused; it has unambiguous KPIs as a result, that do not challenge its members' sense of moral self-worth; and it resorts more quickly to violence when applying punitive sanctions externally and internally.

If these conclusions make depressing reading, we recommend our forthcoming book *The Challenge of Leading an Ethical and Successful Organization* that explains ways to overcome ethical challenges faced by leaders in their search for success.

Book Outline

Chapter 1 explains how states have a critical role in determining where criminality is perceived to sit on the crime continuum. It also examines the behavior of states and shows that some of the worst crimes are committed by states but are then redefined as glorious events by the winners who rewrite the history of the events to justify their actions.

Chapter 2 demonstrates how the state and OC are natural competitors, both promising people security of lives and livelihood in the territories they control, in return for paying taxes, in the case of the state, or "protection" in the case of OC.

Chapter 3 explores criminal harms. Attitudes to criminality and crime reflect the harm and damage they are perceived to cause to groups and individuals. Perception of harm is related to the cost of the damage in pecuniary, or social terms. The greater the societal revulsion, the more severe the punishments.

Chapter 4 makes the case that often the punishment does not fit the crime. There are five factors that make it difficult to fit the punishment to the crime: impunity of the powerful; regulatory capture; weak regulatory "ecosystems"; social indifference to crimes committed; and mainstream and social media's focus on entertainment and outrage.

Chapter 5 explains how OC organizations are subject to the same external strategic considerations as legitimate businesses, except that the law renders their business illegitimate by definition. The six components of the PESTLE framework that affect strategy are discussed separately for the sake of clarity.

Chapter 6 explains how OC organizations are subject to many of the same internal strategic considerations as legitimate businesses. The chapter explains how the "Five P" performance framework applies to both OC and legitimate businesses and how they are aligned to ensure their organizations achieve their agreed missions and visions.

Chapter 7 examines the differences between OC and legitimate enterprises. It uses the "Five P" performance framework introduced in Chapter 6 to highlight the differences in the ways OC and legitimate businesses apply each of the "Five Ps," given their different operating conditions.

Chapter 8 examines the business strategy implications of the PESTLE factors on organizations. In particular, the impact of politics, economics, society, and legislation and how the belief that the purpose of business is to maximize shareholder value contributes to generating behavior in legitimate businesses that is similar in kind to that of OC.

Chapter 9 concludes that 1) differences in criminality of OC and legitimate businesses are only ones of degree and not of kind; 2) states and OC are natural competitors; 3) elites protect their positions of power and privilege at the expense of others; 4) "Black Letter" law matters despite its imperfections; and 5) OC organizations have three decision-making advantages when compared with legitimate businesses: they do not have ambiguity of purpose; they have a greater clarity of purpose, principles, and processes; and they and their members have a greater willingness to embrace risk.

Chapter 1
The Crime Continuum: The Role of the State

When speeding on the highway or receiving a parking ticket, do you feel you have committed a crime? Do directors and senior managers of companies consider they are criminals if their companies pay fines? Or do they regard it as "the cost of doing business," justified by their alleged fiduciary duty to maximize shareholder value, as long as the fines cost less than the cost of following rules that apply to their business? Do organizations that pay fines without admitting wrongdoing feel they have committed crimes?

The honest answer is "No."

Perhaps checking the definition of the words "crime" and "criminal" might help. The *Oxford English Dictionary* defines "crime" as:

> *"An action or omission which constitutes an offence and is punishable by law."* The Oxford Dictionary of Sociology defines crime in a more complex way: *"an offence which goes beyond the personal and into the public sphere, breaking prohibitory rules or laws, to which legitimate punishments or sanctions are attached, and which requires the intervention of a public authority."* The difference between these two definitions goes to the heart of issues surrounding crime. As the Oxford English Dictionary definition makes clear, the law ultimately defines what is and is not crime. While popular definitions approach the law as a given, sociological definitions approach the issue in a more social way – drawing attention not only to the act itself but the law itself and whose interests it seeks to protect. It makes a distinction between private offences (such as arguments or personal disputes) and public offences that offend a broader set of social norms or values.[1]   [Emphases ours]

It also defines "criminal" as:

> A person who has committed a crime.[2]

The reality is that, although we do not regard ourselves as criminals, whenever we pay a fine that is exactly what we are – paying a fine proves that we committed an offense in the public sphere: "breaking prohibitory rules or laws, to which legitimate punishments or sanctions are attached, and which requires the intervention of a public authority."

The reason we do often not consider ourselves as criminals lies in the more nuanced sociological definition and takes into account the levels of harm done and the interests that need to be protected, as well as consideration of the narrow legal definition.

Crimes can vary in severity; and, while all crimes meet the narrow legal definition, there are differences in the degree of criminality, based on the level and type of harms caused, and how crimes are perpetrated that create a "crime continuum." This continuum ranges from state organized crime (SOC), to organized crime (OC), crime that is organized (CTIO), disorganized crime (DC), and criminal behavior (CB), and on down to individual wrongdoing that is antisocial, harmful, or morally offensive, though legal.

https://doi.org/10.1515/9783110712155-001

To make matters more complicated, different cultures have different definitions and levels of acceptance of "crimes," thus broadening the continuum. Moreover, within each of these categories, there are differences in behavior and approaches, reflecting historical contexts, political and economic conditions, and causes of criminal behavior.

State organized crime (SOC) is defined as:

> The most important type of criminality organized by the state consists of acts defined by law as criminal and committed by state officials in the pursuit of their job as representatives of the state

> *the state specifically instructed selected individuals to engage in criminal acts, the law, it must be emphasized, did not change.*[3]   [Emphasis ours]

SOC occurs in two ways. The first is that states have been regarded by some as being founded by successful criminal enterprises. The second is that states commit organized crimes, once successfully established. The state has a third role with respect to criminality: it defines what is and is not criminal behavior.

States as Successful Criminal Enterprises

The proposition of philosophers[i] and historians[ii] and politicians[iii] who believed in "force" or "conflict" theories of how states came to be formed is based on two theories:

"Force" Theory

Force theory argues that the weak are subjected to the strong because, although social in nature, humans are bellicose and capture and enslave the weak, collecting a band of followers in this way:

> *Government is the outcome of human aggression*

> *Once the State had been established, force, which had hitherto been utilized for subjugating others, was used to maintain internal order and make it secure from any kind of external aggression.* But this alone was not sufficient. Force was used as the sinews of war and power and a bid for superiority . . . *the theory of force traces the State's origin and development to conquest and [justifies] its authority, by the proposition that might is right.*[4]   [Emphases ours]

> *[Tilly] starts with the idea that state is a form of "protection racket": its monopoly on the use of force within a territory allows it to charge for this service, which is necessary for the development*

---

i Hobbes, Hegel, Nietzsche.
ii Polybius, Leacock.
iii Mussolini, Hitler.

of commerce and regular commercial exchanges . . . They were the natural result of a process whereby war begat territory, which begat resource extraction, which begat larger military forces, which begat more war and so on. "War making, extraction and capital accumulation interacted to shape European state making,"[5] . . . What sets Tilly apart is that he does not differentiate between the government's monopoly on violence and the monopoly on violence held by other actors in their own territories or spheres of influence, especially as it served the need of a centralized authority and the development of the nation-state itself. *These other actors essentially operate as the state under a different moniker. And in some instances, these actors assist the process of state building, even while they are committing illegal acts to gain and maintain their power.* "Banditry, piracy, gangland rivalry, policing and war making all belong on the same continuum," Tilly argues. *The process by which we could therefore determine who was a "legitimate" and who was an "illegitimate" force came about slowly and was fraught with contradictions.*[6]   [Emphases ours]

We do not usually think of states being originally successful criminal enterprises because history is always written by the winners. However, the prophet Samuel in the Old Testament gave an accurate warning of the expropriation that occurs when a people choose a king:

> This will be the manner of the king that shall rule over you. He will take your sons and appoint them for himself, for his chariots, and to be his horsemen; and some shall run before his chariots.
>
> And he will appoint him[self] captain over thousands, and captains over fifties; and will set them to ear [sow] his ground, and to reap his harvest, and to make his instruments of war, and instruments of his chariots.
>
> And he will take your daughters to be his confectionaries, and to be cooks, and to be bakers.
>
> And he will take your fields, and your vineyards, and your olive yards, even the best of them, and give them to his servants.
>
> And he will take a tenth of your seed, and of your vineyards, and give it to his officers, and to his servants.
>
> And he will take your manservants, and your maidservants, and your goodliest young men, and your asses, and put them to his work.
>
> He will take a tenth of your sheep: and ye shall be his servants.
>
> And ye shall cry in that day because of your king which ye shall have chosen you; and the Lord will not hear you in that day.[7]

As children in England, we were taught that the Norman conquest of England was "a good thing" to quote *1066 And All That: A Memorable History of England.*[8] Yet, for Anglo-Saxons, the Norman Conquest was a disaster of pillage, theft, and ethnic cleansing, culminating in the "Harrowing of the North" in 1069–1070:

> William . . . ordered villages to be destroyed and people to be killed. Herds of animals and crops were burnt. Most people who survived starved to death . . .
>
> *Not only was the population reduced by 75% but land was salted (poisoned) to prevent people growing crops in the future. . . . William had achieved his main aim . . . control of the North, and he had prevented a future rebellion. Now William was able to place loyal nobles in charge to look after his lands*[9] [Emphasis ours]

History records invasions, conquests, piracy, and the establishment of new states and empires that are simply theft of other people's property and lands; and extortion in the form of taxes or tribute payments to guarantee a peaceful existence – behavior similar to that of organized crime organizations like the Mafia, Triads, and Yakuza. However, because history is written by the victors, these actions are not recorded as crimes against their victims, but as glorious actions in the annals of the winners' histories.

We do not regard the conquest and settlement of the Americas, of Australia, and of New Zealand by Europeans as theft of lands that belonged to the Plains Indians, the Aztecs, Incas or Mayans, the Aborigines of the Amazon or Australia, and the Māoris;[iv] nor, do we regard their conquests as theft. Instead, we celebrate the creation of "new civilizations," and we treat them as signs of human progress. As the Duc de la Rochefoucauld wrote:

> Some crimes are become innocent even glorious by their sheer impudence, number, and enormity. This is why public thefts become skilful moves, and *annexing provinces without justification is called making conquests.*[10] [Emphasis ours]

"Conflict" Theory

This argues that since the beginning of time there have been conflicts between groups. Three conditions are required for these conflicts to form a "State":[11]
1. *Social stratification:* A minority gaining and exercising organized control over a majority subject people
2. *Private ownership of property:* Benefits the dominant minority at the expense of the subordinated majority, enabling it to exercise coercive power
3. *Defined settled territory:* Both dominant and subject groups live in the defined territorial area over which the dominant ruling class, embodied as a "State," exercises sovereignty

---

iv We do not mourn the people the Plains Indians, Aztecs, Incas, and Mayans subjugated in their turn, nor all the peoples in Eurasia, displaced or exterminated in its many migrations east, west, and south. We treat this cycle of emigration, displacement, conquest, subjugation, and integration as the being the natural order of survival.

Voltaire summarized this as:

> In general, the art of government consists of taking as much as possible from one class of citizens to give to another.[12]

It is important to remember that conflicts between elite groups are perpetual, reflecting the ebb and flow of economic and political power and the rise and fall of leaders and their supporting cliques. This state of flux exists in all forms of organization, and it determines who are outgroups and who are ingroups and who are outlaws and who are law-abiding, because it is winning elites that decide what is legal and what is not, and the levels of criminality that they will tolerate as part of the art "of taking as much as possible from one class to give to another" in Voltaire's words.

> *Institutional fragility guarantees elites will tolerate grey zones operating in all types of illicit businesses that are oriented towards perpetuating their interests.* In practical terms, elites look to control public politics and, when necessary and convenient, minimize interventions aimed at opening the state to public scrutiny and accountability. In this sense, *the state is less a guardian and generator of common interests, and more an instrument of private groups with private interests.* The mixing and interplay between elites and organized crime grows roughly in proportion to the state's inability to enable processes that foster transparency and accountability.[13]
>
> [Emphasis ours]

The "Jealous" State

> Anarchist thinkers have long identified the jealousy inherent to the modern state; an exclusive sovereignty claimed against other nation states, secessionists, non-state geopolitical actors, and especially against independent organisation by the people themselves.[14]

International Relations experts regard the state as being jealous because:
1. It claims to "own" its citizens, which is why secessionists are not to be tolerated (for example, the US in the Civil War; China's treatment of Tibet, Uyghurs, Taiwan, and more recently Hong Kong; and Russia's annexation of Crimea).
2. It is often hostile toward international "non-state actors" such as religions that do not recognize state boundaries (Islam) and internationalist institutions (for example, the International Court of Criminal Justice or the European Court of Justice).
3. It is suspicious of any powerful independent institutions within the state from fear that separate unions of citizens within the state could form a "state within the state" (for example, President Erdogan of Turkey's treatment of the Gulenists in the government upon whom he had depended to achieve power, once he had succeeded[15]).

The state's demand for exclusive control over its people is often presented as being benevolent, "oriented toward achieving the common good," even though such centralization and control often leads to disastrous results, even in a democracy like the UK:[16]

> The state's failure to meet people's immediate needs in the pandemic crisis was addressed by a blossoming of local-level mutual aid initiatives. Thousands upon thousands of people joined together to support vulnerable neighbours, produce Personal Protective Equipment (PPE), deliver food and medicines, and much more besides. The striking characteristic of these mutual aid groups is their autonomous organisation, quite separate from established charities, political parties, or indeed the state (Covid-19 Mutual Aid UK FAQs). *But of key interest here is how the state, via co-option and suppression, has jealously squeezed out the space for these autonomous expressions of community self-reliance.*[17]   [Emphasis ours]

> Lieffe compares the state to 'an abusive lover who grip[s] ever tighter the more it los[es] control' (2020: 143), and this has been the jealous character of the UK government during the Covid-19 pandemic crisis. The state requires its "subjects and resources [to] be *assets*, serving the imperatives of the state" (King 2019: 3). When people challenge those imperatives by organising independently to meet their own needs, the state rushes to re-assert its sovereignty and control. *This* is the jealousy at the core of the state – not against geopolitical competitors and certainly not against market interests, but against the people's own ability to organise themselves.[18]

Why should the state behave like "an abusive lover" gripping ever tighter when it loses control? The answer, we believe, lies in the fact that the state is made up of competing interests and when one dominant vested interest fears that it is losing ground, it will react to reassert its privileged position at the expense of the common good – especially if it has been behaving as an extractive institution interested only in maximizing its hold over resources at the expense of the common good, achieving this through militias like Hezbollah and Amal in Lebanon[19] or Conservative party chumocracy clientelism in the UK:

> *There is a world of difference between people organising to make demands (becoming part of a process through which interests are brokered, agreement reached) and a government dispensing courtly favours according to its immediate interests.* "Clientelism" (receiving benefits in return for political support) is not citizenship. It widens the gap between people and their politics. *Rather than meaningfully involve us in the democratic process, the government has only to know – from polling, market research and social media sentiment analysis – what to offer to enough social segments, in the right places, to remain in power.* . . . . It has no obligation to work with populations to address fundamental challenges (the climate crisis, inequality, infrastructural decay) and *no incentive to overcome resistance from clients demanding that their self-interest be satisfied. Under such a regime, things don't rapidly fall apart. Uncared for, they slowly become more threadbare.* The public realm is reduced to an endless queue of ambulances for which no doctor waits.

> *To remain in favour with its supporters (voters, donors, second employers) the government needs continuously to reward them. Whatever gets in the way of making ad hoc decisions – constitutional rules or independent overseers – is an obstacle to be overcome.* . . . . As the constitutional expert Meg Russell observes, ignoring independent oversight is a hallmark of this government:

marginalising the Commons; trying to overturn the parliamentary commissioner for standards; ignoring breaches of the ministerial code; weakening the electoral commission. *These are not deviations but steps in a process of making it easier for centralised administration to direct resources to where political calculation deems it necessary.*[20]   [Emphases ours]

People often think of the state or the "government" as a monolithic construct, forgetting the role that elites within it play in the organization and allocation of economic, social, and political power. Under a thin veneer of a stable polity is the permanent jockeying of four different types of elites. The interaction between them affects how societies, politics, and economies operate through the channeling of resources, regulating trade and commerce, defining wrongdoing, and enforcing its punishment. There are occasions when it may suit these elites to engage in corrupt or criminal practices to gain advantage, even if it means weakening the state and legitimate businesses and allowing organized crime (OC) to flourish.[21]

1. *Economic elites* seek to control the means of production. Their power is based on the economic capital they control, influencing labor markets and consumers through their attempts to create and maintain oligopolies or monopolies, and reinforced by dominating the mainstream media and in becoming the "go-to" platforms in social media. They use this power to influence/control political and social elites through the management of public opinion to advance their economic interests.[22]

2. *Political elites* seek to achieve hegemony over their communities using state resources or connections to the state and political parties to play a dominant role in their communities. They are party leaders, members of legislatures with a direct role in determining policy, or consiglieres and lobbyists whose role it is to align political and economic elite interests through the manipulation of public opinion.[23]

3. *Social elites* do not have the same power economically or politically as the previous two elites; instead, they are able to propagate ideas as well as mobilizing people behind those ideas. Typically, they are leading members of civil society, religious leaders, artists, and academics. When they are effective, they can acquire economic and political power, and they are able to use their understanding of the structure and processes of the state in this acquisition. Their positions of leadership are based on their personal authority resulting from their credibility, legitimacy, debating skills, and being trusted by the community. These characteristics are more important in multi-ethnic and multicultural communities where their ability to connect with power-brokers in those communities is critical.[24]

4. *Bureaucratic elites* populate the apparatus of the state. They have the power to make decisions and, as they become more expert, they achieve greater independence from the economic and political elites, increasingly operating to protect their own priorities, resources, and interests (memorably captured in the British TV series "Yes, Minister"). They matter because of the power they hold over the allocation of the state's resources resulting from their understanding of the

state's procedures. The more advanced a society, the greater the specialization in its activities giving these elites more influence and power which reinforces the importance of a specialized bureaucracy when making decisions about complex matters:[25]

> The state is made up of a group of people with a level of specialization, which gives life to a state bureaucracy that acquires power as measured by their level of specialization and their capacity to make decisions.[26] This bureaucracy creates in turn bureaucratic elites with power over state resources, including political resources.[27]

In Japan with its Amakudari,[v] the US, and Europe, these bureaucratic elites were able to become so closely aligned with the political and economic elites through the "revolving door" appointment processes of politicians and senior executives to senior governmental positions that it has become hard to draw the boundary between them.[28,29]

What makes the state jealous is the competition between its four elites at the expense of the common good. This reflects the fluidity of the boundaries between different elites, making them fearful of losing out in what they see as a "win-lose" world within the confines of the state. To gain advantage, they may use new political forces as "useful idiots" in their struggle with other elites. Perhaps the most memorable and disastrous example of such behavior was the German Weimar Republic's economic and financial elite backing Hitler's rise, believing they could use him to defeat the Communist and Socialist movements destabilizing Germany after World War I. In this example, the Weimar government and their puppet President Hindenburg, proved to be Hitler's "useful idiots" to their cost and to the cost of the rest of the world.[30] In extreme cases of competition, the elites are more concerned with preserving their advantages, even if it leads to a collapsed state as a result of their harmful extractive practices:

> Because elites dominating extractive institutions fear creative destruction, they will resist it, and any growth that germinates under extractive institutions will ultimately be short-lived. Second, *the ability of those who dominate extractive institutions to benefit greatly at the expense of the rest of society implies that political power under extractive institutions is highly coveted, making many groups and individuals fight to obtain it. As a consequence, there will be powerful forces pushing societies under extractive institutions toward political instability* [e.g., Afghanistan, Iraq, Lebanon, Libya and Syria].[31]   [Emphasis ours]

---

v "In Japan, the term *amakudari* (literally, "descent from heaven") refers to the post-retirement employment of senior bureaucrats in private and public corporations and non-governmental organizations, particularly those that fall under the jurisdiction of the ministry they retired from." *Investopedia*, https://www.investopedia.com/terms/a/amakudari.asp, accessed on November 29, 2021.

State Committed Organized Crimes

People in government have access to power that can be used for illegal purposes but defended on grounds of national security or the best interests of the state. There are many examples, ranging from Russia's 2014 illegal annexation of Crimea,[32] in violation of their own guarantee to the Ukraine,[vi] to America's 2020 assassination of Qassim Soleimani, leader of Iran's Revolutionary Guard.[33] It is difficult to punish the perpetrators of state committed organized crimes because of their power and position.

The Nuremberg trials at the end of World War II established the principle that state officials of defeated states could be tried for crimes, even when following orders;[34] and since then, the International Criminal Tribunal has successfully tried a number of state officials, including Presidents, for their actions; notably Radovan Karadzic[vii] and Ratko Mladic[viii] for genocide and crimes against humanity in Bosnia during the Bosnia-Herzegovina civil war.

State-sanctioned assassinations,[35,36,37] attempted and successful regime change,[38] the use of proxies,[39] and cyber-attacks by governments[40] are all justified in the name of national security, despite being treated as criminal when undertaken by non-state actors. For example, the logistical support given to the Saudis in their war with the Houthis in the Yemen by the British[41] and Americans[42] has helped create a humanitarian disaster and immense civilian suffering. With the exception of state-sponsored cyber-attacks, all of the above activities have been undertaken by states since the earliest of times.

Cynics could be forgiven for saying that this proves winners get away with bad behavior while losers get punished. Support for such a view comes from the fact that the United States does not recognize the jurisdiction of the International Criminal Court in order to prevent its soldiers being tried for war crimes.[43] The only reason President Assad and the Russians[44] and the Saudis[45] have gotten away with the brutal bombing of civilians in the Syrian and Yemeni civil wars was the decision of the US and British prosecutors at the Nuremberg and Tokyo trials to exclude aerial bombing of civilians as a war crime because they had done so much more of it than the Germans or Japanese:

---

vi "In 1994, the three depository states of the Nuclear Nonproliferation Treaty (NPT) – Russia, the United States, and the United Kingdom – extended positive and negative security assurances to Ukraine. The depository states underlined their commitment to Ukraine's sovereignty and territorial integrity by signing the so-called 'Budapest Memorandum.'" Buderjeryn, M., "Issue Brief #3: The Breach: Ukraine's Territorial Integrity and the Budapest Memorandum," *Wilson Center,* https://www.wilsoncenter.org/publication/issue-brief-3-the-breach-ukraines-territorial-integrity-and-the-budapest-memorandum accessed on February 16, 2021.

vii President of Republika Srpska.

viii Chief of Staff of the Army of Republika Srpska.

The decision not to include terror bombing among the war crimes to be prosecuted at Nuremberg or Tokyo helped to legitimate this behavior. . . . Thus, even the most significant effort in history . . . failed to even define the intentional bombing of civilians as a crime let alone punish the behavior or attempt to deter it in the future with formal sanctions. Thus, *the legal legitimacy conferred upon terror bombing by the International Military Tribunals helped to . . . ensure that it would be a normal and acceptable method of warfare in the future*

During World War II the Allies did not openly violate the laws of war but they simply interpreted them to justify and "legalize" their resort to the aerial bombardment of civilian populations in Germany and Japan.[46]   [Emphases ours]

Realpolitik also makes a difference. For example, although President Biden released a CIA report, long blocked by President Trump, that implicated Saudi Crown Prince Mohammed bin Salman in the gruesome murder of Jamal Khashoggi, a dissident Saudi journalist, no sanctions have been imposed by the US against the Crown Prince because Saudi Arabia is too important an American ally in the Middle East. However, President Biden indicated his disapproval by refusing to deal directly with the Crown Prince and ended his backing of Saudi involvement in the Yemeni war – a form of shaming.[47] Realpolitik is the recognition that the "Arrogance of Power" leads to a culture of impunity where leaders like Putin and the Saudi Crown Prince believe correctly that they can get away with murder.[48] Or, as Presidential candidate Donald Trump said in 2016:

"I could stand in the middle of Fifth Avenue and shoot somebody, and I wouldn't lose any voters, OK?" Trump remarked at a campaign stop at Dordt College in Sioux Center, Iowa. "It's, like, incredible."[49]

A further reason why those in power are able to misbehave with impunity is that electorates seem to have become less interested in leaders demonstrating honesty, decency, and operational competence, and are more interested in leadership based on "charisma."[50]

Perhaps history's most effective drug-related state organized crime was undertaken by William Jardine, the founder of Jardine Matheson.[51] A Scottish surgeon who originally worked for the East India Company in the early 1800s, he learned the importance of the opium trade from India to China and decided to set up business in Canton in 1820. He and his partner, James Matheson, set up their company Jardine Matheson in 1828 to import opium *illegally* into China and wanted the monopoly the East India Company had over the opium trade to end. They lobbied hard and achieved their objective in 1833 when Parliament in London abolished the East India Company monopoly on the tea and opium trades. In 1834, shipments of tea to Britain were up by 40 percent and opium sales to China rose correspondingly, shown in Figure 1.1.

The East India Company had been doing a great trade in tea from China. Unfortunately for the British, the Chinese authorities were only interested in being paid in silver for their tea, and England was short of silver. The East India Company had something that Chinese wanted to buy to pay for the tea: Bengal opium and Indian cotton. The resulting three-way trade with China selling tea to Britain, the East

OPIUM IMPORTS INTO CHINA, 1650–1880

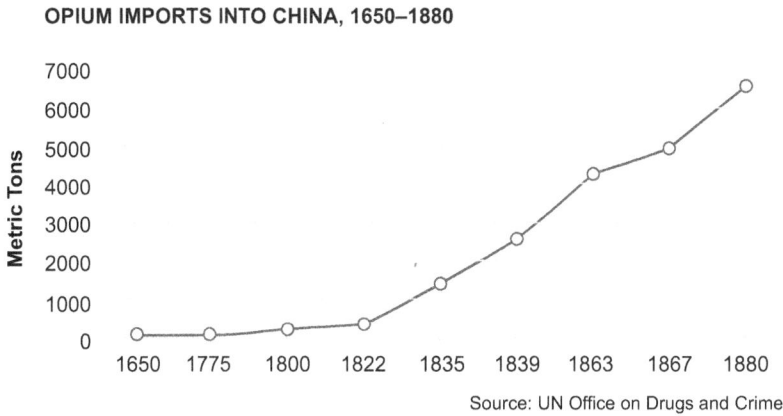

Source: UN Office on Drugs and Crime

Figure 1.1: Annual Opium Imports in Metric Tons (1650–1880).

India Company and associated British merchants in Hong Kong selling opium and cotton to the Chinese to pay for the tea was profitable. This success created its own problems. It helped make the East India Company the largest and most powerful company in history and accounted for getting China hooked on opium grown by the company in India and exported *illegally* to China to pay for the tea.[52]

Recognizing early on the seriousness of the social problems the opium trade created, the Chinese government banned the importation and production of opium in 1800[53] when the volumes were still small. In 1813, it outlawed the smoking of opium, punishing offenders by beating them 100 times. In 1836, the government became serious about enforcing the 1813 ban, and closed opium dens and executed Chinese dealers. Nothing worked and the problem got worse. There was a debate (on familiarly modern lines) about the best way to deal with the scourge. On one side were those Chinese officials who argued for the legalization of opium production and sale, using taxes to price opium out of the market while providing revenues to the government to help pay for the outflow of silver. The winning side, led by Lin Zexu, governor of Canton (modern Guangzhou), however, argued that the opium trade was a moral issue, and an "evil" that had to be eliminated by any means possible. *They argued that instead of targeting opium users, they should stop and punish the "pushers" who imported and sold the drug in China."*[54]

In 1839, Lin Zexu arrived in Canton to oversee the ban. He wrote an open letter to Queen Victoria (which, sadly, she never received) questioning Britain's support for the trade and its morality. He arrested more than 1,600 Chinese dealers, seized and destroyed tens of thousands of opium pipes, and demanded that the foreign companies hand over their supplies of opium. When the British refused, he stopped all foreign trade and quarantined the area where foreign merchants operated. After six weeks, the merchants handed over 20,000 chests (2.6 million pounds) of opium. Lin also seized and destroyed the opium on board British ships. There was an argument about whether they were in international waters. The impounded opium was mixed with lime and salt and dumped in the sea. Lin Zexu put pressure on the Portuguese administration in Macao to expel the recalcitrant British who moved to Hong Kong.

British representatives in Guangzhou asked the merchants to hand over the opium in order to keep British merchants and ships safe in the short term to keep open the extremely profitable China trade in other goods. However, in London, Lin's actions were seen as an affront to British dignity and concepts of trade. William Jardine had left Canton for London just before Lin Zexu's confiscation of the contraband opium. He developed a plan to force compensation from China by using open warfare. To achieve this, he needed to sway opinion of the British public and the government. He was helped by the huge size of the opium liability that was worth millions of pounds sterling and the demands of the merchants in China, India, and London:[55]

> *Those in support of war presented their case . . . that it was Britain's patriotic duty to defend her honor against the insults perpetrated by China.* The debates closed with Lord Palmerston reading a petition that had been signed by representatives of important British trading firms in China. In the petition the merchants declared that, *"unless measures of the government are followed up with firmness and energy, the trade with China can no longer be conducted with security to life and property, or with credit or advantage to the British nation."* . . . In the end patriotism defeated isolationism and the proponents of sending a naval force to China won with a vote of 271 to 262.[56] [Emphases ours]

In June 1840, 16 British warships and merchantmen arrived at Canton. In the next two years the British bombarded forts, seized cities and forced the Chinese to cede Hong Kong, pay an indemnity, and grant Britain full diplomatic recognition.[57] Lin Zexu was exiled. Dozens of Chinese officers committed suicide in an unequal war with the more modern British forces:

> Final death tolls at the end of the war have been estimated at only 500 for the British and over 20,000 Chinese troops. One British officer remarked on these lopsided numbers, *"The poor Chinese had two choices, either they must submit to be poisoned, or must be massacred by the thousands, for supporting their own laws in their own land."*[58] [Emphasis ours]

From the Chinese point of view, the First Opium War was an outrage, profoundly humiliating, and the cause of a deep sense of historic grievance that has lasted until today.

Putting the First Opium War into modern perspective, the Governor of Canton was deeply concerned at the morally and economically damaging effect that opium addiction was having on Chinese society. He was also worried about the balance of payments impact and as a result he confiscated *the smuggled, contraband* opium and had it dumped into the sea, enforcing his country's laws. Exactly as the US DEA or any other modern drug enforcement agency would do when dealing with the cocaine smuggled into their countries by the Colombian or Mexican cartels, and for the same reasons: the harm drug addiction creates to addicts as individuals and to society as a whole. The difference is that today we regard the Cali and Sinaloa cartels as criminal organizations posing a serious public health and organized crime threat to consuming countries and would be just as outraged as the Chinese government was, if the Colombian or Mexican government were to declare war to support their cartels who were breaking our laws. The reason the British opium smugglers got away with it in 1842 was that the British government backed their illegal actions and had the power to defeat the Chinese.

In short, a crime is not a crime if the state declares that it is not; and it is a crime when the state declares that it is. We are forced to agree with the following paradoxical statement:

> Law is a two-edged sword; it creates one set of conflicts while it attempts to resolve another. The passage of a particular law or set of laws may resolve conflicts and enhance state control, but it also limits the legal activities of the state. State officials are thus often caught between conflicting demands as they find themselves constrained by laws that interfere with other goals demanded of them by their roles or their perception of what is in the interests of the state. There is a contradiction, then, between the legal prescriptions and the agreed goals of state agencies. Not everyone caught in this dilemma will opt for violating the law, but some will. Those who do are the perpetrators, but not the cause, of the persistence of state-organized crime.[59]
>
> [Emphases ours]

The other difficulty with using the law alone to define what is or is not a crime is that the law is not concerned with fairness, natural justice, or morality, but seeks to achieve predictability. Good laws keep people out of the courts because the judicial outcomes are predictable and there is no point using lawyers and judges to adjudicate a process which is time-consuming, costly, and uncertain.

Perhaps one of the best illustrations that the law is amoral is the ancient Common Law saying that "Possession is nine points [tenths] of the law." This has been the justification throughout the ages for conquerors keeping the territories they have captured.[60] It is the reason why the Plains Indians live on reservations, Crimea is now part of Russia, and the Palestinians find it so difficult to get the Israelis to leave the Occupied Territories on the West Bank. Fairness, natural justice, and morality have no role to play from a legal perspective, though they clearly do from a political one.

The third role of the state is that of defining what is and is not criminal behavior and of determining what are appropriate punishments. In so doing, states have adopted two different approaches: rule *by* law and rule *of* law.

Defining Criminal Behavior (CB)

Criminal behavior manifests along a continuum defined by the state from felony to misdemeanor,[ix] offense, infraction, and wrongdoing.

Felony

A felony in the US is a crime that is punishable by imprisonment in a state or federal prison for longer than one year. At its most extreme, it is punishable by death in certain states (e.g., Texas). The level of sentencing is a continuum, determined by the seriousness of the felony, typically divided into class A, B, and C; or class 1, 2, and 3; with the severity of the sentencing determined by the distance of the felony from class A or class 1, as these are the most serious. Felonies are tried in state courts. A general list of felonies covers:[61]

1. *Violent offenses:* These include first- and second-degree murder, manslaughter, aggravated assault with a deadly weapon, grievous bodily harm, actual bodily harm, and robbery
2. *Crimes against property:* These include grand theft, arson, and vandalism
3. *Drug offenses:* These include producing, distributing, selling, or trafficking drugs
4. *Sex crimes:* These include sexual assault and human trafficking
5. *White collar crime:* This covers money laundering, embezzlement, securities fraud, criminal breach of trust, and tax evasion.

---

ix "Crimes in England are classified into indictable offenses (which may be tried by a jury) and summary offenses (which may be tried summarily without juries). Indictable offenses are further divided into treasons, other felonies, and misdemeanours. The law of England has employed no consistent principle to determine the classification of an offense as a felony. In some instances, crimes classified as misdemeanours involve greater social peril than many statutory felonies, and penalties for misdemeanours may exceed those for felonies . . . The distinction between felony and misdemeanour is less significant for modern law than formerly, and many commentators have questioned its utility. Classifications distinguishing offenses of greater dangerousness from lesser crimes appear in continental European codes: thus, the French penal code distinguishes between *délits* and *contraventions* . . . The classification of offenses in English and US law has been criticized as capricious and unsatisfactory." The Editors of *Encyclopaedia Brittanica*. "Felony and misdemeanour." *Encyclopedia Britannica*, 16 October 2019, https://www.britannica.com/topic/felony, accessed 27 February 2021.

Misdemeanor

A misdemeanor in the US is a lesser crime punishable by fine or imprisonment in a county jail for less than one year. Misdemeanors are tried in lower courts, such as municipal, police, or justice courts. Typical misdemeanors include:

> Petty theft, disturbing the peace, simple assault and battery, drunk driving without injury to others, drunkenness in public, various traffic violations, public nuisances and some crimes which can be charged either as a felony or misdemeanor depending on the circumstances and the discretion of the District Attorney.[62]

The only exception are misdemeanors in the impeachment statement: "High crimes and misdemeanors," where they are treated as a felony.

Offense

In law, an offense is:

> The doing of that which a penal law forbids to be done, or omitting to do that it commands; in this sense it is nearly synonymous with crime. (q.v.) In a more confined sense, it may be considered as having the same meaning with misdemeanor, (q.v.) but it differs from it in this, that it is not indictable, but punishable summarily by the forfeiture of a penalty. 1 Chit. Prac.14.[63]

Infraction

Infractions are minor offenses, of lesser severity in law than misdemeanors. They are:

> violations or infringements; or breach of statutes, contracts, or obligations. However, the act itself is very minor and hence the resulting penalty is also very minor.

> Examples of infractions include parking overtime, speeding, and tailgating.[64]

Wrongdoing

Wrongdoing differs from the other legal definitions because it introduces morality, in addition to the legal technicalities, and includes codes of conduct. It is:

> a violation which is not of a merely technical or minimal nature of a Federal or State regulation, of a political subdivision ordinance or regulation or of a code of conduct or ethics designed to protect the interest of the public or the employer.[65]

In other words, it is "behavior that is illegal or immoral,"[66] or "the act or an instance of doing something immoral or illegal."[67] Interestingly, in the international English definition, illegality comes first; in the British English definition, immorality comes first, perhaps reflecting a nuanced cultural difference.

Differences of culture place people at different points on the criminality continuum. For example, so-called "honor killings" are regarded as murder in the first degree in most of the world. But for some communities in the Middle East[68] and South Asia,[69] they are an obligation to preserve the family's honor that is so powerful that fathers and brothers have no hesitation to kill their daughters or sisters and, in some cases, the state seems powerless or unwilling to act against them, despite having laws that outlaw honor killings.[70] The same is true of FGM (female genital mutilation) which is a crime in some countries but not in others; and even where it is a crime, some states do not appear to take it seriously or consistently because of the strength of cultural resistance.[x]

Corruption is also culturally determined. In most of Europe and North America, giving preferential treatment to family members either in terms of employment or contracts is regarded as a corrupt conflict of interest. However, in most of Africa, Asia, and Latin America, helping other members of the family is the first duty of someone in a position to help.

It is no accident that OC occurs in countries where obligation to kin and clan comes before the duty to be a law-abiding citizen, and being answerable to the rulings of a state that is held in low regard.

References

1 The Scottish Centre for Justice and Crime Research (2021), "What is crime?" *University of Glasgow, School of Education,* http://www.sccjr.ac.uk/wp-content/uploads/2015/10/SCCJR-What-is-crime.pdf, accessed on February 15, 2021.
2 *Oxford Learner's Dictionary* (2021), "Criminal" (Oxford: Oxford University Press), https://www.oxfordlearnersdictionaries.com/definition/english/criminal_1#:~:text=criminal-,noun,person%20who%20commits%20a%20crime, accessed on February 15, 2021.

---

x "An estimated 55 million girls in Africa under the age of 15 have undergone FGM or are at risk. Somalia has the world's highest FGM prevalence (98 percent of women have been cut), followed by Guinea, Djibouti, Mali and Sierra Leone. 22 of the 28 countries in Africa where FGM is endemic have legislation criminalizing FGM, although enforcement is generally weak and prosecutions rare. Half of all girls who have undergone FGM or are at risk live in three countries – Egypt, Ethiopia and Nigeria – all of which have laws against FGM. Chad, Liberia, Mali, Sierra Leone, Somalia and Sudan, which are home to 16 million girls, have no law, meaning FGM is still effectively legal." Batha, E. (2018), "Factbox: Female Genital Mutilation around the World: A Fine, Jail or No Crime," *Reuters,* September 14, 2018, https://www.reuters.com/article/us-africa-fgm-lawmaking-factbox-idUSKCN1LT2OS, accessed on November 8, 2021.

3 Chambliss, W. (1989), "State-organized crime – The American Society of Criminology," 1988 Presidential Address. *Criminology*, 27, 1, quoted in Kramer, R. C. (2016), "State-Organized Crime, International Law and Structural Contradictions" *Crit Crim* 24, January 4, 2016, pp. 233–234, https://doi.org/10.1007/s10612-015-9306-3, accessed on February 25, 2021.

4 University of Political Science (2021), "Force Theory of Origin of State," *The Encyclopedia of Political Science,* https://www.politicalscienceview.com/force-theory-of-origin-of-state/, accessed on February 16, 2021.

5 Tilly, C. (1991), "War Making and State Making as Organized Crime," Evans, P., Rueschemer, D., and Skocpol, T. (eds.), *Bringing the State Back* (Cambridge, 1991), pp. 169–191, cited in Dudley, S., "Conceptual Framework: Organized Crime" in "Elites and Organized Crime: Introduction, Methodology, and Conceptual Framework," *Insight Crime*, p. 28, https://idl-bnc-idrc.dspacedirect.org/bitstream/handle/10625/55845/IDL-55845.pdf, accessed on November 17, 2021.

6 Ibid, p. 171.

7 Samuel, Chapter 8, verses 11–19, *The Oxford Miniature Coronation Bible* (Oxford: Oxford University Press, June 2, 1953), p. 294.

8 Yeatman, R. J., and Sellar, W. C. (1930), *1066 And All That: A Memorable History of England* (London: Methuen).

9 BBC, "The Harrying of the North in response to rebellion," *The Norman Conquest,* https://www.bbc.co.uk/bitesize/guides/zsjnb9q/revision/5#:~:text=In%20the%20north%2Deast%20of,they%20had%20rebelled%20or%20not, accessed on February 16, 2021.

10 La Rochefoucauld (1678), *Maxims* (Harmondsworth: Penguin Classics, 1979), Maxim 608, p. 120.

11 Becker, H., and Smelo, L. (1931), "Conflict Theories of the Origin of the State," *The Sociological Review*, 23, No. 2, July 1931, p. 65, https://journals.sagepub.com/doi/abs/10.1111/j.1467-954X.1931.tb01784.x?journalCode=sora, accessed on February 16, 2021.

12 Voltaire, https://www.brainyquote.com/quotes/voltaire_124855, accessed on February 16, 2021.

13 Dudley, S., "Elites and Organized Crime: Introduction, Methodology, and Conceptual Framework," *Insight Crime*, p. 44, https://idl-bnc-idrc.dspacedirect.org/bitstream/handle/10625/55845/IDL-55845.pdf, accessed on November 29, 2021.

14 Donaghey, J. (2021), "A Jealous State? The character of Covid Government in the UK," *Academia Letters,* Article 298, February 2021, https://doi.org/10.20935/AL298, accessed on November 25, 2021.

15 "Turkey ramps up Gulen crackdown with nearly 700 arrests," *Reuters*, February 18, 2020, https://www.reuters.com/article/us-turkey-security-gulen-idUSKBN20C0ES, accessed on November 30, 2021.

16 Donaghey, (2021) p. 2.

17 Ibid., p. 3.

18 Ibid., p. 4.

19 Hubbard, B., and Santora, M. (2021), "Deadly Clashes in Beirut Escalate Fears over Lebanon's Dysfunction," *New York Times*, October 16, 2021, https://www.nytimes.com/2021/10/14/world/middleeast/beirut-lebanon.html, accessed on November 30, 2021.

20 Finlayson, A. (2021), "Sleaze is just a symptom- democratic politics in the UK is dying," *The Guardian*, November 29, 2021, https://www.theguardian.com/commentisfree/2021/nov/29/sleaze-uk-politics-democracy-government, accessed on November 29, 2021.

21 Dudley, op. cit., pp. 6–7.

22 Ibid., p. 42.

23 Ibid.

24 Ibid.

25 Ibid.

26 Weber, M. (1993) *Economía y sociedad* (Madrid, 1993) cited in ibid., p. 42.

27 Dudley, op. cit., p. 42.

28 Mosca, G. (2001), "La clase política," in Battle, A., *Diez textos básicos de ciencia política* (Barcelona, 2001), cited in ibid.

29 Mills, C. W. (1957), *La élite del poder* (Mexico, 1957), cited in ibid.

30 Fest, J. C. (1973), *Hitler* (London: Weidenfeld & Nicolson), pp. 298–313.

31 Acemoglu, D., and Robinson, J. A. (2012), *Why Nations Fail: The Origins of Power, Prosperity, and Poverty* (New York: Currency), p. 430.

32 Pifer, S. (2020), "Crimea: Six Years After Illegal Annexation," *Brookings Institution*, March 17, 2020, https://www.brookings.edu/blog/order-from-chaos/2020/03/17/crimea-six-years-after-illegal-annexation/, accessed on February 23, 2021.

33 Alsmadi, F. A. (2020), "A Year without Soleimani: Will Iran retreat regionally?" *Al Jazeera*, January 10, 2021, https://www.aljazeera.com/tag/soleimani-assassination/, accessed on February 16, 2021.

34 History.com Editors (2020), "Nuremberg Trials," https://www.history.com/topics/world-war-ii/nuremberg-trials, accessed on February 18, 2021.

35 Ketchell, M. (2020), "Alexei Navalny poisoning: what the theatrical assassination attempts reveal about Vladimir Putin's grip on power in Russia," *The Conversation*, September 10, 2020, https://theconversation.com/alexei-navalny-poisoning-what-theatrical-assassination-attempts-reveal-about-vladimir-putins-grip-on-power-in-russia-145664, accessed on February 18, 2021.

36 Maier, T. (2019), "The evidence that the US government got into the assassination business," *CNN*, April 17, 2019, https://edition.cnn.com/2019/04/17/opinions/us-assassination-attempt-maier/index.html, accessed on February 18, 2021.

37 David, S. R. (2003), "Israel's Policy of Targeted Killing," *Ethics and International Affairs*, 17, No. 1, https://www.law.upenn.edu/institutes/cerl/conferences/targetedkilling/papers/DavidIsraelPolicy.pdf, accessed on February 18, 2021.

38 Jeffrey, J. (2017), "How to Get Regime Change Right" *The Washington Institute for Near East Policy*, October 3, 2017, https://www.washingtoninstitute.org/policy-analysis/how-get-regime-change-right, accessed on February 18, 2021.

39 Champion, M. (2020), "How Iran Pursues its Interests Via Proxies and Partners," *Bloomberg*, January 6, 2020, https://www.bloomberg.com/news/articles/2020-01-05/how-iran-pursues-its-interests-via-proxies-partners-quicktake, accessed on February 18, 2021.

40 GAO (2005), "Cyber Threat Source Descriptions," *Department of Homeland Security's (DHS) Role in Critical Infrastructure Protection (CIP) GAO-05-434* (Washington D.C.) May 2005, https://us-cert.cisa.gov/ics/content/cyber-threat-source-descriptions, accessed on February 18, 2021.

41 Al Jazeera (2021), "UK approved $1.9bn of arms sales to Saudi Arabia since the ban lifted" *Al Jazeera*, February 9, 2021, https://www.aljazeera.com/news/2021/2/9/uk-approved-1-4bn-of-arms-sales-to-saudi-arabia-post-export-ban, accessed on February 18, 2021.

42 Crowley, M., and Jakes, L. (2021), "Biden Announces End of US Support to Saudi War in Yemen," *The New York Times*, February 4, 2021, https://www.nytimes.com/2021/02/04/us/biden-yemen-saudi-arabia.html, accessed on February 18, 2021.

43 "US Opposition to the International Criminal Court," UN Documents, *Global Policy Forum*, https://archive.globalpolicy.org/us-un-and-international-law-8-24/us-opposition-to-the-icc-8-29.html, accessed on February 18, 2021.

44 Wille, B., and Weir, R. (2020), "Targeting Life in Idlib," *Human Rights Watch*, October 15, 2020, https://www.hrw.org/report/2020/10/15/targeting-life-idlib/syrian-and-russian-strikes-civilian-infrastructure, accessed on February 27, 2021.

45 Roth K. (2020), "Yemen, Events of 2019," *Human Rights Watch*, https://www.hrw.org/world-report/2020/country-chapters/yemen, accessed on February 27, 2021.

46 Kramer (2016), pp. 239–240.

47 Freedland, J. (2021), "From Syria to China, dictators are still getting away with murder," *The Guardian,* February 26, 2021, https://www.theguardian.com/commentisfree/2021/feb/26/syria-china-dictators-crimes-humanity, accessed on February 27, 2021.

48 Miliband, D. (2019), "The new arrogance of power: Global politics in an age of impunity," 2019 Fulbright Lecture, *International Rescue Committee,* June 19, 20, 21, 2019, https://www.rescue.org/press-release/new-arrogance-power-global-politics-age-impunity, accessed on February 27, 2021.

49 Dwyer, C. (2016), "Donald Trump: 'I Could . . . Shoot Somebody, And I Wouldn't Lose Any Voters'," *NPR,* January 23, 2016, https://www.npr.org/sections/thetwo-way/2016/01/23/464129029/donald-trump-i-could-shoot-somebody-and-i-wouldnt-lose-any-voters, accessed on February 27, 2021.

50 Rawnsley, A. (2021), "What does the Salmond v Sturgeon Feud mean for the future of the union?" *The Guardian,* February 28, 2021, https://www.theguardian.com/commentisfree/2021/feb/28/what-does-salmond-v-sturgeon-feud-mean-for-future-of-union?utm_term=ba3f981265683366fb7af3be145ac4b7&utm_campaign=BestOfGuardianOpinionUK&utm_source=esp&utm_medium=Email&CMP=opinionuk_email, accessed on March 2, 2021.

51 Cassan, B. (2005), "William Jardine, Architect of the First Opium War," *Historia,* https://www.eiu.edu/historia/Cassan.pdf, accessed on February 18, 2021.

52 Blakemore, E. (2019), How the East India Company became the world's most powerful business," *National Geographic,* September 6, 2019, https://www.nationalgeographic.com/culture/article/british-east-india-trading-company-most-powerful-business, accessed on February 18, 2021.

53 Hayes, J. P. (2021), "The Opium Wars in China," *Asia Pacific Curriculum,* https://asiapacificcurriculum.ca/learning-module/opium-wars-china, accessed on February 22, 2021.

54 Ibid.

55 Ibid.

56 Cassan (2005), p. 114.

57 Magdoff, H., Nowell, C. E., and Webster, R. A. (2020), "Western colonialism," *Encyclopedia Britannica*, 9 Dec. 2020, https://www.britannica.com/topic/Western-colonialism, accessed February 18, 2021.

58 Newsinger, J. (1997), "Britain's Opium Wars," Monthly Review (October 1997), p. 32, quoted in Cassan, "William Jardine," op. cit.

59 Chambliss (1989).

60 "Possession is Nine Points of the Law and Legal Definition," *USLegal.com,* 2021 https://definitions.uslegal.com/p/possession-is-nine-points-of-the-law/, accessed on February 28, 2021.

61 Wishnia, J. (2020), "What is a Felony? Define Felony and Felony Charges List" *LegalMatch,* October 8, 2020, https://www.legalmatch.com/law-library/article/what-is-a-felony.html, accessed on February 23, 2021.

62 "Misdemeanor," *Legal Dictionary,* https://dictionary.law.com/Default.aspx?selected=1259, accessed on February 23, 2021.

63 Stewart, W. J. (2006), "Offence," *Collins Dictionary of Law,* https://legal-dictionary.thefreedictionary.com/offence, accessed on February 23, 2021.

64 Wex Definitions Team (2020), "Infraction," Legal Information Institute (Utica: Cornell Law School), June 2020, https://www.law.cornell.edu/wex/infraction#:~:text=Infraction%20has%20multiple%20legal%20meanings,penalty%20is%20also%20very%20minor, accessed on February 23, 2021.

65 [Herman v. Carbon County, 2010 U.S. App. LEXIS 19193 (3d Cir. Pa. Sept. 14, 2010)], cited in "Wrongdoing Law and Legal Definition," *US Legal Inc,* 2021, https://definitions.uslegal.com/w/wrongdoing/, accessed on February 23, 2021.

66 "Wrongdoing," *Collins COBUILD Advanced English Dictionary,* https://www.collinsdictionary.com/dictionary/english/wrongdoing, accessed on February 23, 2021.

67 Ibid.

68 Bulos, N. (2020), "After Woman's Brutal Killing by Her Father, Jordan Asks at What Price 'Honor'?," *The Los Angeles Times*, July 28, 2020, https://www.latimes.com/world-nation/story/2020-07-28/jordan-honor-killing-protests-violence-against-women, accessed on February 23, 2021.
69 Bukhari, M. (2019), "Brother Found Guilty of 'Honor Killing' of Pakistan Social Media Star," *Reuters*, September 27, 2019, https://www.reuters.com/article/us-pakistan-honourkillings-idUSKBN1WC0LU, accessed on February 23, 2021.
70 Ijaz, S. (2019), Pakistan Should Not Again Fail 'Honor Killing' Victim: End Impunity of Family Murders of Women," *Human Rights Watch*, August 22, 2019, https://www.hrw.org/news/2019/08/22/pakistan-should-not-again-fail-honor-killing-victim, accessed on February 23, 2021.

Chapter 2
The Crime Continuum – The Role of Organized Crime

A common characteristic of organized crime (OC) is the sense of historical roots that defines the identity of participants, gives meaning to what they do and frames their core values,[1] providing them with anchoring cultural myths, defining how they interact with their external environments,[2] and providing the longevity that exceeds the lifetimes of principal participants.[3]

Despite disagreement in criminological literature about the defining characteristics and prevalence of OC, there is general agreement that the three most prevalent types of OC are Mafia-, Triad-, and Yakuza-type organizations.

Defining Characteristics

There are more than 200 definitions of OC[4] (an indication of the difficulty of defining it). Despite the absence of a generally accepted definition, a number of attributes have been identified that can provide a basis for defining common characteristics: (1) absence of overt political goals; (2) hierarchical organization; (3) limited and exclusive membership; (4) unique subculture; (5) self-perpetuating; (6) use of violence to attain goals; (7) seeks to monopolize geographical areas of operations; and (8) governed by explicit rules, rituals, and regulations.[5]

A definition we like is that of Joseph Albini and Jeffrey McIllwain:

> A form of criminal activity within a social system composed of a centralized or decentralized social network (or networks) of at least three actors engaged in an ongoing criminal enterprise in which the size, scope, leadership and structure of the network is generated by the ultimate goal of the enterprise itself (i.e., how the crime is organized). This goal takes advantage of opportunities generated by laws, regulations, and social customs and mores and can be pursued for financial profit and/or the attainment of some form of power to effect social change and/or social mobility via the leveraging and brokering of the network's social, political and economic capital. Members of the network can be from the underworld or the upperworld. In some forms, force and/or fraud are used to exploit and/or extort victims, while in others illicit goods and services are provided by members of the network to customers in a marketplace where such activity is often permitted through the establishment of practices which foster the compliance and/or acquiescence of corrupt public and private sector officials who receive remuneration in the form of political favors or in the form of direct or indirect payoffs.[6]

We argue that one of two additional external conditions must apply for OC to prosper: either (1) the state must be corrupt, weak, or failing; and/or (2) it is regarded as illegitimate by a significant group of its subjects, who feel alienated from the majority that the state serves well.

https://doi.org/10.1515/9783110712155-002

OC and the state attempt to do the same things in the territories they control. Specifically, they aim to achieve a monopoly on the use of force and on taxing people:

> The protection of property and personal security are obligations assumed by states everywhere both as a means of legitimizing the state's franchise on violence and as a means of protecting commercial interests.[7]

If the state fails to protect property and personal security, it loses its moral claim to monopolize violence. Violence is the modus operandi of OC, as it achieves the same objectives. Recent evidence from Italy suggests that when the state is unable to protect people's livelihoods, as has happened during the Covid-19 pandemic, OC has stepped into the gap and fulfilled people's needs, providing "Mafia welfare," creating an opportunity for OC (1) to expand its reach, and (2) to then extort the people it has helped.[8]

The state and OC are potentially direct competitors. Where the state is strong, OC is weak and vice versa:

> *Think of crime as a competition in state-making. In strong states that effectively address the needs of their societies, the non-state entities cannot outcompete the state.* But in areas of socio-political marginalization and poverty – in many Latin American countries, conditions of easily upward of a third of the population – *non-state entities do often outcompete the state and secure the allegiance of large segments of society.*[9]   [Emphases ours]

There has been a tendency to assess the relationship between the state and OC through the lens of the state's ability to reform or strengthen the judicial system and security forces to deal with OC on the one hand and its programs of action to discourage the young from joining OC on the other. This approach has unfortunate consequences because it encourages governments, civil society, and multilateral agencies to think they must choose between "good guys" and "bad guys" in a zero-sum game. The danger is that large portions of society (both political and economic) who have little option but to operate with or around OC are excluded. It also covers up history in which pirates, smugglers, and outlaws played key roles in the construction of the social, political, and economic foundations of states.[10]

More worrying is that the approach turns a blind eye to OC's undermining of political and social ecosystems in areas (like Central America) where the state is weak or absent. OC undermines them by developing strategies to control elections through allies in key political posts in government ministries and decision-making committees. It simultaneously influences the selection of key people in bureaucratic elites (armed forces and police), and weakens the system of judicial checks and balances. OC changes social and cultural relationships, capturing power by partnering with or threatening religious, indigenous, and intellectual leaders.[11] The willingness to use often extreme violence to maintain internal discipline and external social control, as well as extorting "taxes," puts OC in direct competition with the state whose essential function is to provide protection of life and livelihoods in return for paying taxes:

Organized crime's use of violence can fundamentally undermine that social contract or establish a kind of parallel social contract. In the most extreme cases, criminal groups become the guardians of specific geographic areas, giving these groups immense political and social capital from which they construct a virtual fortress around themselves.[12]

The key to OC's success is the extent to which elites are focused on protecting what Acemoglu and Robinson termed a "parasitic extractive system" that stunts economic and political development through the skewed way in which the state deploys security forces, allocates development resources, taxes citizens, and administers justice.[13] Such a system thwarts creative destruction and economic innovation, leaving few opportunities for outsiders to rise, forcing people (like Pablo Escobar) to seek other ways of leveling the social playing field through OC that allowed him to amass huge amounts of money and corrupt ruling elites:[14]

> *The political capital that comes with these relationships allows criminal groups to exert power in particular ways that permit them to avoid prosecution, advance and expand their business interests, and establish a base from which to exert power over state resources*, as Rawlinson shows in the case of Russia. Finally, organized crime obtains power by intersecting with the communities in which it operates, which allows it to gain important social capital, thereby adding a further layer of protection from prosecution and public scrutiny. This, as mentioned earlier, can come from supplanting the state as neighborhood watchdog, i.e., its police and often its judicial system. In addition, as some of our case studies illustrate, criminal groups build support by providing jobs and services to the community.[15]   [Emphasis ours]

This more sophisticated approach explains the rise of an emerging category of so-called "Mafia states,"[16] where the state collaborates actively with criminals. It is not clear whether these alliances qualify as OC or as CTIO (Crime That Is Organized). We are inclined to treat them as a new type of CTIO (and we discuss them in the last section of this chapter).

Historically, OC has flourished in the US, Southern Italy, China, and Japan. A weak state and an alienated section of the population existed in Southern Italy; in Manchu China, the government was regarded as illegitimate by supporters of the deposed Ming dynasty (who later dispersed to Hong Kong and Taiwan); and in Japan the *burakumin*[i] and *ronin*[ii] were outcasts. Just as important to the success of OC organizations was that, at various times in their history, the authorities in Italy,

---

i "Burakumin (Japanese: "hamlet people"), also called Eta ("pollution abundant"), outcaste, or "untouchable," Japanese minority, occupying the lowest level of the traditional Japanese social system. The Japanese term *eta* is highly pejorative, but prejudice has tended even to tarnish the otherwise neutral term *burakumin* itself." The Editors of Encyclopaedia Britannica (2015), "Burakumin," *Encyclopedia Britannica*, 18 Nov. 2015, https://www.britannica.com/topic/burakumin, accessed 23 February 2021.
ii Ronin is "a lordless samurai, especially one who has been deprived of his territory," *Collins English Dictionary*, https://www.collinsdictionary.com/dictionary/english/ronin, accessed on February 23, 2021.

China, Hong Kong, and Japan collaborated actively with OC to establish or re-establish social control in times of major political change.

The relationship of OC to the state can be categorized in three ways: (1) *preda-tory* where OC expands at the expense of the state; (2) *parasitic* where OC uses the resources of the state to gain and hold on to power; (3) *symbiotic* where OC creates a state within the state.[17] Which strategy or combination of strategies OC adopts de-pends on its relationship with elites of the state (see Chapter 7) because there are four types of elites (economic, political, social, and bureaucratic) that are often in competition for the state's resources (see Chapter 1).[18]

When these elites are hostile to OC, OC cannot flourish (as opposed to crime that is organized), and despite the romantic treatment of OC in novels, TV, and films extolling the virtues (and vices) of OC, it would appear to be in decline, as a result of (1) the state recognizing the potentially existential competitive threat OC may create; and (2) technological changes in the criminal marketplace, undermin-ing the traditional OC business model.

Weak states allow small groups to meet and form hierarchies, until they be-come OC capable of co-opting institutions. Such weakness provokes the emergence of alternative and illegal powers, which fill power and order vacuums.[19]

Mafia

The term "Mafia" indicates a specific form of socially prestigious OC, accepted and/or tolerated by communities, that is also capable of infiltrating the legal economy and politics. Mafias transcend class and the separation of illegal and legal activities. They are able to acquire and use social capital to achieve strategic goals through their members and through the use of political allies.[20]

Mafia-style OC is an Italian, American, and Australian phenomenon, originat-ing in the Kingdom of Naples – mainland Italy south of the Papal States plus Sicily – and arriving later in the US and Australia with Sicilian and Calabrian immigrants. It originated where the state was weak and the landed aristocracy exploited the peas-antry. It was a response to the failure of the Kingdom of Naples to provide security and property protection for agricultural communities; in part the result of a merry-go-round of foreign rulers[iii] who alienated rural communities from the state.

---

iii Sicily was governed by Arabs (954–1060), Normans (1060–1194), Germans (1194–1266), French (1266–1282), followed by the Spanish (1302–1860) when it was unified with the rest of Italy as part of the Kingdom of Naples. https://en.wikipedia.org/wiki/Kingdom_of_Sicily#Hohenstaufen_king dom, accessed on February 28, 2021.

The Kingdom of Naples was governed by the Spanish (1504–1713) and Austrians (1713–1734) and the Spanish (1734–1860). Even after the Kingdom of Naples was unified with the rest of Italy (1860), it was governed by Northern Italians who did not understand its socio-economic structure

Mafia associations aim to exercise the typical functions of a modern political entity: imposing norms of behaviour on the general population, controlling a territory, exerting physical coercion and punishing transgressors and imposing a rudimentary tax system through the practice of generalised extortion.[21]

Even within Mafia-style of OC, "one size does not fit all." The Sicilian Cosa Nostra and its Mafia links in the US and Australia are organized differently from the Camorra, which essentially focuses on Naples and its hinterland, which, in turn, is different from the Calabrian 'Ndrangheta and its dynamic and flexible approach to globalization. The organizational structures and business models are unique to each, reflecting different histories and responses to change.

1 Cosa Nostra ("Our Thing")

Originally, the Mafia and mafiosi (members of the Mafia) had no criminal connotations, and the term "mafioso" was used to describe someone who was suspicious of central authority, given the long line of foreign rulers in Sicilian history. This suspicion set the stage for an "industry of violence." Gangs helped to spread the Gabellotto's[iv] power base either by theft, intimidation, or by doing favors for the local lords, enabling them to become landholders and patrons of the peasants they claimed to protect. The Gabellotti gained further power when Italy established universal suffrage. They now controlled votes that ensured political power as well as social and economic control. They were also the interlocutors for the peasants to express their grievances to the lords and their political representatives.[22] By the middle of the 19th century, these groups had become clan-based, secret private armies that extorted money from large landowners to protect their crops, citrus groves, and flocks. Eventually they became the Mafia that we think of today.[23]

When Sicily became a province of the newly unified Italy, the Piedmontese-led government in Rome asked the Mafia clans to help them deal with independent criminal bands in Sicily. In return, the central government turned a "blind eye" to Mafia extortion of landowners. The central government made a Faustian bargain they believed would be temporary – long enough to allow Rome to gain control. Instead, the Mafia clans expanded and embedded themselves in Sicilian politics and the economy, intimidating voters to support certain politicians who were then

---

and needs. "Naples, Kingdom of," *Encyclopedia.com*, https://www.encyclopedia.com/history/modern-europe/italian-history/kingdom-naples, accessed on February 28, 2021.

iv "Gabellotto – entrepreneurs who leased farm lands from aristocrats. They would hire guards that would both protect the property and have control over the working farmers. These aristocrats would constantly be in debt to the Gabellotto for rent and taxes. This would lead to the loss of their properties entirely, and the Gabellotto became an undeniable power on the island." Tano, D., "The Sordid History of the Sicilian Mafia," https://wearepalermo.com/the-history-of-sicilian-mafia/, *We are Palermo*, accessed on November 30, 2021.

indebted to the Mafia. Even the Catholic Church joined this unholy bargain, relying on Mafiosi to look after its huge property holdings and control its tenant farmers.[24]

> There was no significant middle or even merchant class in Sicily. Nor was there a developed civil society as had existed for centuries in northern Italy

> Not only were there no civil organizations to moderate between the citizen and the state but there was no properly functioning state. *The period in which the Mafia emerged was one in which there was a crisis of state authority.*[25]   [Emphases ours]

The Sicilian clans introduced new practices to become stronger institutionally, with initiation ceremonies where new members swore secret oaths of loyalty, reinforced by "Omerta" – the code of silence and non-cooperation with the authorities – based on the ancient Sicilian practice that people never went to government officials to seek justice and never cooperated with authorities investigating crimes.[26] Cosa Nostra influence grew in Sicily until 1920, when Mussolini came to power. Given Fascism's totalitarian approach to governing, he was not prepared to share power with the mobsters, forcing many to emigrate to the US – where the Mafia was emerging as a powerful force as a result of Prohibition – as well as to Australia.

The Cosa Nostra recovered toward the end of World War II when the American armed forces used Mafiosi as sources of intelligence in the invasion of Sicily.[27] Both the Social Democratic and Christian Democratic governments that followed the end of World War II were in cahoots with the Mafia.[28,29] This allowed the clans to dominate the booming construction industry in the post-war reconstruction of Sicily. During this period, the Mafia expanded its activities, entering the international narcotics trade, so that by the 1970s it was a major player.

In the US, the Mafia built upon its successes during Prohibition, expanding into loan sharking, prostitution, and infiltrating labor unions and legitimate industries such as construction, the New York garment trade, and ice-making. Like their Sicilian counterparts, the US Mafia adopted the code of Omerta, and engaged in bribing and intimidating politicians, public officials, witnesses, and businessmen.

In Sicily, the success of the Mafia in 1970s and 1980s and their close relationship with the politicians in Rome led the Cosa Nostra to assassinate senior officials in the Sicilian administration who were beginning to clean up corruption in Palermo.[30] This was seen as an existential challenge to the government in Rome and cost the Mafia the support of Palermo locals. The resulting reaction and the so-called "maxi trials"[v] of Mafiosi by the state in their heartland territory weakened the hold of the Mafia and led to its decline from the mid-1990s onward.[31]

---

v The so-called "maxi trials" were held in Palermo, Messina, and Catania. 500 members were tried in Palermo in 1987. In 1991 another 241 were tried. This was achieved by adopting US techniques of flipping informants. Before judge Falcone's murder there were hardly any; within six months of his murder, there were 200, and in less than a year there were 600–700. Shelley, L.I. (1994), "Review:

2 Camorra

The Camorra is the oldest of the three Italian secret societies of criminals. It is thought to have originated in Spain as early as the 15th century and was introduced from there to Naples.[32] It became powerful in the 19th century as a result of weakness of the corrupt Spanish Bourbon government of the Kingdom of Naples that allowed it to flourish by co-opting the Camorra:

> As the Camorra grew in influence and power, its operations included criminal activities of various kinds, such as smuggling, blackmail, extortion, and road robberies. *The corrupt Bourbon regime did not interfere with the society; indeed, members of the Camorra were taken into the police service, and the organization became entrenched among both Neapolitan municipal employees and the army.*[33]   [Emphasis ours]

The Bourbon rulers reinforced the Camorra's social standing externally; while it raised its own prestige by adopting aristocratic customs when it became a secret society, renamed "Bella Società Riformata," when the leaders of Naples' twelve districts met in the "Santa Caterina in Formiello" church, and during a solemn ceremony gave a new character to the Society. The chief had to be a native of the "Porta Capuana" where many of the criminals lived.[34]

The initiation ceremony was dangerous. The blindfolded novice had to pick up a coin from the floor while the "Bella Società Riformata" members, each wielding a dagger, circled around him. At a signal, the members stabbed at the coin while the initiate attempted to retrieve it. Hands were slashed, but the test for courage and tenacity was completed. New members became "Giovanotti onorati," honored youths. After serving their apprenticeships, novices were allowed to enter the inner circle of the "Società Maggiore" and subjected to another initiation.

By the light of a single candle, the candidate sat at a table on which lay a dagger, a loaded pistol, and a glass of poisoned wine. Blood was drawn from his hand using the dagger. At this point the candidate put his hand out to his comrades, swearing to obey the orders of the capo and keep the secrets of the "Bella Società Riformata":

> Pointing the pistol to his temple while lifting the wine glass to his lips, he swore to kill himself if he received the order to do so. At this point the capo took the pistol, fired it into the air and smashed the glass to the floor. The youth knelt. The capo, putting his hand on the youth's head, pronounced the final words, "You are now a man!" It was understood that to speak the name of the "Bella Società Riformata" chief at any time meant death.[35]

Naples in the early 1800s was a wild and filthy city. The Camorra flourished in this disorder, initially by organizing gambling and taking 20% of the earnings. Collectors included baggage handlers at the port, hotel clerks, street vendors, cabmen, and

Mafia and the Italian State: The Historical Roots of the Current Crisis," *Sociological Forum*, December 1994, Vol 9, No 4, Special Issue: Multiculturalism and Diversity (December 1994), p. 670, https://www.jstor.org/stable/685007, accessed on January 22, 2021.

thieves. In return for taxing the populace, the Camorra provided a long list of services that the government and judiciary failed to offer: acting as middlemen and arbitrators, they kept the peace, settled disputes between buyers and sellers, tenants and landlords, creditors and their debtors, and employers and employees. Most important of all, they settled matters of family honor – that could lead to death if not resolved – usually by negotiating a wedding. Camorra justice was personal, speedy, and regarded as fairer than the justice the corrupt and disinterested government could provide.[36] As a result, there were entire neighborhoods where the government could not enter.

The Camorra's formal entry into politics came in 1860 when the chief of police asked it to help provide security for Garibaldi's entry into Naples. The state endorsed Camorra control until the early 1900s, even allowing the Camorra to be responsible for law and order in the jails.[37]

3 'Ndrangheta

For much of the historical analysis of OC, the Calabrian 'Ndrangheta was regarded incorrectly as an offshoot or "poor cousin" of the Sicilian Mafia. Maybe that was a result of Calabria being just across the Straits of Messina from Sicily. However, since 1931, when the name 'Ndrangheta was first used, law enforcement and criminologists have gradually come to realize, not merely that it has independent origins and a quite different and much more adaptive organizational strategy, but that it is in fact the most powerful and wealthiest of Southern Italy's OC organizations.[38]

> The 'Ndrangheta – whose name comes from the Greek for courage or loyalty – has a tight clan structure which has made it famously difficult to penetrate.
>
> With its network of hundreds of family gangs based around the southern region of Calabria, it is even more feared and secretive than the Sicilian mafia.
>
> Its roots go back to a criminal association specialised in gambling, the Garduna, which was created in the Spanish city of Toledo in 1412.
>
> It spread to Calabria, one of Italy's poorest regions, and started building up as a crime network based on kidnapping for ransom.[39]

Before 2010, when the 'Ndrangheta was added to article 416 *bis* of the Italian Criminal Code as a mafia criminal organization, with the Italian Supreme Court confirming it as having a unified and precise structure, the general perception of the 'Ndrangheta was:

> that organised crime in Calabria was simply a group of uncivilised, uncultured shepherds interested only in their own profits and their own lands but essentially not dangerous beyond their own territories . . . the 'Ndrangheta . . . today identifies a specific and complex structure made of over 150 family clans – is not only powerful for its criminal status within and beyond national boundaries, but is also one of the prime engines of the political scene in Calabria – where its control is broadly undisputed – as well as nationally.[40]   [Emphasis ours]

An additional reason for the misperception of the relative significance of the 'Ndrangheta is the continuing lack of clarity about its organizational structure. However, what is clear is that it is no longer the same as it was originally:

> Whether or not the 'Ndrangheta is today one organisation or a brand name for a multitude of clans enjoying independency and autonomy from one another, today's composition of Calabrian organised crime is very distant from the origins[41]

It has successfully metastasized while strengthening its organization in its homeland (Calabria) by a series of kidnappings as well as infiltration into the organs of local government in Reggio Calabria and East and West Calabria. This change was achieved by a policy of "colonization" in Northern Italy, the European Union,[42] and Australia[43] through the use of settled emigrants from Calabria who brought the culture of the 'Ndrangheta with them; and global reach was achieved through its representatives dealing with local drug traffickers as result of their pre-eminence in drug trafficking.[44] However, as with all true Mafia-type organizations, territorial control remained essential and was not forgotten.[45]

Despite its success in establishing profitable "colonies" outside Calabria,[46] and beachheads through connections with local drug traffickers, its spiritual DNA remains firmly Calabrian, centered on the sanctuary of the "Madonna de Polsi."[47]

Recently, the Italian state has targeted 'Ndrangheta in the same way it set about diminishing the Cosa Nostra when provoked by Totò Riina's war against it in the early 1990s,[48] and it appears to be having similar success in cutting the organization down to size, using the same "maxi-trial" method, leading to the conviction of 70 of its leaders so far.[49] More trials are expected over the next two years with the most important leaders choosing to face the longer trials rather than opting for the expedited version:

> While 355 people have yet to be judged in proceedings expected to last two years or longer, those judged on Saturday had opted for a speedy trial . . .

> The biggest fish in the prosecution's case – Mancuso "The Uncle," 67, considered the leader of the 'Ndrangheta families who dominated the Vibo Valentia province of Calabria; and ex-senator and lawyer Giancarlo Pittelli, 68, accused of being Mancuso's white-collar fixer – have opted for the longer trial.

> Of the eight defendants in the fast-track trial who faced a maximum of 20 years, six received the full sentence. They included Gallone, 62, who helped orchestrate his boss Mancuso's three years on the run beginning in 2014. Mancuso had only recently been released from prison after serving 19 years.[50]

Chinese Triads

The conquest of China (1618–1683) by the invading Manchu, to end the Ming dynasty and establish their own Qing dynasty, led to the foundation of the Hung Mun,

Tien Tei Wei (Heaven and Earth Society), and San Hwo Hui (Three United Society) triads, to overthrow the Qing dynasty and restore the Ming dynasty in China:

> *Guided by a strong patriotic doctrine, the triad maintained a rigid central control over the behavior and activities of its members, who regarded themselves as blood brothers and were expected to be loyal and righteous. The early triad society still maintained its secret and cultural features, as reflected in its paraphernalia, organizational structure, recruitment mechanism, initiation ceremony, oaths, rituals, secret codes, and communication system.* There were clear rules, codes of conduct, and chains of command. In the early 1900s, the Hung Mun gradually disintegrated into many triad societies or gangs that operated independently from each other in different parts of China. *With the Chinese Communist Party in power in 1949, many triad members escaped to Hong Kong, Macau, Taiwan, and Chinatowns in overseas countries* together with thousands of refugees. In the beginning, refugees from the same ethnic groups united themselves to protect their own interests against other ethnic groups in a definite neighborhood. *With the infiltration of triad elements, some of these groups were gradually transformed into triad societies (or tongs in Chinatowns overseas), which used violence to protect them in a dominated territory*"[51]   [Emphases ours]

After 1949, when the mainland Chinese Communist Party cracked down on all independent organizations that could threaten its control on power, Hong Kong became the triad capital, with as many as 16 percent of its three million inhabitants estimated by the Hong Kong police to be triad members.[52] Given their traditions and enforced hierarchical and cohesive subcultures, triads were effective in controlling local territories, but less suited to dealing with the fluid and dynamic nature of international OC.

Triads have been co-opted by governments because of the perception that they were patriotic. The Chinese Kuomintang government had a close relationship with triads before World War II and used them in their battles with the Communists in Shanghai in 1927. The Japanese succeeded in using some Hong Kong triads during their occupation of Hong Kong by appealing to anti-European feelings and resentment against the British colonial power. The British, in turn, sought the help from triads in order to re-establish their control after World War II. This perception of triads being patriotic organizations has been the basis of their durability, whether it was in China or Hong Kong, and helped the authorities overlook their long-term criminality in return for their short-term help.[53]

There is a legend about the origin of triads in China that explains why the triads turned against the Qing dynasty, after having helped it get established. Legend has it that 128 Shaolin monks helped either the Kangxi or Qianlong Emperor defeat invading Xi Lu barbarians. They were then accused of plotting a rebellion against the Emperor who ordered the Shaolin monastery be destroyed. Only five of the monks survived and vowed to avenge their comrades; and so, they founded the lodges to foment a mass uprising against the Qing.

The reality is somewhat different in that triads were also connected to peasant mutual aid societies involved in rebellions by poverty-stricken peasants.[54] For example, in 1796, the Buddhist White Lotus sect, established under the Mongols, led a rebellion over tax that lasted until 1804. Although it was suppressed, it damaged the Qing dynasty by showing that Manchu troops could be defeated, and encouraged the rise of movements to "oppose the Qing and restore the Ming."[55]

The leading triad organization, the Tin Tei Wui, however, was established around 1761, not as an effort to overthrow the Qing, but as a brotherly fraternity and mutual aid society in Zhangzhou prefecture in Fujian province. It was only one of the 199 secret societies that were formed in the century following the end of the Qianlong Emperor's reign. However, it became a source of uprisings including those in 1768 and 1769 in the south of Fujian province, motivated by rebellion against the Qing, but also by robbing wealthy households. It adopted a secret initiation ceremony with binding blood oaths as well as a code and hand signals to ensure survival, given that multi-surname brotherhoods were banned under the Qing. It prospered and spread from Zhangzhou across Fujian province and into Taiwan.[56]

Triads became more important with the rise of the Kuomintang (KMT) and the overthrow of the Qing in 1911.[57] The association of triads with the KMT became even closer once the Revolution had succeeded, in particular with the Shanghai-based "Green Gang," led by "Big-Eared Du" (Du Yusheng), the KMT's enforcer in Shanghai. The relationship was so close that Chiang Kai Shek is believed to have become a member when he was working in Shanghai in 1919.

According to a Shanghai Special Branch report, Tu Yueh-Sung (Du Yusheng) was a major distributor of opium through his "Black Stuff Company" which got $3,000–$10,000 a month from every opium trader in the French Concession in return for being granted the freedom to sell opium openly. He then paid $180,000 a month to the French authorities.[58] The report went on to state:

> His relations with the Kuomintang were first established in about 1924, when important members of the Party, which was considered to be a secret organ in Shanghai, requested him to afford protection.[59]

In April 1927, Special Branch reported that Du and the Green Gang provided Chiang Kai Shek with 2,000 men to help the 26th Army massacre 5,000 members of the Communist-controlled unions in Shanghai during the "White Terror," increasing Du's influence with the Nationalist army. The level to which Du had influence with the Nationalist government was demonstrated in 1935 when the Minister of Finance, Dr H. H. Kung, asked him to negotiate with the shareholders of the Bank of China and the Bank of Communications when they were nationalized.[60] Chiang Kai Shek also used the Green Gang to kidnap wealthy Shanghainese businessmen, whose ransoms helped make good the financial shortfalls of the KMT government. In addition, the KMT issued government bonds that local people had to buy or face being kidnapped or beaten by the Green Gang.[61]

The Communist Party of China (CPC) was initially sympathetic to the rural secret societies as part of their strategy of gaining peasant support in the countryside. Before 1949, the CPC was favorably disposed toward the "Red Spears" in the north of China, and in July 1936, Mao praised the "Association of Elder Brothers" (Ko Lao Hui) for their patriotic participation in the 1911 revolution, and pointed out their shared values in that both they and the CPC were oppressed by the ruling class and were actively resisting the Japanese. He went so far as to avow that the Ko Lao Hui could operate legally under the Chinese Soviet government. However, once they won the civil war, the Communists culled triads ruthlessly in 1950 because the defeated Kuomintang continued to use triads in their anti-Communist struggle. This caused the triads to flee to Hong Kong, Macao, and Taiwan.[62]

With the introduction of the "Open Door" policy in the 1980s, Triads were encouraged to re-enter mainland China from Hong Kong. However, in 1989, the triads helped smuggle democratic leaders out of China to Hong Kong after the Tiananmen Square crackdown. As a result, the mainland authorities applied a "united front" tactic to co-opt the triads, once they regained sovereignty over Hong Kong in 1997, and recruit them to the communist camp.[63]

Hong Kong Triads

Despite popular perceptions of Hong Kong Triads, they represent only around three percent of criminal activity[64] and have become loosely organized cartels with members often undertaking their own opportunistic activities without reference to their bosses. Membership is fluid with members able to move from one triad gang to another:

> Although various societies are symbolically part of the triad family, they are decentralized in that no one central body is able to unite all triad societies, or to give universal commands. *The triads' organizational structure has become flexible and decentralized. The traditional rank system has been largely reduced to three levels.* These are called Red Pole, 49, and Blue Lanterns. The initiation ceremony has been simplified. Most people join a triad society based on an oral agreement with their Big Brother. *Today it is no longer possible for many triad societies to enforce strict discipline over their members. Transfer of membership between triads can also be done quite easily. Triad Big Brothers have no obligation to look after their followers when they encounter problems.*[65]   [Emphases ours]

Three trends have affected all triads in Hong Kong: (1) members of different triads cooperate in running profitable criminal projects that are not bound to one particular territory, such as underground casinos which have to keep moving but which still need to be protected from extortion or competition; (2) they team up with legitimate entrepreneurs to monopolize new markets, such as interior design, realty, and intimidating actors; and (3) they invest in legitimate hospitality businesses.[66]

Perhaps the most significant change is the attitude of the CPC regarding triads since the 1997 handover of Hong Kong to China. Even before 1997, the CPC recognized the potential benefits of working with triads in Hong Kong as part of their

United Front when Tao Siju, as Minister of Chinese Public Security said at a press conference in 1993, after meeting members of the Sun Yee On that:

> As for organizations like the triads in Hong Kong, *as long as these people are patriotic, as long as they are concerned with Hong Kong's prosperity and stability, we should unite with them. I believe that the more people we unite with the better.* . . . Our public security organs have broad links and ties with different strata in society, including such groups. . . . I may as well tell you a story from my own experience. . . . *When a state leader visited a foreign country, an organization that is similar to the triads you mentioned dispatched 800 of its members to guard our state leader against any danger.*[67]   [Emphases ours]

In May 1997, a former deputy secretary-general of the mainland's New China News Agency was quoted as saying at a forum at Hong Kong's Baptist University that:

> I told them [triad leaders] that what the administration wanted was a peaceful return and that they could not attempt to do anything to upset Hong Kong's prosperity and stability.[68]

In 2014, a self-professed triad member said in a news interview that:

> All the existing triad groups in Hong Kong are patriotic and follow the country's orders. . . . There is a public security ministry . . . they are not talking about cooperating with triads. . . . *Triads can only follow what they are told to do.*[69]   [Emphasis ours]

The most important triads in Hong Kong are the Sun Yee On, Wo Shing Wo, and 14K (Tak, Ngai and Hau "factions"), but other active groups include Shui Fong and Luen Ying She.[70]

1 Sun Yee On

The Sun Yee On was founded by the Teochew (Chui Chau) minority in Hong Kong. These days it has members from different Chinese groups and even some locally born Indians and Pakistanis as junior members. It used to have full initiation ceremonies but has stopped doing so to avoid police detection. Compared with the other triads in Hong Kong, it is relatively structured and disciplined, with members helping each other when in legal trouble. Although there are members in Australia, Canada, the UK, and the US, this was not the result of an organized program of emigration by the Sun Yee On, but rather an opportunistic consequence of Hong Konger emigration pre-1997. Despite fears to the contrary, there has been no mass triad emigration before or after 1997.[71]

Members of Sun Yee On are allowed to undertake private investments and build personal connections abroad and in Hong Kong without permission. Connections overseas are based on personal networks, and involvement in Hong Kong in drugs, street-selling of pirated VCDs/DVDs, stock market speculation, money laundering, vehicle theft, prostitution, loan sharking, and extortion are private investments.[72]

Members were active in the international drug trade in the past, in particular the importing of heroin from Thailand, where there is a large Teochew community, into Hong Kong and some drug smuggling to western countries. There is insufficient evidence to suggest that Sun Yee On still plays an important role, as this business requires capital, connections, and the necessary skills to undertake it, making it more opportunistic.[73]

Sun Yee On members have been increasingly involved in legitimate businesses (catering, films, and the stock market) though it is not clear whether this is the result of money laundering or legal activities where they have used their reputation as triads to monopolize the activity. It is clear, however, that when compared with other triads, members tend to participate more in non-violent crime and have more legitimate relationships with legitimate entrepreneurs, lawyers, and accountants. Since 1997, the Sun Yee On has kept a low profile.[74]

2 Wo Shing Wo
Originally an offshoot of the Wo Hop To triad established in 1908, it broke away in 1930 to become an independent society. Its membership is diverse. It has a Central Committee made up of influential and senior officials with a Chairman (Cho Kun) and Treasurer (Cha So), usually elected from the Central Committee at an annual or biannual meeting. Although the leadership helps settle internal and external disputes, they do not dictate which criminal activities their members may undertake. There are members in Canada, the UK, and the US; and there are connections with the Big Circle Gangs in the Netherlands. However, as was the case with the Sun Yee On, these were not the result of a deliberate emigration plan. The overseas connections and contacts are largely personal and have little to do with the society. There are no indications that mass Wo Shing Wo migration took place before or after 1997.[75]

At a personal level, Wo Shing Wo members invest in the same criminal activities as members of the Sun Yee On and 14K, but with one addition, the manufacture of pirated VCD/DVDs. They do not transfer part of their profits to the society.[76]

Compared with other triad groups, Wo Shing Wo members tend to participate in more violent crime, attempting to dominate street-level organized crime. Although there are indicators that individual Wo Shing Wo members have been involved in some specific legitimate businesses such as the catering and entertainment business, their roles in the legitimate economy are not clear.[77]

3 14K
The 14K was established in the early 1950s by members with a KMT (Nationalist Party) background from Guangdong in China. Compared with other triads, 14K is relatively disorganized, with different subgroups that have become separate triads in their own right[vi] that often fight each other.[78]

---

vi The Tak, Ngai, and Hau factions.

14K members are found in Australia, Canada, the Netherlands, the UK, and the US. According to police sources, some individual members may have connections with the Big Circle Gangs in Holland, Yakuza in Japan, and the United Bamboo Gangs in Taiwan.

At a personal level, 14K members invest in the same criminal activities as members of the Sun Yee On and Wo Shing Wo, but with one addition: the London gold bullion scams they organized and operated, where investors were encouraged to invest in scams that promised high returns in the London bullion market.

Compared with other triad groups, 14K members tend to participate in traditional street-level organized crime. Some 14K members in Hong Kong continued to have a close relationship with senior Nationalist Party members in Taiwan in the 1960s and 1970s. Today, however, 14K members in Hong Kong no longer appear to be interested in political movements.[79]

Taiwanese Triads

The Chinese Nationalist government regained sovereignty over Taiwan from the Japanese, who had ruled the island since 1895, in 1945 when the Japanese surrendered at the end of World War II.[80] In 1949, Chiang Kai Shek's defeated Nationalist government (KMT) fled to Taiwan, taking some two million mainland Chinese (Waishengren) supporters with them and settled in Taiwan. The KMT takeover of the island was deeply resented by the majority Hoklo inhabitants, following the so-called "228 Incident" when Nationalist soldiers from the mainland killed between 18,000 and 20,000 Hoklo who had been protesting at the harsh treatment by the KMT in the "White Terror" that lasted from February 27 to March 8, 1947.[81]

Chiang Kai Shek was accustomed to working with triads and using them as an instrument of political enforcement in return for turning a blind eye to their criminal activities, ever since he had worked closely with the Green Gang in Shanghai's "White Terror" in 1927; and it was second nature for the KMT to work closely with the Bamboo Union founded in 1957 during the KMT's rule by martial law that lasted until 1987.

In a reversal of fortunes, given their KMT affiliated origins, the Mainland CPC has been attempting to co-opt both of the most important triads in Taiwan, the Bamboo Union and the Four Seas to help them regain Taiwan and promote integration with China, providing funds to the Bamboo Union of US$ 4.5million a year and to Chang An-Lo ("White Wolf"), their former leader who is pro-China with US$ 750,000 a year.[82]

Certain characteristics appear to be shared between the Bamboo Union and their arch-rival the Four Seas.[83] Both were established by outsider Waishengren (mainland Chinese) for protection from bullying by Hoklo (indigenous Taiwanese) gangs. They had links to the KMT government. Their sources of capital accumulation were originally from protection, debt collection, gambling, prostitution, and

extortion. In the booming 1990s, they diversified into legitimate businesses in entertainment, investment companies, land development, realty, and waste disposal.
The operating principles of both gangs were opportunistic and violent. There were
no lawyers or accountants or other professionals involved in their organizations.

1 Bamboo Union

The Bamboo Union was founded in 1957 by Chen Chi-Li with two other outsider
Waishengren teenagers, who joined to secure a place for themselves in Taiwan and
to protect themselves from threats by Hoklo (indigenous Taiwanese) children who
rejected and bullied them. Its original goal was to gain social acceptance through
street fighting.[84] By the late 1960s, the gang expanded into extortion, gambling,
drugs, and prostitution when Waishengren nightclub owners welcomed the gang to
protect them from Hoklo gangs in the flourishing R&R industry, created by well-
paid American GIs on leave from the Vietnam War.[85]

The Bamboo Union and the "Iron Blood Patriots" were endorsed by Chiang
Hsia-Wu, son of the then President Chiang Ching-Kuo, who deputized them as instruments of Taiwanese foreign policy. He personally sanctioned them as a paramilitary branch of the secret police to undertake "black ops" that would embarrass the
government if discovered. In return, they were granted a share of the global heroin
trade funneled from the Golden Triangle by KMT elements in Thailand.[86]

The Bamboo Union became a key part of the mechanism of government control
until 1984. Members were knowingly employed by the National Security and Intelligence Bureau, as advisers to Chiang Hsiao-Yung, admitted into the police, military,
and intelligence academies, and even to the top of government.[87] Their association
with the "Iron Blood Patriots" ended with the murder by Chen Chi-Li and two associates of Sino-American journalist Henry Liu in 1984 in San Francisco for having written an unauthorized critical biography of President Chiang Ching-Kuo.[88] Chen Chi-Li
testified at his trial in Taiwan that he had been instructed by the Head of Military
Intelligence to kill Liu because he was a Communist spy and that he agreed to do it,
pro bono, as a patriotic act.[89] This was the most prominent example of the KMT
using the Bamboo Union in a number of other political killings in the early 1980s.[90]

The unique social standing the Bamboo Union achieved under its founder-
leader Chen Chi-Li is demonstrated by his funeral after he died of cancer in 2007.
Membership at the time of his death was 10,000. There were more than 10,000
mourners, including Taiwanese politicians, representatives of the Four Seas and Ce-
lestial Way, Japanese Yakuza, Hong Kong, Macao, Malaysian, and Thai triads, all
under the gaze of thousands of police;[91] and according to local news the family
spent more than NT$20 million to ensure the funeral was held in grand style.[92]

Fellow gangsters said that Chen never understood why the government would
treat a patriot like him as a criminal. He believed he was not a normal gangster, but
an idealist who had made money by doing the right thing.[93] After his release from

prison in 1991 for the murder of Henry Liu, Chen declared he wanted to transform Bamboo Union into a legitimate enterprise and invested successfully in construction inside and outside Taiwan, including a RMB 10 billion resort in China's Moon Lake area.

2 Four Seas

The origins of the Four Seas are similar to those of the Bamboo Union, and for the same reasons – outsider Waishengren teenagers joining to get respect and protection from indigenous Hoklo teenagers. In 1997, Four Seas had only 11 tongs (subsidiary gangs), but by 2005, law enforcement was targeting more than 40. Recruitment was indiscriminate, with candidates coming from high schools or dropouts, resulting in a high level of churn among junior members (after a three-month probation). However, the senior membership remained constant, with law enforcement noting an increase in senior persons of interest of only 50 in the same period.[94]

Unlike Bamboo Union, Four Seas has an initiation process that requires bowing to Kuan Kung, a legendary warrior featured in "The Romance of the Three Kingdoms" idolized by the Chinese underworld (and the police), taking oaths, pricking fingers, drinking wine mixed with blood, announcing gang rules, and introducing new recruits to old members. There are ten gang rules, all prohibiting (1) drug use; (2) rape and kidnapping; (3) eating free meals; (4) creating trouble; (5) cheating and fraud; (6) resisting orders; (7) robbery and theft; (8) victimizing good people; (9) compromising national interests; and (10) betraying the gang and its members.[95]

Violence between gangs and between the Four Seas' own tongs is a feature of Four Seas, with their "killers" coming from within the gangs rather than subcontracting the violence to outside hitmen.[96]

Like the Bamboo Union, Four Seas has extensive political operations. They established close relationships with politicians by helping them run for the legislature, city and council elections, town and township elections, representing ward leaders, donating money, participating in campaigns, and providing protection in return for immunity from prosecution as well as political help to expand their influence campaign activities.[97]

Yakuza

The Yakuza date back 400 years. Even though they are an important manifestation of OC, they have never been a Japanese version of the Italian Mafias:

> The yakuza are not secret societies, and aren't banned by the government. In fact, *you can find the address of each group's headquarters on the National Police Agency website. They are regulated. They have offices, business cards and corporate emblems.* There are two monthly yakuza fan magazines reporting on the groups.[98] [Emphases ours]

Historically, their alienation did not arise from the weakness or illegitimacy of the Japanese state, unlike in Italy and China. Instead, it was the result of the first Yakuza being Burakumin – social outcasts, untouchables because of their occupational status, preventing them from physical contact with other human beings. They were executioners, butchers, leather workers, and undertakers by trade – people whose daily contact with death meant that, in Buddhist and Shinto society, they were unclean.[99]

The Burakumin had been excluded from Japanese society since the 11th century, but in 1603 at the start of the Tokugawa Shogunate, they became outcasts: forced to leave major cities, sent to live in their own communities, their children denied education. Even today, people with Burakumin names find it difficult to get good jobs.

The Tokugawa Shogunate (1603–1857) intervened in the gang wars between different groups of peddlers (tekiya) between 1735 and 1749 to bring calm and to reduce the amount of fraud being practiced by creating and appointing "oyabun" or officially sanctioned bosses. The honor of carrying a sword and using a surname was extended to these "oyabun"[100] (translated it means foster-parent) to signify that they were the heads of the tekiya families.[101] *The Yakuza have been regulated ever since.*

The second group of people who became Yakuza were gamblers (bakuto), which was illegal in the Tokugawa period and remains illegal to this day:

> Even today, specific yakuza gangs may identify themselves as tekiya or bakuto, depending on how they make the majority of their money. They also retain rituals used by the earlier groups as part of their initiation ceremonies.[102]

Soon the Yakuza were well-established criminal organizations with their own customs and strict codes of loyalty, silence, and obedience. Joining the Yakuza meant more than joining a gang. It was a home for the new member and his boss became his new father. Loyalty required him in some gangs to cut ties with his biological family. This cutting of ties was part of the appeal, finding a family with members that could be brothers.[103]

Loyalty required Yakuza to cover their bodies with painfully acquired tattoos and any disloyalty would lead to them having to cut off the fingers of their left hands (starting with the little finger), weakening their ability to hold a sword, making them more dependent on their gang for protection.

For a long period, the Yakuza were tolerated by the government that valued their unique skills. The government occasionally called on them to help with military activities, including acting as bodyguards to US President Eisenhower when he visited Japan in 1960. The fact that their codes formally forbade them from stealing showed that Yakuza considered themselves "businessmen," even though their activities were not legal.

Historically, they were involved in drug-dealing, extortion, and prostitution. However, the Yakuza also traffic women. The government turned a blind eye to these activities. It was only when the Yakuza diversified into "white collar" crime in the 1980s that it cracked down on them.[104] Since 1991, when the government passed the "anti-Yakuza" law, membership has fallen, with gangs letting their members leave because they no longer have enough money to pay them to stay:

> Crackdowns have forced them to operate on a steadily reduced scale. At the start of the 1990s, crime organizations had a total of almost 70,000 members, but this had fallen to around 18,000 by the end of 2016. The Yamaguchi-gumi was dubbed "an army of 40,000," including associates, but the split has helped it dwindle to a quarter of that size.[105]

The visible part of Japan's OC has shrunk as the Yakuza adapt to a changing environment, resulting from the government's unwillingness to let Yakuza flaunt their traditions and behavior in public. As a result, Yakuza are changing how they behave publicly, moving out of some of their traditional lines of business into less visible ones, as what is, in effect, a franchise system that is being rendered obsolete.[106]

The Japanese government has never really been interested in eliminating the Yakuza; instead, it has been interested in keeping them under control and out of sight.[107] However, the effect of the 2011 ordinances has been to destroy the effectiveness of the Yakuza franchises, driving their members out of the organizations and underground:

> A yakuza boss formerly affiliated with the Sumiyoshi-kai explains, "The yakuza are a franchise. You pay your association dues to borrow the power and menace of the group – fear makes people pay you. *But if you can't use the name or the symbol, why even stay? It's like running a McDonald's without being able to use the golden arches. Better to cut expenses and leave. We're not vanishing. We're restructuring.*"[108]   [Emphasis ours]

Meanwhile, to try to change the deteriorating public perception of the Yakuza, they have practiced their Ninkyo code which forbids them to allow other people to suffer:

> In the spring of 2011, Japan was devastated by one of the most brutal tsunamis and earthquakes in the country's history.

> But then help arrived. A fleet of more than 70 trucks poured into the towns and cities of Tōhoku, filled with food, water, blankets, and everything they could possibly hope to stitch their lives back together

> *This wasn't the only time that the Yakuza had come to the rescue. After 1995's Kobe earthquake, the Yakuza had again been the first on the scene. And not long after their 2011 Tōhoku relief effort started winding down, the Yakuza sent men into the deadly Fukushima nuclear reactor to help ameliorate the situation resulting from the meltdown* that had been caused there by the tsunami as well.[109]   [Emphasis ours]

The verdict is still out regarding the purity of their motives in adopting the Ninkyo code, given that they did not treat the people well that they sent to help out in

Fukushima. They were treated as disposable: not provided with health insurance or radiation meters, and got rid of when they had received large doses of radiation. Yakuza leaders insist they were doing their best to help a society that has shunned them for nearly a thousand years, but it may be that as gangsters they just did not know any other way.[110]

1 Yamaguchi-gumi

Yamaguchi-gumi is a government designated "boryokudan" (criminal organization) with its members placed on watchlists, preventing them from taking loans or renting apartments. Founded in 1915 by former fisherman Yamaguchi Harukichi, who controlled the dispatching of Kobe dockers for his boss Oshima Hideyoshi, he broke away, taking fifty dockers with him.

> Harukichi subsequently cultivated close ties with city councilmen and used those ties to secure a commercial foothold in the *naniwabushi* world of dramatic recitation. His son and successor, Noboru, expanded the family business greatly, extending its influence into the music industry and into the realm of sumō wrestling.
>
> The Yamaguchi-gumi thus focused under its first- and second-generation leaders on more or less legal undertakings. It embarked on the criminal path that has since characterized the organization under the third-generation head, Taoka Kazuo.[111]

Taoka Kazuo took over in 1946 when the Yamaguchi-gumi had only 33 members. He was angered at the way the Taiwanese, Chinese, and Korean gangsters were running amok in defeated Japan, as if the law did not apply to them. He focused on stevedoring and entertainment as a way of countering these foreign elements. This focus on stevedoring paid off handsomely with the declaration of the Korean War and the resulting American demand for stevedoring work. Under Taoka's leadership, the Yamaguchi-gumi became the dominant force in entertainment through a ruthless policy of "carrot and stick," so that by 1975, its membership had grown to 11,000 from the 33 at the start of his reign.[112]

Based in Kobe, this is still Japan's largest criminal organization, but with only 5,200 members in 2016, despite having split into three separate organizations, all based in Kobe. The Kobe Yamaguchi-gumi, split from the original Yamaguchi-gumi in 2015 to become the third largest gang in Japan with 2,600 members, before the Ninkyo Dantai Yamaguchi-gumi broke away from it because some members were unhappy with the membership fees.[113]

In the past, such a split would have led to internecine wars. However, tightened legislation has made it difficult for Yakuza to act; and so, the leaders of the three factions in Kobe have a precarious balance of power that has undermined the traditional rules of the Yakuza world. The memories of the bitter Yama-Ichi gang war in the 1980s that occurred when 3,000 members of the Yamaguchi-gumi followed an unsuccessful claimant to lead the organization to found the now defunct Ichiwa-kai

prevented a repeat performance. Competition between the groups continues, but not through violence on the streets.[114]

2 Sumiyoshi-kai

Sumiyoshi-kai, like the Yamaguchi-gumi, is a government designated "boryokudan.". It was founded as a Tokyo-region gambler union in the early Meiji era, and is the oldest of the three Yakuza organizations. Following the end of World War II, its third supreme leader, Shigesaku Abe, expanded by attracting various gambling and racketeering groups in the Tokyo region. In 2016, it had 3,100 members.[115]

> Unlike the other two largest organizations (Yamaguchi-gumi and Inagawa-kai), the Sumiyoshi-kai operate more like a loose federation of many gangs [centered] around the Sumiyoshi-ikka, while the other two have a rigid hierarchical structure. Therefore, the inner workings of the Sumiyoshi-kai are often difficult to ascertain. Recently, the Sumiyoshi-kai has strongly advocated a peaceful route; some sources even claim that usage of handguns is prohibited. Instead, the Sumiyoshi-kai claims to be fostering friendly relations with neighboring organizations. However, the continuing gun conflicts between other organizations seems to indicate this peaceful message hasn't penetrated lower ranks, and just how fragmented the organization is.[116]

3 Inagawa-kai

Also a government designated "boryokudan," Inagawa-kai's members are placed on watchlists preventing them from taking loans or renting apartments. Founded in 1949 in Atami,[117] it is the third largest organization with 2,500 active members in 2015.[118] It is also the youngest and it drew many of its members from local bakuto (gamblers). Under the leadership of Susumu Ishii, it became known as the "business yakuza":

> Ishii expanded the Inagawa-kai's base from prostitution and gambling to include more white-collar crimes such as labor rackets and speculation fraud, even acquiring several legitimate businesses. He pioneered many of the business practices associated with the yakuza today, maintaining cordial relationships with many of the top CEOs of the country. He invested overseas and even bought a golf course, where he had various executives purchase millions in memberships. Ishii also made forays into politics. He maintained a very close relationship with former PM Junichiro Koizumi's campaign manager, who was from a district controlled by the Inagawa-kai, and is even seen pictured with Shinjiro Koizumi, Junichiro Koizumi's son and Japan's most popular politician.[119]

The Inagawa-Kai has been careful to maintain good relations with the Yamaguchi-gumi, with several of its senior members becoming blood brothers.[120]

Crime That Is Organized (CTIO)

The boundaries between OC and CTIO are blurred.[121] OC is used by politicians and the media as a powerful sound-bite, usually to advance a political agenda. Some criminologists use OC to cover all complex illicit markets: arms, drug and human trafficking, extortion, corruption, and money laundering.[122] Others argue that only arms, drugs, and human trafficking represent OC,[123] yet others believe that OC best describes extortion, corruption, and money-laundering.[124] What is clear is that both types of offenses are "serious crimes" and they need to be organized, as opposed to being spontaneous crimes of opportunity. Violence against persons to achieve monopolistic territorial control, which we believe is a key feature of OC does not apply to all types of illicit markets, such as cigarette smuggling, stolen cars, gambling, prostitution, and extortion of multinational companies.[125] However, such activities do need to be organized; hence our CTIO categorization of activities, typically undertaken by gangs:

> Gangs and their specific "culture," sometimes consisting of rituals, symbols, and the like, seem to impart a sense of identity,[126] status, and solidarity, which the use of violence and "turf wars" . . . serve to strengthen. It can be said that *gang violence is mainly of a tactical nature to achieve short-term goals, whereas criminal organizations use violence more strategically to consolidate long-term goals.*[127] . . . *Criminal organizations often emerge out of gangs . . . and may also recruit members of street gangs to spread violence or provide other services.*[128] Indeed, *there are well-structured gangs that represent quite permanent associations and professionally commit serious and even transnational crimes.*[129] It might therefore be argued that *the distinction between organized crime, gangs, and gang violence is artificial and of little use.*[130]
>
> [Emphases ours]

CTIO overlaps with OC in terms of the illicit markets it serves. The difference between the two approaches depends on characteristics of OC that do not necessarily apply to all forms of CTIO:

1. An alienated section of community based on ethnicity, clan, or family that seeks to provide protection services to its members for security of property, person, and livelihood that the state has failed to provide for them.
2. Both OC and CTIO have networks, but OC is characterized by defined command and control structures, the use of secret codes, complex initiation ceremonies, emphasis on loyalty to the organization, and the use of skilled personnel – including economists, accountants, lawyers, and technicians – and behaves like legal enterprises; whereas CTIO often brings skilled criminal technicians together for a particular crime, who then disband after it has been committed.[131]
3. Institutional survival appears to be a distinguishing feature of OC as opposed to CTIO. The three Mafia-type organizations, the Triads, and the Yakuza have long outlived their founders, unlike the Medellin and Cali cartels in Colombia that were badly damaged by the death of Pablo Escobar and the capture of the Orejualas;[132] though the imprisonment in the US of El Chapo appears not to have damaged the Sinaloa cartel in Mexico because of the relative weakness of the Mexican state.[133]

References

1 Van der Leeuw, S., and Folke, C. (2020), "The Social Dynamics of Basins of Attraction," unpublished paper, p. 11.

2 Ibid., pp. 6–7.

3 Adamoli, S. et al. (1998), "Organised Crime Around the World," *European Institute for Crime Prevention and Control* (Helsinki: Academic Bookstore), p. 9.

4 von Lampe, K. (2021), "Definitions of Organized Crime," February 16, 2021, www.organized-crime.de/organizedcrimedefinitions.htm, accessed on February 23, 2021.

5 Adamoli et al, (1998), p. 9.

6 Albini, J., and McIllwain, J. (2012), *Deconstructing Organized Crime: A Historical and Theoretical Study* (London, 2012), pp. 81–82, quoted in Dudley, S., "Conceptual Framework: Organized Crime," in "Elites and Organized Crime: Introduction, Methodology, and Conceptual Framework," *Insight Crime,* p. 22, https://idl-bnc-idrc.dspacedirect.org/bitstream/handle/10625/55845/IDL-55845.pdf, accessed on November 17, 2021.

7 Chambliss, W. (1989), "State-organized crime – The American Society of Criminology," 1988 Presidential Address. *Criminology*, 27, 1 quoted in Kramer, R. C. (2016), "State-Organized Crime, International Law and Structural Contradictions" *Crit Crim* 24, January 4, 2016, p. 234, https://doi.org/10.1007/s10612-015-9306-3, accessed on February 25, 2021.

8 Johnson, M. (2021), "Italian Mafia tightens grip on small businesses during lockdown," *Financial Times*, February 24, 2021, https://www.ft.com/content/e691bdae-ce58-4b59-aab7-9a0b2778856b, accessed on February 26, 2021.

9 Felbab-Brown, V., "Conceptualizing Crime as Competition in State-Making and Designing an Effective Response," from a speech given to the Conference on Illicit Trafficking Activities in the Western Hemisphere: Possible Strategies and Lessons Learned, 21 May 2010, quoted in Dudley, "Conceptual Framework," pp. 41–43, https://idl-bnc-idrc.dspacedirect.org/bitstream/handle/10625/55845/IDL-55845.pdf, accessed on November 17, 2021.

10 Dudley, op. cit., p. 10.

11 Ibid., p. 12.

12 Ibid., p. 23.

13 Acemoglu, D., and Robinson, J. A. (2012), *Why Nations Fail: The Origins of Power, Prosperity, and Poverty* (New York: Currency), p. 81.

14 Dudley, "Elites and Organized Crime," p. 33, https://idl-bnc-idrc.dspacedirect.org/bitstream/handle/10625/55845/IDL-55845.pdf, accessed on November 29, 2021.

15 Ibid., p. 35.

16 Naim, M. (2012), "Mafia States: Organized Crime Takes Office," *Foreign Affairs,* May/June 2012, https://www.jstor.org/stable/23217970, accessed on February 25, 2021.

17 Dudley, "Elites and Organized Crime," p. 24, https://idl-bnc-idrc.dspacedirect.org/bitstream/handle/10625/55845/IDL-55845.pdf, accessed on November 17, 2021.

18 Dudley, "Conceptual Framework," pp. 41–43, https://idl-bnc-idrc.dspacedirect.org/bitstream/handle/10625/55845/IDL-55845.pdf, accessed on November 17, 2021.

19 Ibid., p. 44.

20 Sergi, A. (2015), "Mafia and Politics as Concurrent Governance Actors. Revisiting Political Power and Crime in Southern Italy," in van Duyne, P. C., Maljević, A., Antonopoulos, G. A., Harvey, J., von Lampe, K. (eds.), *The Relativity of Wrongdoing: Corruption, Organised Crime, Fraud and Money Laundering in Perspective* (Oisterwijk: Wolf Legal Publishers), pp. 43–70.

21 Fijnaut, C., and Paoli, L., (eds) (2004), *Organised Crime in Europe: Concepts, Patterns and Control Policies in the European Union and Beyond* (Dordrecht, The Netherlands: Springer), p. 49.

22 Dudley, "Elites and Organized Crime."

23 History.com Editors (2019), Origins of the Mafia, *A&E Television Networks*, May 28, 2019, https://www.history.com/topics/crime/origins-of-the-mafia, accessed on January 22, 2021.

24 Ibid., pp. 26–27.

25 Shelley, L. I. (1994), "Review: Mafia and the Italian State: The Historical Roots of the Current Crisis," *Sociological Forum*, December 1994, 9, No. 4, Special Issue: Multiculturalism and Diversity (December 1994), p. 666, https://www.jstor.org/stable/685007, accessed on January 22, 2021.

26 History.com Editors, "Origins of the Mafia."

27 Shelley (1994), p. 668.

28 Ibid., p. 662.

29 Ibid., p. 669.

30 Ibid., p. 665.

31 Ibid., p. 669.

32 Peluso, P. (2013), "The Roots of the Organized Criminal Underworld in Campania," *Sociology and Anthropology*, 1, No. 2, p. 119, https://www.researchgate.net/publication/260834618_The_Roots_of_the_Organized_Criminal_Underworld_in_Campania/link/02e7e532781f326e95000000/download, accessed on March 3, 2021.

33 The Editors of Encyclopaedia (2011), "Camorra," *Encyclopedia Britannica*, 8 Nov. 2011, https://www.britannica.com/topic/Camorra, accessed March 3, 2021.

34 Peluso (2013), p. 119.

35 Ibid., p. 120.

36 Ibid.

37 Ibid., p. 121.

38 Sergi, A., "'Ndrangheta and Gangster Politics in Calabria. The local side of a global threat," *Centre for Criminology*, Department of Sociology, University of Essex.

39 Agence France Press (2014), "'Ndrangheta mafia 'made more money last year than McDonald's and Deutsche Bank," *The Guardian*, March 26, 2021, https://www.theguardian.com/world/2014/mar/26/ndrangheta-mafia-mcdonalds-deutsche-bank-study, accessed on November 16, 2021.

40 Ibid., p. 2.

41 Ibid., p. 6.

42 Ibid.

43 Sergi, A. (2019), "The 'Ndrangheta Down Under: Constructing the Italian Mafia in Australia," *The European Review of Organised Crime*, 5, No. 1, pp. 60–84, https://www.academia.edu/38695998/Sergi_The_Ndrangheta_Down_Under_Constructing_the_Italian_Mafia_in_Australia, accessed on March 3, 2021.

44 Sergi, A., "'Ndrangheta and Gangster Politics in Calabria," Centre for Criminology, Department of Sociology, University of Essex., pp. 6–7.

45 Ibid., pp. 7–8.

46 Johnson, "Italian Mafia."

47 Ibid., p. 8.

48 Longrigg, C. (2017), "How Totò Riina's war on the Italian state almost destroyed Cosa Nostra," *The Guardian*, November 18, 2017, https://www.theguardian.com/world/2017/nov/18/how-toto-riinas-war-on-the-italian-state-almost-destroyed-cosa-nostra, accessed on November 7, 2021.

49 Agence France Presse (2021), "Italian 'Maxi Trial' Results in Conviction of 70 'Ndrangheta Suspects," *The Guardian*, November 6, 2021, https://www.theguardian.com/world/2021/nov/06/italian-maxi-trial-results-in-conviction-of-70-ndrangheta-suspects, accessed on November 7, 2021.

50 Ibid.

51 Lo, T. W., and Kwok, S. T. (2017), "Chinese Triad Society," *Oxford Bibliographies,* September 27, 2017, https://www.oxfordbibliographies.com/view/document/obo-9780195396607/obo-9780195396607-0115.xml, accessed on March 5, 2021.

52 Ibid.

53 Purbrick (2019), "Patriotic Chinese Triads and Secret Societies: From the Imperial Dynasties, to Nationalism, and Communism," *Asian Affairs,* August 15, 2019, https://www.scienceopen.com/document?vid=a61f8c1b-d473-4032-9a6c-af2d655bb80a, accessed on March 5, 2021.

54 Ibid.

55 Ibid.

56 Ibid.

57 Ibid.

58 Special Branch, Shanghai Municipal Police, *Information on Mr. Tu Yueh-sung alias Tu Yuin,* in the Shanghai Municipal Police files, cited in ibid.

59 Ibid.

60 Ibid.

61 Maguire, K. (1997), "Modernisation and Clean Government: Tackling Crime, Corruption and Organised Crime in Modern Taiwan," *Crime, Law and Social Change,* 28, p. 75, https://link.springer.com/article/10.1023%2FA%3A1008204328221, accessed on March 11, 2021.

62 Purbrick, (2019).

63 Ibid.

64 Chu, Y. K. (2005), "Hong Kong Triads after 1997," *Trends in Organized Crime,* 8, No. 3, Spring 2005, p. 6, https://doi.org/10.1007/s12117-005-1033-9, accessed on March 8, 2021.

65 Ibid., p. 5.

66 Ibid., p. 7.

67 Kristof, N. D. (1993), "China Police Have Gang Link in Hong Kong, Official Says," *New York Times,* April 9, 1993, https://www.nytimes.com/1993/04/09/world/china-police-have-gang-link-in-hong-kong-official-says.html, accessed on June 18, 2019, quoted in ibid.

68 "Triads and China do Hong Kong Deal," *The Independent,* October 22, 2011, https://www.independent.co.uk/news/triads-and-china-do-hong-kong-deal-1261085.html, accessed on March 7, 2021.

69 Ejinsight (2014), "HK Triads Turned 'Patriotic' After 1997 Handover," December 10, 2014, http://www.ejinsight.com/20141210-hk-triads-turned-patriotic-after-1997-handover-says-michael-chan/, accessed on March 7, 2021.

70 Broadhurst, R., and Wa, L-K. (2009), "The Transformation of Triad 'Dark Societies' in Hong Kong: The Impact of Law Enforcement, Socio-Economic and Political Change," *Security Challenges,* Summer 2009, 5, No. 4 (Summer 2009), pp. 1–38, https://www.jstor.org/stable/26460067?seq=1&cid=pdf-, accessed on January 22, 2021.

71 Chu, (2005) p. 9.

72 Ibid.

73 Ibid.

74 Ibid., p. 10.

75 Ibid.

76 Ibid.

77 Ibid., p. 11.

78 Ibid.

79 Ibid.

80 Ibid.

81 Shattuck, T. J. (2017), "Taiwan's White Terror: Remembering the 228 Incident," *Foreign Policy Research Institute,* February 27, 2021, https://www.fpri.org/article/2017/02/taiwans-white-terror-remembering-228-incident/, accessed on March 10, 2021.

82 "The Bamboo Union Gang: China's Latest Weapon Against Taiwan," *Asia Sentinel,* October 6, 2017, https://www.asiasentinel.com/p/bamboo-union-gang-china-weapon-vs-taiwan, accessed on March 10, 2021.

83 National Central Police University (2005), "Organized Crime Gangs in Taiwan," *Trends in Organized Crime,* 8, No. 3, Spring, March 2005, pp. 13–23, https://doi.org/10.1007/s12117-005-1034-8, accessed on March 10, 2021.

84 Huang, H-L. (2007), "From the Asian Boyz to the Zhu Lian Bang (the Bamboo Union Gang): A Typological Analysis of Delinquent Asian Gangs," *Asian Criminology* 2, 2007, pp. 127–143, https://doi.org/10.1007/s11417-007-9033-0, accessed on March 10, 2021.

85 Kyne P. (2000), "Blood and Drugs – A Guide to the Bamboo Union," *Phnom Penh Post,* July 21, 2000, https://www.phnompenhpost.com/national/blood-drugs-guide-bamboo-union, accessed on March 10, 2021.

86 Ibid.

87 Yang, S. (2020), "Declassified Secret Documents Show Close Ties between Taiwan KMT, Bamboo Union before 1984," www.taiwannews.com.tw, June 25, 2020, https://www.taiwannews.com.tw/en/news/3953426, accessed on March 10, 2021.

88 Maguire, (1997).

89 Mathews, J., Oberdorfer, D. (1985), "Taiwan Admits Role in Murder of U.S. Author," *The Washington Post,* January 16, 1985, https://www.washingtonpost.com/archive/politics/1985/01/16/taiwan-admits-role-in-murder-of-us-author/5e98e4eb-6c60-47e7-8e51-8ac38c0d6dbf/, accessed on March 10, 2021.

90 Hille, K. (2007), "Killer's death haunts Taiwan party," *The Financial Times,* November 2, 2007, https://web.archive.org/web/20110711045920/http://us.ft.com/ftgateway/superpage.ft?news_id=fto110220071519221533, accessed on March 10, 2021.

91 Liu, W. L. (2007), "Death of a Triad Boss," *Time,* November 12, 2007, https://world.time.com/2007/11/12/death_of_a_triad_boss/, accessed on March 10, 2021.

92 Chung, L. (2007), "Grand mafia-style funeral for boss of Taiwanese gang," *South China Morning Post,* October 19, 2007, https://web.archive.org/web/20170405171448/http:/www.scmp.com/article/612105/grand-mafia-style-funeral-boss-taiwanese-gang, accessed on March 10, 2021.

93 Chang, R. (2007), "The Rise and Fall of Crime Boss Chen Chi-Li," *Taipei Times,* October 22, 2007, http://www.taipeitimes.com/News/taiwan/archives/2007/10/22/2003384236, accessed on March 10, 2020.

94 National Central Police University (2005), p.21.

95 Ibid., p. 22.

96 Ibid.

97 Ibid., p. 23.

98 Adelstein, J. (2017), "Opinion: Japan's Yakuza aren't Disappearing. They're Getting Smarter," *The Washington Post,* April 9, 2017, https://www.washingtonpost.com/news/global-opinions/wp/2017/04/08/japans-yakuza-arent-disappearing-theyre-getting-smarter/, accessed on March 4, 2021.

99 Oliver, M. (2020), "Inside the Yakuza: The 400-Year-Old Japanese Criminal Syndicate," July, 16, 2020, https://allthatsinteresting.com/yakuza-history, accessed on January 22, 2021.

100 Ibid., p. 1.

101 Szczepanski, K. (2019), "History of Japanese Organized Crime, the Yakuza," *ThoughtCo,* July 17, 2019, https://www.thoughtco.com/the-yakuza-organized-crime-195571, accessed on March 4, 2021.

102 Ibid.

103 Ibid., p. 2.

104 Ibid., p. 3.

105 Power News (2017), "Fragmented Yamaguchi-gumi a Sign of Changing Yakuza Times," *Society,* September 4, 2017, https://www.nippon.com/en/features/c04201/, accessed on March 4, 2021.

106 Adelstein (2017).

107 Ibid.

108 Ibid.

109 Oliver (2020).

110 Ibid., p. 5.

111 Kenji, I. (2015), "Yamaguchi-gumi Split Signals Changes in the Yakuza World," *Society*, December 7, 2015, https://www.nippon.com/en/currents/d00205/, accessed on March 4, 2021.

112 Ibid.

113 Power News (2017).

114 Kenji (2015).

115 Power News (2017).

116 "Sumiyoshi-kai," *The Yakuza: Pinkyless and Tattooed,* December 14, 2015, https://yakuzahistory.wordpress.com/sumiyoshi-kai/, accessed on March 4, 2021.

117 "Inagawa-kai," *The Yakuza: Pinkyless and Tattooed,* December 14, 2015, https://yakuzahistory.wordpress.com/inagawa-kai/, accessed on March 4, 2021.

118 Power News (2017).

119 "Inagawa-kai, op. cit."

120 Ibid.

121 Woodiwiss, M., and Hobbs, D. (2009), "Organized Evil and the Atlantic Alliance: Moral Panics and the Rhetoric of Organized Crime Policing in America and Britain," *British Journal of Criminology*, 49, pp. 106–128, cited in Hauck, P., and Peterke, S. (2010), "Organized Crime and Gang Violence in National and International Law," *International Review of the Red Cross,* 92, No. 878, June 2010, p. 408, https://www.icrc.org/en/doc/assets/files/other/irrc-878-hauck-peterke.pdf, accessed on March 3, 2021.

122 Wright, A. (2006), *Organised Crime* (Cullompton, Devon/Portland, Oregon: Willan Publishing), p. 49, cited in ibid., p. 409.

123 van Dijk, J. (2007), "Mafia Markers: Assessing Organized Crime and its Impact on Societies," in *Trends in Organized Crime*, 10, p. 40, cited in ibid., p. 409.

124 Buscaglia, B., and van Dijk, J. (2003), "Controlling Organized Crime and Corruption in the Public Sector," *Forum on Crime and Society*, 3, Nos. 1 and 2, 2003, cited in ibid., p. 409.

125 Naylor, T. R. (2009).

126 Siegel, L. J., and Welsh, B. C. (2009*), Juvenile Delinquency: Theory, Practice, and Law* (California: Wadsworth) pp. 312–315; Morash, M. (1989), "Gangs, Groups and Delinquency," in *British Journal of Criminology*, 23, No. 4, 1989, pp. 309–331, cited in ibid., p. 412.

127 Decker, S. H., and van Winkle, B. (1996), *Life in the Gang: Family, Friends, and Violence* (Cambridge, Cambridge University Press), pp. 23–25; cited in ibid., p. 412.

128 Ianni, F. A., with Reuss-Ianni, E. (1972), *A Family Business: Kinship and Social Control in Organized Crime* (New York: Russel Sage Foundation), p. 53, cited in ibid., p. 412.

129 Franco, C. (2008), "The MS–13 and 18th Street Gangs: Emerging Transnational Threats?" *CRS Report for Congress* (Washington, D.C.: Congressional Research Service), p. 6; cited in ibid., p. 410.

130 Hauck and Peterke (2010), p. 412.

131 Williams, P. (2002), "Transnational Criminal Networks," in Aquilla, J., and David F. Ronfeld, D. F. (eds), *Netwars and Networks: The Future of Terror, Crime, and Militancy* (Santa Monica, CA, 2001: RAND), p. 65; UNODC (2002), *Global Programme against Transnational Organized Crime: Results of a Pilot Survey of Forty Selected Organized Criminal Groups in Sixteen Countries* (Geneva: United Nations Office on Drugs and Crime), p. 30, cited in ibid., p. 412.

132 Woody, C. (2017), "Pablo Escobar's Death Cleared the Way for a Much More Sinister Kind of Criminal in Colombia," *Insider,* March 28, 2017, https://www.businessinsider.com/colombia-criminal-cartel-world-changes-after-pablo-escobar-was-killed-2017-2, accessed on March 3, 2021.
133 Garcia, D. A. (2019), "In Mexico, El Chapo's Sons Add Brash New Chapter to Crime Family," *Reuters,* October 23, 2019, https://www.reuters.com/article/us-mexico-violence-sinaloa-feature-idUSKBN1X12RD, accessed on March 3, 2021.

Chapter 3
The Criminal Harm Continuum

Attitudes to criminality and crime reflect the harm and damage it causes to groups and individuals. Perceived harm is related to the cost of the damage in pecuniary or social terms, and the greater the revulsion people experience. Revulsion is expressed in the severity of the punishments assigned to crimes. Mitigating circumstances (whether crimes were premeditated or committed on the spur of the moment, and whether perpetrators could be expected to understand the impact of their actions) play a part in deciding what sanctions are imposed in particular societies. Just as there is a crime continuum of how crimes are committed (see Chapters 1 and 2), there is a criminal harm continuum that reflects the perceived severity of crimes.

The continuum of criminal harm ranges from threatening existential harm to the state, through a breakdown in law and order, and to the economic, social, and environmental costs resulting from actions undertaken by criminals and organizations, and how they are organized. National differences can mean that in one jurisdiction actions are criminal and in another they are not, primarily because the perception of harm differs.

Political authority can only be maintained consensually when a significant majority of the total community agrees on the basic principles of a regime, a shared ideology reflecting interlocking values, interests, and beliefs. These agreements are often based on ancient customs, religion, common historical experience, and fears of dislocation or a common enemy. The coming together of these elements is the basis of patriotism; and it is this agreement that civil wars destroy.[1] This explains why governments spend time and effort to strengthen a sense of ideological attachment to their rule through education and the provision of law and order. Education reinforces social cohesion and support for authority via religious education (in theocracies) or class-based education (as in England), or secular education based on the written constitution (as in the US).[2] Civil wars fracture the institutions of law and order and the assumptions underlying the educational system in a way that interstate wars do not. The winning side are "patriots" and the losers are "traitors," and in such a binary situation both sides have every incentive to fight. As Sir John Harington observed in Elizabethan times:

> Treason doth never prosper; What's the reason?
>
> For if it prosper, none dare call it treason.[3]

Breakdown in Law and Order

Hobbes illustrated in *Leviathan* the compact people have with the state; in return for surrendering their freedom to compete without limitation, the state will provide

https://doi.org/10.1515/9783110712155-003

law, order, and enforcement to allow subjects to enjoy the fruits of their labor. If the sovereign (the state) fails in its fundamental duty, it forfeits the loyalty of its subjects.[4]

In Chapter 2, we saw how the state and OC are rival providers of law, order, and enforcement. Where the state is weak, corrupt or absent, OC steps in to take over the role of providing security of the person, protection of property, and settlement of disputes. Where the state is strong, transparent, and present, there is little scope for OC to flourish.

Preserving the authority of the state requires an administration capable of imposing its jurisdiction on every part of the national territory. Achieving this involves maintaining good communications, employing police forces capable of controlling demonstrations, responding swiftly to crimes against property and person, through a justice system that provides timely and transparent decisions. How the police and the justice system operate reflects the character of the regime and whether the public is served and protected,[5] or oppressed and terrorized (as in the examples of Nazi Germany's Brownshirts, known as the "battering ram" of the Nazis,[6] or Lenin's Cheka, responsible for the "Red Terror" of 1918-22,[7] the Soviet NKVD responsible for carrying out Stalin's "White Terror in 1937-8,[8] and the current Russian FSB that botched poisoning Alexei Navalny[9]).

There have been times when the state and OC have worked together to ensure stability in the face of rapid change or political upheaval (see Chapter 2). However, there are limits to state toleration of its OC competitor. Whenever OC presents an existential threat to the establishment, the establishment has fought back and crushed the ambitions of OC—for example, in China, Hong Kong, Japan, and in Italy during Mussolini's rule and more recently with the dismantling of the Cosa Nostra in the 1990s[10] and the current maxi-trials in Calabria targeting the 'Ndrangheta.[11] OC has not always been beaten back by the state, that clearly has not been the case in Mexico where despite the government using the army in their battle with the cartels in Northern Mexico, the corruption of the police and polity has led to a stalemate.[12]

The definition of the laws and the kind of order to be maintained and its limits are in the hands of the state, but this power can be used criminally to suppress all dissent. The avoidance of inconvenience is not considered by the Universal Declaration of Human Rights to be a sufficient justification for the erosion of fundamental rights, however annoying processions, demonstrations, and protests might be to the majority. The practice of maintaining public order sits on a continuum from totalitarian, criminal suppression of human rights in the name of law and order (as practiced by Hitler's Brown Shirts, Lenin's Cheka, Stalin's NKVD, and Putin's FSB at one extreme), and Machiavelli's endorsement of the Roman Republic's contentious and noisy political process[13].

Governments usually seek a balance between restricting freedoms in the name of law and order and ensuring that the system allows citizens to enjoy the fruits of their labors and to pursue their own goals without harming others. Law-and-order enforcement is complicated because one person's terrorist is another's freedom fighter, turning legitimate enforcement into a provocation and a potential cause for further violence, as happened in France in May 1968's student riots, with unforeseen long-term consequences.[14] It may result in civil war when mishandled by the establishment, as in Syria in 2011.[15] Illegitimate enforcement, as in the repression of protests after election results have been ignored, as in Belarus[16] or Myanmar[17] is the behavior of "criminal" governments.

Economic Harm

The economic harms of criminal behavior manifest across a continuum, ranging from economic losses caused by wars and civil wars, to the costs of bribery and corruption, and the costs of illegal activities of OC. The economic harm continuum extends from harms caused by criminal activities to those that are caused by harmful legal, but immoral, activities.

Wars

In addition to the humanitarian costs of interstate wars and civil wars, there are economic costs. Attempts have been made, notably by Glick and Taylor, to quantify the costs of wars. Although estimates suffer from problems of data availability and the assumptions that have to be made, they do offer some insight into the magnitude of financial harm caused. The financial harms fall disproportionately on the losers in war.

Glick and Taylor estimated the negative economic impacts of World Wars I and II on world trade as follows:

> In the case of WWI, war among adversaries reduced world trade by roughly 12% in 1914–1915 and by almost 15% in 1916–1918; the effects then dampened monotonically. The impact on neutrals reduced world trade by an additional 5–6% in the period 1914–18.

In the case of WWII, war among adversaries reduced world trade by 15% in 1941 and by almost 20% in 1945, as more countries entered the war. The impact on neutrals accounts for a fall off in trade of an additional 8–9% during 1939–41; this effect then decays as the United States and other countries shift from neutral to belligerent status.[18]

World War I and World War II had serious negative economic effects on international trade. World War I's impact was greater than that of World War II because the world economy was much more globally interdependent in 1913 than it was in 1939, shown in Tables 3.1 and 3.2.

Table 3.1: World War I Impact on International Trade.

Trade Loss	Globally (%)	Combatants (%)	Neutrals (%)
With combatants			
a. Permanent flow loss of trade	**1.21**	4.87	1.61
b. Permanent flow loss of GDP	**2.22**	2.28	2.09
With Neutrals			
a. Permanent flow loss of trade	**1.33**	1.61	—
b. Permanent flow loss of GDP	**0.33**	0.46	—
Total trade losses			
a. Permanent flow loss of trade	**2.54**	6.48	1.61
b. Permanent flow loss of GDP	**2.55**	2.74	2.09

Source: Based on Glick, R., and Taylor, A. M., (2005), "Collateral Damage: Trade Disruption and the Economic Impact of War," Working Paper, *Federal Reserve Bank of San Francisco*, p.41, https://www.frbsf.org/economic-research/files/wp05-11bk.pdf, accessed on March 24, 2021.

Table 3.2: World War II Impact on International Trade.

Trade Loss	Globally (%)	Combatants (%)	Neutrals (%)
With combatants			
a. Permanent flow loss of trade	**1.57**	6.30	2.13
b. Permanent flow loss of GDP	**1.24**	1.27	0.36
With Neutrals			
a. Permanent flow loss of trade	**1.99**	2.13	—
b. Permanent flow loss of GDP	**0.30**	0.36	—
Total trade losses			
a. Permanent flow loss of trade	**3.56**	8.43	1.99
b. Permanent flow loss of GDP	**1.54**	1.64	0.30

Source: Glick and Taylor (2005), p. 43.

The disruption to global trade caused by the collapse of the pre-World War I global economy was exacerbated by protectionist and autarkic policies adopted by major trading nations after the 1929 crash.[19]

They estimated that output after World War I as a percentage of global GDP fell by 3.4% and after World War II by nearly twice as much at 6.6% as a result of extensive collateral damage caused by the targeting of non-battlefield assets (cities, industrial capacity, and civilians), whereas World War I focused on battlefields. The extent of the impact in lost future GDP varied considerably by country, though the US appears to have been relatively untouched by either war.

The latest estimates, for 2016, from the World Economic Forum estimate the cost of conflict at $14.3 trillion a year for the global economy. This spending breaks down as follows: military $5.6 trillion, internal security $4.9 trillion, losses from conflict $1.0 trillion, and from crime and interpersonal violence $2.6 trillion.[20] If such costs could be reduced, the opportunity to spend more on pro-social projects, such as health, environmental issues, or education, would rise.

Civil Wars

Major civil wars have proved expensive to losers even where there is a strong moral imperative underlying the conflict:

1 Thirty Years War (1618–1648)
The Thirty Years War in Germany led to the death of 20% of the German population, and in the corridor from Pomerania to the Black Forest to the death of 50% of the population.[21]

2 American Civil War (1861–1865)
In the American Civil War, based on the latest estimates, between 752,000 and 851,000 soldiers were killed, roughly two percent of the American population.[22] It should be remembered that for every three soldiers killed, another five died of disease during the war,[23] bringing the total possible number of deaths to 2.0–2.3 million, or roughly 3.2 percent of the American population.

3 Spanish Civil War (1936–1939)
Recent estimates put the total dead from the Spanish Civil War at 500,000. There were war crimes on both sides. The dead represented 3.3% and the wounded 7.5% of the Spanish population.[24,25]

4 *Korean War* (1950–1953)
By the time the Korean War armistice was signed in July 1953, some 5 million soldiers and civilians had died. Nearly 10,000 North and South Korean troops died in border skirmishes before the war started. By the time the fighting ended, 2.5 million of the dead were civilians, representing 10% of Korea's pre-war population.[26] In the short term, the war destroyed the economies of both the North and South,[27] although the South recovered quickly. The unending state of truce has led to levels of continued military spending in the North that might be better deployed elsewhere—

North Korea spent 21.9–24.4% of its GDP on its military in 2007–2017[28] (South Korea spent 2.7% of its GDP in 2019[29]).

5 *Vietnam War* (1954–1975)

The Vietnam War cost the Vietnamese 3,350,000 lives: 2,000,000 civilians in the North and South, 1,100,000 North Vietnamese and Vietcong troops, and between 200-250,000 South Vietnamese troops;[30] as well as the Americans' 58,220 lives.[31] The economic costs of the war were $843.6 billion (in 2019 dollars) or 2.3% of GDP spent by the Americans and peak US inflation of 6.1% in 1969,[32] and it destroyed the trust Americans had in their government.[33] The war spilled over into Laos and Cambodia so that casualties were higher still. Between 1965 and 1973, 1 in 30 Indochinese were killed, 1 in 12 wounded and 1 in 5 became a refugee (14,305,000 people).[34]

6 Lebanese Civil War (1975–1990)

After fifteen years of fighting, the Lebanese Second Republic was established. The cost to the Lebanese was more than 100,000 dead, nearly one million displaced out of a population of around four million, and several billion dollars' worth of damage to property and infrastructure.[35] The long-term harm to Lebanese institutions is reflected in the government's inability to govern effectively, demonstrated most obviously by its failure to provide a functioning economy,[36] inability to deal with the impact of the Covid-19 pandemic,[37] and its incompetence to deal with the consequences of the Beirut port explosion in 2020.[38] Lebanon has lost its reputation for being the "pearl of the Mediterranean."

7 *Syrian Civil War* (2011–ongoing)

By 2019, after eight years of fighting, the damage from the Syrian Civil War was estimated as 511,000 Syrians killed or missing,[i,39] of which civilians killed or missing were 204,911;[40] 13,145,000 displaced (62.4% of the total population), 6,495,000 internally and 6,650,000 were refugees outside Syria in: Turkey (3,586,070),[ii,41] Lebanon (1,500,000),[42] Jordan (666,294),[43] Germany (532,000),[44] Iraq (253,000),[45] Egypt

---

i The latest 2021 estimates suggest that the death toll is more likely to be 600,000. Anadolu Agency (2021), "Syrian Civil War Cost More than $1.2 trillion: Aid Group," *Daily Sabah*, March 5, 2021, https://www.dailysabah.com/world/syrian-crisis/syrian-civil-war-cost-more-than-12-trillion-aid-group, accessed on March 20, 2021.

ii Syrian refugees represented 21.8% of Lebanon's population, 10.7% of Jordan's population, and 5.1% of Turkey's population, creating severe stresses for the host countries and desperate poverty and poor working conditions for the refugees themselves. Christopherson, E. (2020), "These ten countries receive the most refugees," *Norwegian Refugee Council*, November 1, 2020, https://www.nrc.no/perspectives/2020/the-10-countries-that-receive-the-most-refugees/, accessed on March 20, 2021.

(133,000),[46] Sweden (109,000),[47] and Austria (49,000).[48] Although Syria accounts for less than one percent of the world's population, Syrians make up nearly one-third of the world's refugees.[49]

So far, the war has cost more than $1.2 trillion and there are estimated future costs of US$ 41.4 trillion through to 2035. If the additional remedial health and education costs for displaced children (40% of those displaced) is taken into account, the cost rises to US$ 41.7 trillion.[50]

Financial Harm

Financial criminal harm covers: fraud, bribery, corruption, and money laundering.

Fraud

Fraud is "a knowing misrepresentation of the truth or concealment of a material fact to induce another to act to his or her detriment."[51] Fraud can be committed internally by employees, also known as "occupational fraud," or externally by customers, suppliers, or other third parties. "Occupational fraud" occurs when a person uses their occupation for personal enrichment by misusing, or misapplying, organizational resources and/or assets.[52]

External fraud comes in many forms: dishonest vendors might collaborate in bid-rigging tenders, or charge for goods and services that have not been provided or are of inferior quality; dishonest customers might use bad checks or false accounts when paying, or return stolen, knock-off, or used products for refunds. Other types of external fraud include hacking, theft of intellectual property, and tax, bankruptcy, insurance, and healthcare frauds. Criminals defraud individuals through Ponzi schemes, identity theft, and advanced-fee frauds.[53]

The estimated total cost of fraud has risen by 56% in the period 1997–2018 to reach £130 billion each year in the UK alone, and globally to £3.9 trillion (US$ 5.127 trillion), equivalent to 6.05% of global GDP.[54] Since 2008, average company losses have risen from 4.57% to 7.15%. The average organization should expect losses to be between 3% and 6% but can go as high as 10%.[55]

Bribery

The definition of bribery is "the offering, giving, soliciting, or receiving of any item of value as a means of influencing the actions of an individual holding a public or legal duty. This type of action results in matters that should be handled objectively being handled in a manner best suiting the private interests of the briber. Generally, bribery constitutes a crime and both the offeror and the recipient can be criminally charged."[56] Bribery takes a number of forms: kickbacks, secret commissions, facilitation payments, influence peddling, and electoral bribery.[57]

1. *Kickbacks* are paid by companies to secure profitable contracts or contracts on favorable terms. Part of the benefit from the contract is paid (or "kicked back") to the decision maker granting the contract. The organization granting the contract is not aware of the payment to its official.[58]

2. *Secret commissions* occur when an agent requests or accepts a payment to influence contracts for the benefit of the payer, without the knowledge or consent of their principal. This may be to secure a contract, to gain favorable terms, or even to prevent a contract being entered into with a competitor.[59]

3. *Facilitation payments* are made to a government official in order to encourage or ensure that the official performs his or her normal duties in processing documents or advancing a file quickly. In many countries, facilitation payments are legal and treated as the "cost of doing business."[60]

4. *Influence peddling* occurs where officials look for payment to use their influence to secure an undue advantage or favor for the payer. It also occurs when payers ask officials to use their influence to obtain an unfair advantage in return for the consideration. It is rare in business contracts, but often happens with politicians.[61]

5. *Electoral bribery* is a crime in some countries if a donation has been made to promote a political party of candidate with the intent of influencing the result of an election in the hope of retaining or securing a commercial advantage.[62] The difference between this and legal lobbying or providing political donations, as practiced in the US, for example, seems rather blurred.

The problem with bribery is that the individual who receives the bribe is incentivized to make a decision that may not be in the best interests of his or her employer.

In a sense, there is no difference in objectives between paying extra to get better service from flying first class and paying a bribe to expedite the treatment of documents. Both aim to jump the queue. The difference lies in the transparency of the former and the opacity of the latter. In the former case, there is a published service level agreement in return for the extra payment, and the money goes to the airline. In the latter case, there is no guarantee of "specific performance" and the money goes to the individual rather than the organization which may in addition incur extra costs to do what the briber is asking for, being harmed twice as a result of receiving less income and paying more to deliver it.

Based on World Bank estimates, bribes paid globally totalled US$ 1 trillion.[63]

Corruption

According to Transparency International:

> Corruption is the abuse of entrusted power for private gain. It can be classified as grand, petty and political, depending on the amounts of money lost and the sector where it occurs.
>
> Grand corruption consists of acts committed at a high level of government that distort policies or the central functioning of the state, enabling leaders to benefit at the expense of the public good. Petty corruption refers to everyday abuse of entrusted power by low- and mid-level public officials in their interactions with ordinary citizens, who often are trying to access basic goods or services in places like hospitals, schools, police departments and other agencies.
>
> Political corruption is a manipulation of policies, institutions and rules of procedure in the allocation of resources and financing by political decision makers, who abuse their position to sustain their power, status and wealth.[64]

Transparency International goes on to explain the economic harms of corruption:

> *Economically, corruption depletes national wealth.* Corrupt politicians invest scarce public resources in projects that will line their pockets rather than benefit communities, and prioritise high-profile projects such as dams, power plants, pipelines and refineries over less spectacular but more urgent infrastructure projects such as schools, hospitals and roads. *Corruption also hinders the development of fair market structures and distorts competition, which in turn deters investment.*[65]   [Emphases ours]

From an economic perspective, corruption does harm in the following ways: It *increases the costs of doing business.*

> The costs are not just financial. Corruption brings with it risks of prosecution, penalties, black-listing, and reputation damage. It distorts market mechanisms, rewarding inefficiency, stifling growth, investments, and future growth. IMF research shows that there is almost five percent less investment in countries deemed to be corrupt and the World Economic Forum estimates corruption increases the cost of doing business by up to 10 percent on average.[66]

It also leads to waste and inefficient use of scarce resources. Corruption leads to poor value for money, misallocation of resources, deliberately slowed down approval processes, and nepotism; all of which undermine the effectiveness of the state, and enterprises:

> "Investments are not allocated to sectors and programmes which present the best value for money or where needs are highest, but to those which offer the best prospects for personal enrichment of corrupt politicians. Thus, *resources go into big infrastructure projects or military procurement where kickbacks are high, to the detriment of sectors like education and health care.* Moreover, public tenders are assigned to the highest bribe payer, neglecting better qualified companies not willing to bribe, *which undermines the quality of the projects carried out.* In some instances, *public funds are simply diverted from their intended use, embezzled and exploited for private enrichment.* Corruption also slows down bureaucratic processes, as *inefficient bureaucracies offer more leverage for corrupt public officials: the longer the queue for a*

service, the higher the incentive for citizens to bribe to get what they want. Finally, nepotism—in both private and public organisations—*brings incompetent people into power*, weakening performance and governance.[67]   [Emphases ours]

Table 3.3 lists the ways in which corruption creates direct and indirect economic costs:

Table 3.3: Direct and Indirect Costs Created by Corruption.

Source of Loss/Damage	Project owner	Project funder	Suppliers
Theft/Waste of project funds	✓		✓
Increased price of project	✓	✓	✓
Increased maintenance, repair, and replacement	✓		
Additional finance costs	✓	✓	✓
Bribes paid	✓	✓	✓
Reduced operating profit	✓	✓	✓
Increased operating costs	✓		✓
Loss of business opportunities and investment	✓	✓	✓
Damages for civil liability	✓	✓	✓
Fines for criminal liability	✓	✓	✓
Legal fees	✓	✓	✓
Loss and damage to officers and employees	✓	✓	✓
Reputation damage	✓	✓	✓

Source: Based on "Cost of Corruption," *Global Infrastructure Anti-Corruption Centre*, https://giac centre.org/the-cost-of-corruption/, accessed on March 24, 2021.

Money Laundering

It is noteworthy that "money laundering" has only recently become a crime; an example of the changing definitions of "crime." According to the following definition by the European Commission:

> Money laundering includes the following:
> 1. The conversion or transfer of property, knowing that such property is derived from criminal activity or from an act of participation in such activity, for the purpose of concealing or disguising the illicit origin of the property or of assisting any person who is involved in the commission of such activity to evade the legal consequences of his action
> 2. The concealment or disguise of the true nature, source, location, disposition, movement, rights with respect to, or ownership of property, knowing that such property is derived from criminal activity or from an act of participation in such activity
> 3. The acquisition, possession or use of property, knowing, at the time of receipt, that such property was derived from criminal activity or from an act of participation in such activity
> 4. Participation in, association to commit, attempts to commit and aiding, abetting, facilitating and counselling the commission of any of the actions mentioned above.[68]

Typical criminal money laundering activities are shown in Table 3.4.

Table 3.4: Typical Criminal Money Laundering Activities.

Organized crime and racketeering	– Drugs – Prostitution – Sexual exploitation of minors – Kidnap and ransom – Blackmail and extortion – Theft, burglary, and robbery
Trafficking	– Arms – Stolen goods – Human trafficking, smuggling immigrants, and refugees – Smuggling
Financial crime	– Insider trading and market manipulation – Tax evasion – Fraud – Forgery – Exchange control evasion – Counterfeiting currency – Bribery and corruption

Source: Based on: Black Sea Trade and Development Bank (2020), *Anti-Fraud, Corruption, Money Laundering and Terrorism Financing Policy and Domiciliation of BSTDB Counterparties,* p.18, October 29, 2020, https://www.bstdb.org/Antifraud_pol icy.pdf, accessed on March 25, 2021.

Money laundering has three steps:[69]
1. *Placement:* Funds are deposited in a financial institution or cash is converted into negotiable instruments. To disguise criminal activity, launderers route cash through a front operation—a business such as a check cashing service or jeweler. Another option is to convert cash into negotiable instruments such as cashier's checks, money orders, or traveler's checks.
2. *Layering:* This involves the wire transfer of funds through a series of accounts in order to hide the true source of the money. This often means transferring funds to countries with strict banking secrecy laws. Once deposited in a bank in such a country, the funds can be moved through the accounts of shell companies which exist just to launder money. The huge daily volumes of wire transfers make it difficult for law enforcement agencies to track the laundered money as it moves from one account to the next.
3. *Integration:* This involves moving the layered funds into the regular financial world, once they are no longer traceable to their original criminal source. They are then mixed with funds whose source is legitimate. At this point, the launderer can invest the funds in legitimate business ventures, real estate, or luxury assets.

In The Global Threat Assessment report on money laundering in 2020, it was estimated that financial crime had risen from US\$ 2.1 trillion or 3.4% of global GDP to
US\$ 5.8 trillion or 6.7% of global GDP in 2018.[70] Money laundering alone had risen
from US\$ 1.6 trillion in 2009 to US\$ 4.4 trillion in 2018, of which OC was responsible
for a rise from US\$ 0.87 trillion in 2009 to US\$ 2.4 trillion by 2018. The top five
countries reporting money laundering were the US, Germany, Canada, Japan, and
the UK, in that order, accounting for 53% of the total financial crime in 2018, with
the next fifteen countries generating 27%, and the rest of the world 20%.[71]

Criminal Economic Harm

Criminal economic harms are substantial and various, shown earlier in Table 3.4.
Data collected between 2009 and 2015 estimated annual global economic harm created by these activities totaled US\$ 1,213.9 billion; broken down into counterfeit prod-
ucts (US\$ 541.3 billion), drugs (US\$ 411.62 billion), prostitution (US\$ 186.0 billion),
illegal gambling (US\$ 140.0 billion), piracy and theft (US\$ 131.53 billion), and trafficking and human smuggling (US\$ 57.3 billion).[72]

   This does not include the cost of cybercrime which was expected to exceed US\$
1 trillion in 2020.[73] Nor does it include the economic domino effects of the activities
involved in terms of the costs incurred in public health and lost productivity as a
result of sickness, the cost of law-and-order enforcement, the loss in tax revenues
to the state, or the lost productivity caused by defective counterfeit products.

Social Harm

Social harm is caused by organized crime, the shadow economy, and legal, but immoral behavior (see Chapter 5).

Organized Crime

The harms caused by OC are political, legal, public-health-related, and environmental. They impact both society and individuals. Chapter 2 showed the extent to which
OC has, at times, had a symbiotic relationship with the political process. It also has
an indirect effect on the political process as a consequence of political concerns
about OC involvement in illicit drugs, smuggling immigrants, and financial crime.[74]

   The main anxiety expressed about the harm OC inflicts on the political process
is concerned with the corrosive effect of corruption and influence peddling:

On the political front, corruption is a major obstacle to democracy and the rule of law. In a democratic system, offices and institutions lose their legitimacy when they're misused for private advantage. This is harmful in established democracies, but even more so in newly emerging ones. It is extremely challenging to develop accountable political leadership in a corrupt climate[75]

OC attempts to influence the political process by the use of corruption or violence to get laws changed—either by targeting politicians associated with the laws, or by attempting to ensure the election of a political party sympathetic to the objectives of OC, as has been the case in Sicily since the end of World War II.[76]

Corruption impacts societies in a multitude of ways. In the worst cases, it costs lives. Short of this, it costs people their freedom, health or money. The cost of corruption can be divided into four main categories: political, economic, social and environmental.

Corruption corrodes the social fabric of society. It undermines people's trust in the political system, in its institutions and its leadership. A distrustful or apathetic public can then become yet another hurdle to challenging corruption.[77]   [Emphasis ours]

The rise of "Mafia states" since the Global Financial Crisis (GFC) and the collapse of the Soviet Union is a worrying new development. In some jurisdictions, politicians and OC have come together to create a new type of actor in which senior government officials are key players in criminal enterprises, and where defending the interests of such enterprises becomes a state priority.[78]

Indeed, top positions in some of the world's most profitable illicit enterprises are no longer filled only by professional criminals; they now include senior government officials, legislators, spy chiefs, heads of police departments, military officers, and, in some extreme cases, even heads of state or their family members.[79]

The scale and scope of OC supported by "Mafia states" now match that of the largest multinational corporations. This increased access to the power of state organs is new. Government officials and criminals often work together through legal business conglomerates with ties to political leaders, their families, and friends, leading to them holding controlling interests in strategic sectors of the national and, in some cases, the global economy, for example in aluminum, nickel, and natural gas.[80]

Shadow Economy

In 2018, the global shadow economy was estimated to typically represent 31.9% of the GDP of 158 countries in the world.[81] It includes:

all economic activities which are hidden from official authorities for monetary, regulatory, and institutional reasons. *Monetary reasons include avoiding paying taxes and all social security contributions, regulatory reasons include avoiding governmental bureaucracy or the burden of regulatory framework, while institutional reasons include corruption law, the quality of political institutions and weak rule of law.* For our study, the shadow economy reflects mostly legal economic and productive activities that, if recorded, would contribute to national GDP, therefore the definition of the shadow economy in our study tries to avoid illegal or criminal activities, do-it-yourself, or other household activities.[82]   [Emphasis ours]

In the 31 European countries covered in the research, the shadow economy—that is, untaxed economic activity, which includes illegal activities (on average)—represented 17.1% of recorded GDP; Switzerland being the lowest at 6.0% and Bulgaria being the highest at 29.6%. After making allowances for criminal activities, and DIY, and other household activities, the size of the shadow economy was estimated at 11.1% on average; Switzerland falling to 3.9% and Bulgaria to 19.2%.[83]

The substantial illegal activities in the shadow economy are made possible by:

the actions of average members of society: for example, the millions of citizens involved in China's counterfeit consumer-goods industry and in Afghanistan's drug trade, the millions of Westerners who smoke marijuana regularly, the hundreds of thousands of migrants who every year hire criminals to smuggle them to Europe, and the well-to-do professionals in Manhattan and Milan who employ illegal immigrants as nannies and housekeepers. *Ordinary people such as these are an integral part of the criminal ecosystem.*[84]   [Emphases ours]

References

1 Heslop, D. A. (2020), "Political System: The Functions of Government," *Encyclopedia Britannica*, 30 Oct. 2020, https://www.britannica.com/topic/political-system, accessed on March 22, 2021.
2 Ibid.
3 Harington, J., *Epigrams*, https://www.britannica.com/biography/John-Harington -:~:text=Treason doth never prosper%3A what's,none dare call it treason, accessed on March 14, 2021.
4 Hobbes, T. (1651) (London: Penguin Classics, 1968).
5 Heslop (2020).
6 "Stormtroopers: A New History of Hitler's Brownshirts," *Military History,* November 30, 2018, https://www.military-history.org/books/stormtroopers-a-new-history-of-hitlers-brownshirts.htm, accessed on March 22, 2021.
7 Walker, S. (2017), "Stalin's Secret Police Finally Named but Killing Still Not Seen as Crimes," *The Guardian*, February, 6, 2017, https://www.theguardian.com/world/2017/feb/06/stalin-secret-police-killings-crimes-russia-terror-nkvd, accessed on March 22, 2021.
8 Blakemore, E. (2020), "How the Red Terror Set a Macabre Course for the Soviet Union," *National Geographic*, September 3, 2020, https://www.nationalgeographic.com/history/article/red-terror-set-macabre-course-soviet-union, accessed on March 22, 2021.
9 Antanova, N. (2021), "Russia's Security Agencies Are Both Terrifying and Incompetent," *FP News*, January 15, 2021, https://foreignpolicy.com/2021/01/15/russia-security-agencies-terrifying-incompetent-fsb/, accessed on March 22, 2021.
10 Longrigg, C. (2017), "How Totò Riina's War on the Italian State Almost Destroyed Cosa Nostra," *The Guardian,* November 18, 2017, https://www.theguardian.com/world/2017/nov/18/how-toto-riinas-war-on-the-italian-state-almost-destroyed-cosa-nostra, accessed on November 7, 2021.

11 Agence France Presse (2021), "Italian 'Maxi Trial' Results in Conviction of 70 'Ndrangheta Suspects," *The Guardian,* November 6, 2021, https://www.theguardian.com/world/2021/nov/06/italian-maxi-trial-results-in-conviction-of-70-ndrangheta-suspects, accessed on November 7, 2021.

12 Ernst, F. (2020), "Time to End the Lethal Limbo of the U.S.-Mexican Drug Wars," October 7, 2020, https://www.crisisgroup.org/latin-america-caribbean/mexico/time-end-lethal-limbo-us-mexican-drug-wars, accessed on March 22, 2021.

13 Machiavelli, N. (1531), *The Discourses on Livy* (Harmondsworth: Pelican Classics, 1970).

14 Beardsley, E. (2018), "In France, The Protests Of May 1968 Reverberate Today—And Still Divide the French," *NPR,* May 29, 2018, https://www.npr.org/sections/parallels/2018/05/29/613671633/in-france-the-protests-of-may-1968-reverberate-today-and-still-divide-the-french, accessed on March 24, 2021.

15 Ozcan, E. E. (2021), "10 Years since Start of the Syrian Civil War," *Anodolu Agency,* March 14, 2021, https://www.aa.com.tr/en/middle-east/10-years-since-start-of-syrian-civil-war/2175768, accessed on March 24, 2021.

16 Klobets, V., and Kramer, D. (2021), "Lukashenko's Brutal Crackdown Has Lethal Help From Moscow," *FP,* March 4, 2021, https://foreignpolicy.com/2021/03/04/belarus-lukashenko-protests-election-russia-putin-brutal-crackdown-weapons-ammunition-bypol/, accessed on March 24, 2021.

17 "Myanmar Protests: Demonstrators Killed in Bloody Yangon Crackdown," *BBC News,* March 14, 2021, https://www.bbc.com/news/world-asia-56395085, accessed on March 24, 2021.

18 Glick, R., and Taylor, A. M. (2005), "Collateral Damage: Trade Disruption and the Economic Impact of War," Working Paper, *Federal Reserve Bank of San Francisco,* p. 18, https://www.frbsf.org/economic-research/files/wp05-11bk.pdf, accessed on March 24, 2021.

19 Ibid., p. 26.

20 Smith, R. (2018), "Conflict Costs the Global Economy $14 trillion a Year," *World Economic Forum,* January, 15, 2018, https://www.weforum.org/agenda/2018/01/conflict-costs-global-economy-14-trillion-a-year/, accessed on March 24, 2021.

21 Daley, J. (2017), "Researchers Catalogue the Grisly Deaths of Soldiers in the Thirty Years War," *Smithsonian Magazine,* June 6, 2017, https://www.smithsonianmag.com/smart-news/researchers-catalogue-grisly-deaths-soldiers-thirty-years-war-180963531/, accessed on March 14, 2021.

22 Ibid.

23 "Civil War Casualties," *American Battlefield Trust,* 2021, https://www.battlefields.org/learn/articles/civil-war-casualties, accessed on March 20, 2021.

24 Simkin, J. (2020), "Spanish Civil War: Casualties," *Spartacus Educational,* January 2020, https://spartacus-educational.com/SPcasualties.htm#:~:text=About%203.3%20per%20cent%20of,7.5%20per%20cent%20being%20injured, accessed on March 16, 2021.

25 Del Arco Blanco, M. A., and Anderson. P. (eds.) (2021), *Franco's Famine: Malnutrition, Disease and Starvation in Post-Civil War Spain* (London: Bloomsbury Academic), https://www.bloomsbury.com/us/francos-famine-9781350174658/, accessed on March 20, 2021.

26 History.com Editors (2020), "Korean War," *History,* May 11, 2021.

27 Bitesize, "The Korean War," https://www.bbc.co.uk/bitesize/guides/zqqd6yc/revision/7, accessed on March 16, 2021.

28 "World Military Expenditures and Arms Transfers," *US State Department,* cited by Jo, H. (2020), "North Korea: Sidelining Economic Development to Prioritize Strategic Weapons?" *Military Balance Blog,* July 10, 2020, https://www.iiss.org/blogs/military-balance/2020/07/north-korea-defence-policy-strategic-weapons#:~:text=The%202019%20World%20Military%20Expenditures,military%20between%202007%20and%202017, accessed on March 16, 2021.

29 "Military expenditure (% of GDP)," *World Bank,* 2021, https://data.worldbank.org/indicator/MS.MIL.XPND.GD.ZS?most_recent_year_desc=false, accessed on March 16, 2021.

30 Ibid.

31 Harrington, J., and Suneson, G. (2019), "What Were the 13 most Expensive Wars in U.S. History?," *USA Today*, June 13, 2019, https://www.usatoday.com/story/money/2019/06/13/cost-of-war-13-most-expensive-wars-in-us-history/39556983/, accessed on March 17, 2021.

32 Riddell, T. (1989), "Inflationary Impact of the Vietnam War," *Vietnam Generation*, 1, No. 1, Article 4 https://digitalcommons.lasalle.edu/cgi/viewcontent.cgi?article=1003&context=vietnamgeneration, accessed on March 17, 2021.

33 Amadeo, K. (2020), "Vietnam War Facts, Costs and Timeline," *The Balance*, February 19, 2020, https://www.thebalance.com/vietnam-war-facts-definition-costs-and-timeline-4154921#:~:text=The%20Vietnam%20War%20cost%20%24168,in%20aid%20to%20South%20Vietnam, accessed on March 17, 2021.

34 Shannon, P. (2000), "The ABCs of the Vietnam War," *Indochina Newsletter*, Special Issue pp. 93–97, cited in "Cost of the Vietnam War," *Vietnam Agent Orange Responsibility and Relief Campaign*, April 2000, https://www.vn-agentorange.org/edmaterials/cost_of_vn_war.html, accessed on March 17, 2021.

35 Ibid.

36 Blair, E. (2020), "Explainer: Lebanon's Financial Meltdown and How it Happened," *Reuters*, September 17, 2020, https://www.reuters.com/article/uk-lebanon-crisis-financial-explainer-idUKKBN268223, accessed on March 17, 2021.

37 "Covid-19 Worsened Lebanon's Economic Crisis—Leading Macroeconomic Influencers," *Pharmaceutical Technology*, March 16, 2021, https://www.pharmaceutical-technology.com/features/covid-lebanon-economic-crisis/, accessed on March 17, 2021.

38 Bazzi, M. (2020), "The Corrupt Political Class That Broke Lebanon," *Foreign Affairs*, August 14, 2020, https://www.foreignaffairs.com/articles/lebanon/2020-08-14/corrupt-political-class-broke-lebanon, accessed on March 17, 2021.

39 Roth, K. (2019), "Syria Events of 2018," *Human Rights Watch World Report 2019*, https://www.hrw.org/world-report/2019/country-chapters/syria, accessed on March 20, 2021.

40 "Why Has the Syrian War Lasted 11 Years?," *BBC News*, March 12, 2021, https://www.bbc.com/news/world-middle-east-35806229, accessed on March 20, 2022.

41 Tekin-Koru, A. (2020), "Precarious Lives: Syrian Refugees in Turkey in Corona Times," *Vox^{EU} CEPR*, April 6, 2020, https://voxeu.org/article/precarious-lives-syrian-refugees-turkey-corona-times#:~:text=The%20General%20Directorate%20of%20Migration,of%20age%20(Figure%203), accessed on March 20, 2021.

42 Roth (2019), "Lebanon Events of 2019," *Human Rights Watch World Report 2020*, https://www.hrw.org/world-report/2020/country-chapters/lebanon, accessed on March 20, 2021.

43 Roth (2019).

44 Todd, Z. (2019) "By the Numbers: Syrian Refugees Around the World," *Frontline*, November 19, 2019, https://www.pbs.org/wgbh/frontline/article/numbers-syrian-refugees-around-world/, accessed on March 20, 2021.

45 Ibid.

46 Ibid.

47 Ibid.

48 Ibid.

49 "10 Facts About Refugees," *UNHCR Global Trends 2018*, August 30, 2019, https://www.unhcr.org/cy/wp-content/uploads/sites/41/2019/09/10-Facts-About-Refugees.pdf, accessed on March 20, 2021.

50 Anadolu Agency (2021), "Syrian Civil War Cost More than $1.2 trillion: Aid Group," *Daily Sabah*, March 5, 2021 https://www.dailysabah.com/world/syrian-crisis/syrian-civil-war-cost-more-than-12-trillion-aid-group, accessed on March 20, 2021.

51 Garner, B. (ed.) (2004), *Black's Law Dictionary, 8th edition,* quoted in "Fraud 101: What is Fraud?" *Association of Certified Fraud Examiners,* https://www.acfe.com/fraud-101.aspx, accessed on March 25, 2021.

52 Ibid.

53 Ibid.

54 Gee. J., and Button, M. (2019), "The Financial Cost of Fraud 2019: The Latest Data from around the World," *Crowe and University of Portsmouth,* p.6, http://www.crowe.ie/wp-content/uploads/2019/08/The-Financial-Cost-of-Fraud-2019.pdf, accessed on March 25, 2021.

55 Ibid., p. 7.

56 "Bribery," Legal Information Institute, *Cornell Law School,* https://www.law.cornell.edu/wex/bribery, accessed on March 25, 2021.

57 OECD (2013), "What are Bribery and Corruption?," in *Bribery and Corruption Awareness Handbook for Tax Examiners and Tax Auditors* (Paris: OECD Publishing), p. 11, https://www.oecd-ilibrary.org/docserver/9789264205376-3-en.pdf?expires=1616649405&id=id&accname=guest&checksum=370A8CB4F859F1DC76E13BC853AF3CC8, accessed on March 25, 2021.

58 Ibid., p. 11.

59 Ibid.

60 Ibid.

61 Ibid.

62 Ibid.

63 Ibid., p. 9.

64 Transparency International (2018), "What is Corruption?" https://www.transparency.org/what-is-corruption, accessed on October 3, 2019.

65 Ibid.

66 Zinkin, J. (2020), *The Challenge of Sustainability: Corporate Governance in a Complicated World* (Boston/Berlin: De Gruyter), p. 135.

67 Yermo, J., and Schroeder, H. (2014), "The Rationale for Fighting Corruption," *CleanGovBiz,* OECD, p. 2, https://www.oecd.org/cleangovbiz/49693613.pdf, accessed on October 3, 2019.

68 Directive 2005/60/EC of the European Parliament and of the Council – 26 October 2005, consistent with the definition adopted by the United Nations Convention Against Illicit Traffic in Narcotic Drugs and Psychotropic Substances (1988) (*Vienna Convention*), the United Nations Convention Against Transnational Organized Crime (2000) (*Palermo Convention*), and the United Nations-Office of Drugs and Crime and IMF Model Legislation On Money Laundering and Financing of Terrorism (2005).

69 "Money Laundering," http://legal-dictionary.thefreedictionary.com/Money+Laundering, accessed on 1 April 2015.

70 Cusack, J. (2020), "The Global Threat Assessment," *Financial Crime News,* June 6, 2020, https://thefinancialcrimenews.com/global-threat-assessment-to-download-read/, accessed on April 13, 2021.

71 Ibid.

72 "The Black Market," *Havocscope.com,* https://havocscope.com/, accessed on March 27, 2021.

73 "Cost of Cybercrime to Exceed $1trn in 2020," *Finextra,* December 8, 2020, https://www.finextra.com/newsarticle/37109/cost-of-cybercrime-to-exceed-1trn-in-2020, accessed on March 27, 2021.

74 Shaw, M., and Reitano, T. (2016), "Organised Crime has Affected Politics, but Not in the Way We Have Come to Expect," *Global Initiative Against Transnational Organized Crime,* November 10, 2016, https://globalinitiative.net/analysis/op-ed-organised-crime-has-affected-politics-but-not-in-the-way-we-have-come-to-expect-now-is-the-time-to-build-a-new-agenda/, accessed on March 26, 2021.

75 Transparency International (2018).

76 Alesina, A., Piccolo, S., and Pinotti, P. (2019), "Organized Crime, Violence, and Politics," *The Review of Economic Studies*, Volume 86, Issue 2, March 2019, pp.457–499, https://academic.oup.com/restud/article/86/2/457/5060718, accessed on March 26, 2021.
77 Transparency International (2018).
78 Naim, M. (2012), "Mafia States: Organized Crime Takes Office," *Foreign Affairs,* May/June 2012, 91, No. 3, p. 101, https://www.jstor.org/stable/23217970, accessed on March 27, 2021.
79 Ibid., p. 101.
80 Ibid., p. 103.
81 Medina, L., and Schneider, F. (2018), "Shadow Economies Around the World: What Did We Learn Over the Last 20 Years?" *IMF Working Paper,* WP/18/17, January 24, 2018, p. 23, https://www.imf.org/en/Publications/WP/Issues/2018/01/25/Shadow-Economies-Around-the-World-What-Did-We-Learn-Over-the-Last-20-Years-45583, accessed on March 28, 2021.
82 Ibid., p. 4.
83 Ibid., p. 18.
84 Ibid., p. 102.

Chapter 4
Does the Punishment Fit the Crime?

The word *sanction* has two different meanings depending on whether it is used as a noun or a verb.

1. As a noun, defined by the Oxford English Dictionary as:
   A threatened penalty for disobeying a law or rule[1]
   Measures taken by a state to coerce another to conform to an international agreement or norms of conduct, typically in the form of restrictions on trade or official sporting participation[2]
   Official permission or approval of an action[3]
   Official confirmation or ratification of a law[4]
   A consideration operating to enforce obedience to any rule of conduct[5]

2. As a verb, defined as:
   Give official permission or approval for (an action)[6]
   Impose a sanction or penalty on[7]

Reconciling these two meanings requires treating the concept of sanction/sanctioning as points on a continuum that ranges from disapproval (and resulting punishments) to indifference to approval of outcomes. Sanctions, and sanctioning as punishments, are the responsibility of governments, regulators, judges, cultures, theologians, philosophers, media, society, organizations, and individuals who decide what is unacceptable and acceptable behavior. These groups indicate their views by agreeing and implementing approvals and punishments to achieve desired outcomes.

Government

Governments are human institutions, not divinely ordained ones:

> In this way of thinking, government is not a divine fiat to reign, a synonym for "society," or an avatar of the national, religious, or racial soul. It is a human invention, tacitly agreed to in a social contract, designed to enhance the welfare of citizens by coordinating their behavior and discouraging selfish acts that may be tempting every individual but leave everyone worse off . . .

> *Criminal punishment . . . is not a mandate to implement cosmic justice but part of an incentive structure that discourages antisocial acts without causing more suffering than it deters. The reason the punishment should fit the crime, for example, is not to balance some mystical scale of justice but to ensure that a wrongdoer stops at a minor crime rather than escalating to a more harmful one.* Cruel punishments, whether or not they are in some sense "deserved," are no

https://doi.org/10.1515/9783110712155-004

more effective at deterring harm than moderate but surer punishments, and they desensitize spectators and brutalize the society that implements them.[8]   [Emphasis ours]

Governments prescribe acceptable and unacceptable behavior for their citizens through written constitutions,[i] statutes regulating markets and industries, through the judicial interpretation of statutes, and regulators determining and administering appropriate punishments.

Chapter 1 showed how the state defines crimes on a continuum – ranging from felonies, to offenses, misdemeanors, infractions, and wrongdoings. It also defines what sanctions (penalties) are applicable for particular crimes, allowing the criminal justice system some flexibility when sentencing.

Different regimes have different types of sanctions and different definitions of criminal behavior, which can change over time.

Enforcement of Sanctions

Enforcement itself is a continuum, ranging from the "No Broken Windows" approach that prosecutes infractions and misdemeanors, no matter how small,[9] to regimes that only go after "big fish," used by the Chinese government to target and jail powerful, corrupt politicians like Zhou YongKang and Bo Xilai[10] in order to "kill a chicken to scare the monkeys" – that is, to set an example to deter others.

The intention to enforce can be undermined by various factors, including impunity, regulatory capture, bribery and corruption, an inappropriate "ecosystem," and indifference. Each of these is described in the sections below.

Impunity

When powerful people believe that the rules do not apply to them, and if sanctions (penalties) do not apply to all regardless of their status and standing, the difference in treatment is regarded as (1) unfair, and (2) as a license to break rules. Candidate Donald Trump declared he could stand in the street and shoot someone and would get away it.[11] He was not held accountable during his presidency and this allowed his belief that he had impunity to grow. He maintained that he did not lose the 2020 Presidential election in the face of facts. In the UK, prime ministerial adviser Dominic Cummings broke the Covid-19 "stay at home" rules, driving to Barnard Castle to "test his eyesight." He was not punished for doing so because of his position. The resulting sense of outrage and unfairness led to many more people in the UK defying the lockdown rules.[12] The belief that there was one rule for those close

---

i The UK is an exception in that it has no written constitution.

to Prime Minister Boris Johnson and another for everybody else was given further credence by the Prime Minister's botched attempt to rewrite the rules to protect a Conservative MP from being suspended by Parliament after he had been found to have been in egregious breach of its rules on lobbying.[13] This sense that there is one law for him and another for the rest of the country was exacerbated by the covid-related scandal of "partygate" and in part led to resounding defeats for the Conservatives in the June 23, 2022 bye-elections.[ii] This and other scandals finally led to his party forcing him to resign on July 7, 2022.[iii,iv] Prince Mohammed bin Salman was not sanctioned by the US after the murder Jamal Khashoggi.[14]

There are many examples, notably white-collar crime:[v]

> The control of white-collar crime is inhibited by the entrenched interests of the legitimate sector of government officials, lobbyists and elites, who benefit from exploiting the financial holes in the existing system allowing for fraud, tax evasion, and money laundering. The control of organized crime is similarly compromised, especially when it is used as a tool of business and government for corrupt purposes.[15]

Regulatory Capture

Regulatory capture is not the same as corruption or control. It does not include threats of being re-appointed for gain, nor does it include the promise of a lucrative role in the regulated entity once the regulator has retired. Those are acts of corruption.

> Regulatory capture is characterized by the regulator's attitude, not the regulated entity's actions. A regulator is "captured" when he is in a constant state of "being persuaded": persuaded based on a persuader's identity rather than an argument's merits. *Regulatory capture is reflected in a surplus of passivity and reactivity, and a deficit of curiosity and creativity.* It is evidenced by a body of commission decisions or non-decisions – about resources, procedures,

ii Moore, J., (2022), "'One rule for us, another rule for them' will be Boris Johnsons' legacy", *The Independent*, January 13, 2022, https://www.independent.co.uk/voices/boris-johnson-one-rule-tory-party-b1992319.html, accessed on June 25, 2022.
iii Guy. J., McGee, L., and Kottosova, I., (2022), "UK Prime Minister Boris Johnson resigns after mutiny in his party", *CNN*, July 8, 2022, https://edition.cnn.com/2022/07/07/europe/boris-johnson-resignation-intl/index.html, accessed on July 10, 2022.
iv Adam, K. (2022), "Boris Johnson's Tories suffer fresh electoral defeat: party chair quits", *The Washington Post*, June 24, 2022, https://www.washingtonpost.com/world/2022/06/24/britain-by-election-tory-loss/, accessed on June 25, 2022.
v "White-collar crime, manifested by tax evasion by legitimate businesses and wealthy individuals, is rampant and increasingly global, in order to "park" large amounts of cash in low-tax and tax-free jurisdictions. This tax-haven "shopping" is also very important for corrupt public officials stealing from their own jurisdictions, who need foreign locations to hide the money." Albanese, J. (2021), "Organized Crime Versus White-Collar Crime: Which is the Bigger Problem?" *Academia Letters*, Article 310, p. 2, March 2021, https://doi.org/10.20935/AL310, accessed on July 6, 2021.

priorities, and policies, *where what the regulated entity wants has more influence than what the public interest requires*

Regulatory capture is enabled by those who ignore it, tolerate it, accept it or encourage it: *legislators who under-fund the commission or restrict its authority, presidents and governors who appoint commissioners unprepared for the job,* human resource officials who classify staff jobs and salaries based on decades-old criteria unrelated to current needs, intervenors who treat the agency like a supermarket where they shop for personal needs, and who treat regulatory proceedings like win-loss contests rather than building blocks in a policy edifice.[16]

[Emphases ours]

The first sign of capture is a regulator failing to ask pertinent questions, such as what products and services and what standards and quality serve the public interest best? This lack of focus on the public interest leads to a failure of the regulatory process in the face of regulated organizations' lobbyists and litigation. The companies and their lobbyists are better resourced, better qualified, better paid, and more motivated because of the clearly-defined impact of their actions on profit. The regulators' officers are trying to defend a goal that can appear to be an abstraction.[17] This can lead to the "revolving door" problem that drains regulatory agencies of talented personnel, who may hesitate before offending the companies they regulate for fear of having the revolving door closed on them.

This difference in credentialing produces, and reinforces, a difference in salaries; leading to a difference in motivation and morale; leading, unremarkably, to a *difference in tenure for the talented. They spend their formative years learning on the taxpayer dime, then move to the regulated sector.* No one with the power to fix the problem notices or reacts. *The 'revolving door' then becomes a one-way door: more agency staff move to jobs with the regulated than the other way around. That's capture.* It is neither corruption nor conflict of interest; it is simply the natural economic result of the agency failing to insist on high-quality professionals and pay them their worth.[18]

The second sign of capture is how issues that come before the regulator are framed. The regulated will attempt to frame issues in a way that benefits them at the expense of other parties by arguing that what is good for the company is good for the jurisdiction, making it hard to separate what is, and is not, in the public interest.[19]

Matters are aggravated when regulators are funded by legislatures that are willing to cut financial support for the agencies as a result of political pressure to find cost savings, lobbying from companies that fund political campaigns to overturn policies that the companies find unhelpful, or as result of changes in political ideology following a change of government.

An example of regulatory capture to benefit vested interests was the repeal in 1999 of the US Glass-Steagall Act to allow the combination of banks with securities firms and insurance companies:

On November 12th 1999, President Clinton signed into law the Gramm-Leach-Bliley Act *repealing Glass-Steagall and opening the doors to the abuses that led directly to the Global Financial Crisis. This was the result of the need to legalize the creation of Citigroup – the merger of Citicorp with Travelers in 1998, which had been done in violation of Glass-Steagall*[20] – and Clinton was persuaded by intensive lobbying by Wall Street, Alan Greenspan and the Treasury Secretary, Robert Rubin.[21] *The repeal of Glass-Steagall has been blamed for causing a replay of the run up to the Crash in 1929 in 2008*:

> "The oldest propaganda technique is to repeat a lie emphatically and often until it is taken for the truth. Something like this is going on now with regard to banks and the financial crisis. The big bank boosters and analysts who should know better are repeating the falsehood that repeal of Glass-Steagall had nothing to do with the Panic of 2008.
>
> *In fact, the financial crisis might not have happened at all but for the 1999 repeal of the Glass-Steagall law that separated commercial and investment banking for seven decades. If there is any hope of avoiding another meltdown, it's critical to understand why Glass-Steagall repeal helped to cause the crisis.* Without a return to something like Glass-Steagall, another greater catastrophe is just a matter of time."[22,23]   [Emphases ours]

Glass-Steagall was designed to keep the two cultures of banking and investing separate. Its repeal was designed to commingle the two in the hope of creating a financial institution that would be the best of both worlds (BOBW):

> Yet instead of creating a BOBW financial institution, the result was a hybrid TBTF [Too Big to Fail] monster that put the system at risk, holding governments to ransom as a result. Although initially very surprising, it is perhaps no accident that Sandy Weill, the architect of the demise of Glass-Steagall, has come to the view that it should not have been repealed because the problems of cultural incompatibility are just too great. In an interview with the Financial Times,[24] John Reed, fellow architect of the repeal of Glass-Steagall concluded it was a mistake for the same reason.[25]

Bribery and Corruption

Chapter 3 explored the impact of bribery in terms of its financial harm which was estimated by the World Bank to amount to US$1 trillion per year.[26] An OECD report in 2013 broke bribery down into a number of parts: kickbacks, secret commissions, facilitation payments, influence peddling, and electoral bribery.[27] As far as bribery's impact on *enforcement* is concerned, two of those types matter: influence peddling and electoral bribery. They affect the political process which, in turn, affects regulatory policy and the "revolving door" that creates regulatory capture.

There are no figures for the costs of bribery in influencing regulatory and judicial decisions that affect enforcement. However, there are figures for spending in the US on lobbying, which is a legal activity, designed to influence lawmakers and regulators to benefit the profitability of regulated organizations. In addition to the direct costs of lobbying, economic, social, and public health costs, the impact on communities of organizations engaging in harmful, but legal activities should be added.

The direct costs of lobbying in the US in 2019 came to more than US$ 3.4 billion.[28] The return on investment of such lobbying is impressive. Over a period of four years, the Fortune 100 companies spent US$ 2 billion to receive US$ 400 billion of taxpayer money in return.[29] A US$ 325 million investment by the top ten companies[vi] yielded US$ 338 billion in federal contracts and grants. Eight companies[vii] spent US$ 190 million on lobbying to receive US$ 16.9 billion in contracts, and nearly US$ 1 billion in grants; yet they paid US$0 in corporation taxes.[30]

Election bribery occurs in two forms. The first is when political parties pay voters to cast their votes for their candidates. The second, less brazen, method occurs when donors (private individuals or companies) give money to political campaigns expecting favors in return once the candidate they have supported gets elected. The sums involved depend on state limits on the costs of elections, or the absence of them (as in the US, where the 2020 elections for the White House, Senate, and House of Representatives cost US$ 14.4 billion). Large individual donors gave 42.59% of this sum.[31]

Corruption is tolerated because many people in power benefit from it and many people believe, wrongly, that it is a victimless crime. Such indifference undermines the political will to prosecute perpetrators:

> The same justifications and excuses for bribery and corruption, like other white-collar crimes, are heard time and time again. *"Everybody does it," "it's a cost of doing business," "it doesn't really matter," "nobody gets hurt." This is not true.* The corruption of public or private officials and decision makers, and the payment of bribes, raise serious moral and political concerns. *These are not victimless crimes, and in fact exact a heavy economic and social cost. Bribery and corruption create an unlevel playing field for honest businesses, and cut deep into the social fabric of developed and developing countries alike.* They can translate into inferior and dangerous products allowed onto the market place, substandard building materials used in infrastructure projects that can endanger people's health and welfare, and the diversion of vital money required for education, health and welfare services. *In the end, we all pay the bill.*[32]
>
> [Emphases ours]

Some of the most corrupt countries have excellent written constitutions and regulatory frameworks, but in practice the laws are used as an opportunity to negotiate work-arounds to the private benefit of corrupt officials.

---

vi Lockheed Martin, Boeing, McKesson, General Dynamics, Humana, Centene, United Technologies, UnitedHealth Group, Honeywell, and General Electric.
vii Amazon, Chevron, Delta Airlines, General Motors, Honeywell International, IBM, Prudential Financial, and Tech Data.

Inappropriate "Ecosystem"

The failure of effective enforcement is frequently an issue of a weak "ecosystem" caused by insufficient investment in the institutional capacity needed to create effective enforcement or of social attitudes toward malpractices.

If the criminal justice system and regulatory investigations are slow because of a shortage of judges and magistrates, inadequacies in the courts' administrative systems, or staffing, then the deterrence effect is reduced. In the case of non-violent, or white-collar crime, perpetrators remain free for a long time before being sentenced – which changes their risk-reward calculations. If the likelihood of getting caught is low and if getting people to testify is difficult, then deterrence is greatly weakened.

A 2021 review of global money laundering in *The Economist*[33] suggested why global efforts to reduce money laundering globally were ineffective. Money laundering is a recently defined crime. Before 1980 it was legal in most countries. American efforts after the terrorist attacks on 9/11 in 2001 pressured countries to declare it illegal. As a result, big banks like HSBC, and JPMorgan Chase employ between 3,000 and 5,000 specialists to track laundered money and more than 20,000 overall to oversee risk and compliance. This has led to the end of the most glaring malpractices, but they have been replaced by others.[34]

Several factors contribute to the failure to prevent money laundering:

1. The rise of "trade-based" money laundering where the opportunities to fiddle the paperwork and insufficient customs checks has hindered the progress resulting from the abolition of the glaring sources of money laundering. While some countries have introduced laws to deal with money laundering, enforcement is often ineffective.[35]

2. Enforcement agencies are under-resourced because the public does not appear to care about non-violent crime. They do not appreciate its impact on them because there is no physical violence or visible property damage involved; and yet its costs to society are great. For example, in the UK, fraud makes up more than one-third of all reported crime, yet gets less than one percent of the resources deployed to combat crime.[36] Many agencies lack the resources needed to screen the "suspicious activity reports" which reduces the likelihood of getting caught. Matters are made worse by the difficulties agencies face when it comes to sharing data across jurisdictions, with only the US and UK banks sharing data. This is unfortunate as:

> The value of information coming from a network of banks is thousands of times higher than the information any one bank has, because you can see not just where the money came from, but where it went, and where it went from there, and so on. It gives you a picture of the network.[37]

3. The natural tendency to blame the banks alone for the growth in money laundering and financial crime overlooks the nature of the financial crime "ecosystem":

> lawyers who set up dodgy shell companies, accountants who sign off on their fishy filings and the like have been getting away with slaps on the wrist. Britain's revenues and customs agency, for instance, supervises more than 30,000 accountants, estate agents and other businesses for money-laundering purposes; in the 2019–20 financial year it issued just 31 fines, averaging £290,000. Governments also need to get to grips with the AML implications of cryptocurrencies, and the firms and exchanges that hawk them.[38]

> American regulators have long worried about the enablers, but thanks to effective lobbying they have managed to crawl through loophole after loophole. Estate agents, luxury-goods vendors and others, for instance, won "temporary" exemptions from the Patriot Act (a post-9/11 law with strong anti-money-laundering provisions), which then became permanent. American lawyers are pretty much free to work with whomever they want – in many ways "the perfect friend to have if you're a kleptocrat."[39]

4. If the penalties are not perceived to be commensurate with the harm, if organizations pick up the fines for breaches and those committing them walk away with their bonuses intact, then the regulatory sanctions will not stop malpractice. If the taxpayer foots the bill for the damage caused by malpractice as happened in the aftermath of the Global Financial Crisis (GFC), enforcement will not change behavior. If costs imposed by the sanctions and penalties are less than the pecuniary benefit of criminal behavior, we should not be surprised that enforcement fails. If malpractice is punished by fining the organization without admission of wrongdoing, then senior management and shareholders will conclude that malfeasance is just "the cost of doing business" as long as shareholder value is not obviously impacted.

5. Another area where firms flout the law is in the rise of casual employment (the gig economy) because of weak enforcement of labor laws:

> Many of the most egregious violations relate to gig-economy companies, which pretend that their workers are self-employed contractors when they are in fact more like employees. *These firms have not found loopholes in existing employment law,* as is often believed. Instead, *they act with impunity mainly because enforcement of existing labour law is weak and punishment is feeble.* That calls for more inspections of suspicious firms and tougher fines for rule-breakers.[40]
> [Emphases ours]

6. Getting multinationals, in particular the big tech companies, to pay their fair share of corporate taxes has been dogged by global tax-collecting structural problems resulting from governments pursuing "beggar my neighbor" policies that have meant firms can, to an extent, choose where to park their profits with a view to minimizing the tax burden:

> Breakneck globalisation allowed multinationals to replace fears of double taxation with the joys of double non-taxation, using havens to game the system. By exploiting mismatches between countries' tax laws, taxable profits could be cut or even made to disappear. The game

became easier with the rise of intangible assets, which can be shifted between jurisdictions more easily than buildings or machinery. *Big tech has been a big beneficiary: the five largest Silicon Valley giants paid $220bn in cash taxes over the past decade, just 16% of their cumulative pre-tax profits.*[41]   [Emphasis ours]

Indifference

A damaging cause of weak enforcement arises when society does not agree with the regulations and the state's definition of criminal behavior. During Prohibition in the US, people who were sentenced suffered few social sanctions; the media lionized them (as with the 1932 film "Scarface" about Al Capone in the 1920s, or more recently the American Mafia in "The Godfather" films and Jordan Belfort in the film "The Wolf of Wall Street"). In recent years, malefactors have earned large sums of money by writing about their crimes, in the name of minimizing fraud, like Andrew Fastow, former CFO of Enron,[42] or Nick Leeson of Barings.[43] Such actions seriously undermine enforcement.

Social Axioms and Assumptions

All social behavior is the result of the interplay between culture, religion, ideology, and the media and what it chooses to focus on.

Culture

Culture is complicated. It can be compared to an envelope of heuristics that frame the meaning and purpose of collectives – a set of inherited or passed-down wisdom and rules of thumb to help guide members of the collective, be it an empire, nation, tribe, or organization; to know what to do, when, and how to do it.

Although cultures appear slow to change, constrained as they are by tradition and the speed at which they can respond to changed circumstances, they do change, mutate, and adapt. They must do so to compete with cultures with which they come into contact. The pressure for change is constant and the changes are often incremental so that they are imperceptible if measured over the span of a year. However, when we compare the changes in the manifestations of culture over a generation, a lifetime, a century, or a millennium, we see great changes. For example, the fearsome warrior culture of the Vikings that terrified Western Europe, what is now Russia, and the Mediterranean, has been replaced by the kinder, peace-loving social democracies of Scandinavia.

Just as successful collectives compete for resources by adapting when needed, so it is with cultures.

What people mean by culture depends on whether they are considering it from an anthropological, organizational, or artistic perspective. Anthropologists have many definitions, and the three we like best are:

> Culture is the collective programming of the human mind that distinguishes the members of one human group from those of another. *Culture in this sense is a system of collectively held values.*[44] [Emphasis ours]

> Believing, with Max Weber, that man is an animal suspended in webs of significance he himself has spun, *I take culture to be those webs, and the analysis of it to be therefore not an experimental science in search of law but an interpretive one in search of meaning.*[45] [Emphasis ours]

> Explicit culture is the observable reality of the language, food, buildings, houses, monuments, agriculture, shrines, markets, fashions, and art. They are the symbols of a deeper level of culture. Prejudices mostly start on this symbolic and observable level

> *Explicit culture reflects deeper layers of culture, the norms and values of an individual group.* **Norms** are the mutual sense a group has of what is "right" and "wrong." Norms can develop on a formal level as written laws, and on an informal level as social control. **Values**, on the other hand, determine the definition of "good and bad," and are therefore closely related to the ideals shared by the group.

> *While the norms, consciously or subconsciously, give us a feeling of "this is how I normally* **should** *behave," values give us a feeling of "this is how I* **aspire** *or* **desire** *to behave."* A value serves as a criterion to determine a choice from existing alternatives

> *Culture is man-made, confirmed by others, conventionalised and passed on for younger people or newcomers to learn. It provides people with a meaningful context in which to meet, to think about themselves and to face the outer world.*

> In the language of Clifford Geertz, *culture is the means by which people "communicate, perpetuate, and develop their knowledge about attitudes towards life. Culture is the fabric of meaning in terms of which human beings interpret their experience and guide their action."*[46]
>
> [Emphases ours]

If the anthropological definition of culture can be regarded as a very large envelope of heuristics (rules of thumb), then the organizational approach to culture can be viewed as a smaller packet of heuristics within the larger anthropological envelope, concerning itself more with answering "How?" questions as opposed to "Why?" and "What?" questions. As a result, from an organizational perspective, the definition of culture is more focused. The key difference between the anthropological definition and the organizational definition is the search for meaning in the anthropological definition, highlighted in what differentiates norms and values. Norms reflect a collective's views of what **is**, whereas values reflect its beliefs of what **ought to be**.

A company's culture is the environment created by the priorities it sets.

Sometimes those priorities are made explicit: in a company's formal mission statement, for example, or in the structure of the organisation and the power given to different departments and functions. *Sometimes they are implicit:* what the *Financial Times* once called "the large number of unspoken assumptions and beliefs which managers in the organisation share about 'the way we do things around here'."[47]   [Emphases ours]

Culture is the deeper level of basic assumptions and beliefs that are shared by members of an organization, that *operate unconsciously and define in a basic 'taken for granted' fashion an organization's view of itself and its environment.*[48]   [Emphasis ours]

Organizations are more concerned with what **is**, focusing on short-term performance and ways of achieving results; only occasionally thinking about what **ought to be**, when developing their mission, vision, and values or having to think about ESG (environmental, social, and governance) issues.

Currently, there is a debate on whether legitimate businesses should maximize shareholder value or stakeholder value,[49] and whether these two concepts are in conflict. If the boards and senior management of legitimate businesses believe their fiduciary duty requires them to maximize shareholder value, they will focus on maximizing share value; even being prepared to break the law and pay the resulting fines, as long as the fine-based "cost of doing business" is less than the pecuniary gain of breaking the law. In this sense, there is no difference between the cultures of OC and legitimate businesses.

The fact that regulators and shareholders regard these outcomes as acceptable undermines the purpose of sanctions and encourages a culture of impunity because the company pays the fine rather than individual malefactors themselves.

We will return to issues of organizational culture and its impact on rewards and penalties in Chapter 6 where we discuss the strategy continuum and its similarities in both OC and legitimate businesses.

Media

Governments regard the media as channels for propaganda to glorify the achievements of rulers and reinforce cults of personality, regardless of the truth. In Soviet Russia, *Pravda*, ironically meaning "Truth" was the official organ of the communist party from 1918 to 1991, always toeing the party line. The media see themselves as businesses concerned with the creation of shareholder value. Facebook (now rebranded as Meta[50]) is clearly more interested in maximizing growth and profits than promoting the truth, and according to whistleblower testimony to Congress, prior to the rebranding, has consistently used algorithms that have encouraged conspiracy theories and division regardless of the truth and the harm they create.[51]

To sustain democracies, an active free press has to report truthfully and hold leaders to account. The rise of social media and the unwillingness of these platforms to be responsible for the veracity of what is broadcast has facilitated the dissemination of conspiracy theories and "alternative facts." It has become hard to know what is really happening. The trend has been enabled by politicians and mainstream media pandering to their audiences, regardless of the untruths that are being promulgated. Propagators of conspiracies are not held accountable, nor are the platforms or politicians. Irresponsible, socially divisive behavior is sanctioned (allowed) instead of being sanctioned (penalized) by the media. The concept of being held to account and being responsible for one's actions is replaced by a reality TV show mentality where name recognition and maximized outrage are exploited to increase profits.

In short, the media's revenue-driven focus on bad news and outrage have created an increasingly hostile environment for those who wish to encourage socially responsible behavior, sanctioning (allowing) destructive behavior instead.

The media can only shine a light on government and organizational malpractice through investigative journalism. The media can only do this if it is independent of those about whom it writes, and confident that when malpractice is uncovered, corrective action will be taken; and that requires those in power to have a strong sense of the importance of accountability.

References

1 *Oxford English Dictionary* (2021), "Sanction," *Lexico 2021*, https://www.lexico.com/definition/sanction, accessed on April 4, 2021.

2 Ibid.

3 Ibid.

4 Ibid.

5 Ibid.

6 Ibid.

7 Ibid.

8 Pinker, S. (2018), *Enlightenment Now: The Case for Reason, Science, Humanism and Progress* (Allen Lane) p. 12.

9 Fox, J. (2019), "'Broken Windows' Theory was Right . . . About the Windows," *Bloomberg*, October 16, 2019, https://www.bloomberg.com/opinion/articles/2019-10-16/what-broken-windows-theory-got-right-about-crime, accessed on April 6, 2021.

10 Choi, C-Y., and Ma, J. (2019), "Zhou YongKang, Bo Xilai among Elite Prisoners in China's 'Tigers' Cage' Qincheng Growing Vegetables and Wearing Suits," *SCMP*, January 13, 2019, https://www.scmp.com/news/china/politics/article/2181862/elite-prisoners-chinas-tigers-cage-qincheng-grow-vegetables-and, accessed on April 6, 2021.

11 Diamond, J. (2016), "Trump: I Could Shoot Someone and I Wouldn't Lose Voters," *CNN*, January 24, 2016, https://edition.cnn.com/2016/01/23/politics/donald-trump-shoot-somebody-support/index.html, accessed on April 6, 2021.

12 Weaver, M. (2020), "'People Won't Forget Dominic Cummings' Visit': Barnard Castle Learns to Live with the Notoriety," *The Guardian* December 17, 2020, https://www.theguardian.com/lifeand

style/2020/dec/17/people-wont-forget-dominic-cummings-visit-barnard-castle-learns-to-live-with-notoriety, accessed on April 6, 2020.

13 Cecil, N. (2021), "Owen Paterson: Humbled Boris Johnson in Massive Sleaze U-turn," *Evening Standard*, November 5, 2021, https://www.standard.co.uk/news/politics/owen-paterson-suspension-standards-boris-johnson-rees-mogg-b964337.html, accessed on November 10, 2021.

14 Dozier, K., and Henigan, W. J. (2021), "Here's Why the US Didn't Sanction Mohammed Bin Salman for His Role in the Jamal Khashoggi Killing," *Time*, March 4, 2021, https://time.com/5944070/us-sanction-mohammed-bin-salman/, accessed on April 6, 2021.

15 Albanese, J. (2021), "Organized Crime Versus White-collar Crime: Which is the Bigger Problem?" *Academia Letters*, Article 310, p. 3, March 2021, https://doi.org/10.20935/AL310, accessed on July 6, 2021.

16 Hempling, S. (2014), "'Regulatory Capture': Sources and Solutions," *Emory Corporate Governance and Accountability Review*, https://law.emory.edu/ecgar/content/volume-1/issue-1/essays/regulatory-capture.html, accessed on April 6, 2021.

17 Ibid.

18 Ibid.

19 Ibid.

20 "The Long Demise of Glass-Steagall: A Chronology Tracing the Life of the Glass-Steagall Act, from its Passage in 1933 to its Death Throes in the 1990s, and How Citigroup's Sandy Weill Dealt the Coup de Grâce," *PBS Frontline*, http://www.pbs.org/wgbh/pages/frontline/shows/wallstreet/weill/demise.html, accessed on January 12, 2013, cited in Zinkin, J. (2014), *Rebuilding Trust in Banks: The Role of Leadership and Governance* (Singapore: John Wiley & Sons), p. 206.

21 Ibid., p. 242.

22 Rickards, J. (2012), "Repeal of Glass-Steagall Caused the Financial Crisis," *US News, Economic Intelligence*, August 27, 2012 http://www.usnews.com/opinion/blogs/economic-intelligence/2012/08/27/repeal-of-glass-steagall-caused-the-financial-crisis, accessed on January 12, 2013, quoted in Zinkin, *Rebuilding Trust in Banks*, p. 206.

23 Zinkin (2014), p. 206.

24 Authers, J. (2013), "Culture Clash Means Banks Must Split, Says Former Citi chief," *The Financial Times*, September 8, 2013, https://www.ft.com/content/2cfa6f18-1575-11e3-950a-00144feabdc0, accessed on September 14, 2013, cited in Zinkin (2014), p. 224.

25 Zinkin (2014), p. 224.

26 OECD (2013), "What are Bribery and Corruption?" in *Bribery and Corruption Awareness Handbook for Tax Examiners and Tax Auditors* (Paris: OECD Publishing), p. 11, https://www.oecd-ilibrary.org/docserver/9789264205376-3-en.pdf?expires=1616649405&id=id&accname=guest&checksum=370A8CB4F859F1DC76E13BC853AF3CC8, accessed on March 25, 2021.

27 Ibid.

28 Wilson, M. R. (2020), "Lobbying Spending in 2019 Reached Second Highest Point of Decade," *Bloomberg Government*, January 24, 2020, https://about.bgov.com/news/lobbying-spending-in-2019-reached-second-highest-point-of-decade/, accessed on April 8, 2021.

29 Andrzejewski, A. (2019), "How the Fortune 100 Turned $2 Billion in Lobbying Spend Into $400 Billion of Taxpayer Cash," *Forbes*, May 14, 2019, https://www.forbes.com/sites/adamandrzejewski/2019/05/14/how-the-fortune-100-turned-2-billion-in-lobbying-spend-into-400-billion-of-taxpayer-cash/?sh=426ff95954ff, accessed on April 8, 2021.

30 Ibid.

31 Evers-Hillstrom, K. (2021), "Most Expensive Ever: 2020 Election Cost $14.4 billion," *OpenSecrets.org*, February 11, 2021, https://www.opensecrets.org/news/2021/02/2020-cycle-cost-14p4-billion-doubling-16/, accessed on April 8, 2020.

32 OECD "What are bribery and corruption?" p. 9, https://www.oecd-ilibrary.org/docserver/9789264205376-3-en.pdf?expires=1617814695&id=id&accname=guest&checksum=1DC3D7DB929660F0474B34F8C5A61D11, accessed on April 8, 2021.

33 Finance and Economics (2021), "The War against Money-laundering is being Lost," *The Economist*, April 12, 2021, https://www.economist.com/finance-and-economics/2021/04/12/the-war-against-money-laundering-is-being-lost, accessed on August 12, 2022.

34 Ibid.

35 Ibid.

36 Ibid.

37 Ibid.

38 Ibid.

39 Books & Arts (2021), "Two Books Assess the Fight against Global Corruption," *The Economist*, November 13, 2021, https://www.economist.com/books-and-arts/2021/11/13/two-books-assess-the-fight-against-global-corruption, accessed on November 13, 2021.

40 "Pessimism about the Labour Market is Overdone," *The Economist Special Report*, April 10, 2021, https://www.economist.com/special-report/2021/04/08/pessimism-about-the-labour-market-is-overdone, accessed on April 10, 2021.

41 "Janet Yellen Calls for a Global Minimum Tax on Companies. Could it Happen?" *The Economist*, April 10, 2021, https://www.economist.com/finance-and-economics/2021/04/08/janet-yellen-calls-for-a-global-minimum-tax-on-companies-could-it-happen, accessed on April 10, 2021.

42 Tompor, S. (2018), "Former Enron exec Talks about Ethics, GE and Hillary Clinton," *Detroit Free Press*, March 24, 2018, https://www.freep.com/story/money/personal-finance/susan-tompor/2018/03/24/enron-andrew-fastow-fraud-investments/442203002/, accessed on April 8, 2020.

43 CMI (2018), "5 Lessons on Bouncing Back From Ultimate Rogue Trader Nick Leeson," *Chartered Management Institute*, August 27, 2018, https://www.managers.org.uk/knowledge-and-insights/article/5-lessons-on-bouncing-back-from-nick-leeson/, accessed on April 8, 2021.

44 Geert Hofstede et al. (2010), *Cultures and Organizations: Software of the Mind (3rd edition)* (New York: McGraw Hill, 2010), p. 6.

45 Geertz, C. (1973), *The Interpretation of Cultures* (New York: Basic Books), p. 5.

46 Trompenaars, F., and Hampden-Turner, C. (1997), *Riding the Waves of Culture: Understanding Cultural Diversity in Business, Second Edition* (London: Nicholas Brealey Publishing), pp. 21–24.

47 Hindle, T., quoted in "Culture," *The Economist*, September 17, 2009, https://www.economist.com/news/2009/09/17/culture, accessed on April 13, 2021.

48 Schein, E., "What is Culture?" in *Changing Minds*, http://changingminds.org/explanations/culture/what_is_culture.htm, accessed on July 25, 2012.

49 "CEO Activism in America is Risky Business," *The Economist*, April 14, 2021, https://www.economist.com/business/2021/04/14/ceo-activism-in-america-is-risky-business, accessed on April 16, 2021.

50 Dwoskin, E. (2021), "Facebook is Changing its Name to Meta as it Focuses on the Virtual World," *The Washington Post*, October 28, 2021, https://www.washingtonpost.com/technology/2021/10/28/facebook-meta-name-change/, accessed on November 14, 2021.

51 Slotnik, D. E. (2021), "Whistle-Blower Unites Democrats and Republicans in Calling for Regulation of Facebook," *The New York Times*, October 5, 2021, https://www.nytimes.com/live/2021/10/05/technology/facebook-whistleblower-frances-haugen, accessed on November 14, 2021.

Chapter 5
The Criminal Strategy External Continuum

Organized crime organizations are subject to the same strategic factors as legitimate businesses, except that the law renders their business illegitimate by definition. Strategic decisions are affected by the external environment, changes in it, and how such changes impact competition.

"PESTLE" Framework

The PESTLE framework considers six factors in an organization's external environment (political, economic, social, technological, legal, and environmental) that affect its ability to execute strategy. The framework is widely taught and treats the six components as independent of each other.[1] However, in reality, they interact.

The classical view of Adam Smith in his *Wealth of Nations* (1776), and of John Stuart Mill in his *Principles of Political Economy* (1848), was that economics and politics cannot be discussed in isolation from each other.[2] The economic environment is affected by domestic and international politics – this is still true in today's interconnected world.[3] Social considerations, impacted by technology, affect politics and economics. There have been dramatic consequences on economic growth rates, job opportunities, the structure of society, and the distribution of wealth. The Industrial Revolution reconfigured social and political structures of agrarian economies. These changes impacted the economic outlooks and expectations of countries. The ICT (information and communication technologies) revolution similarly changed both economic and political opportunities and problems. "Industry 4.0"[i] will in turn change political, economic, and social environments. The "economy" is not independent of environment. In the words of Sir Crispin Tickell, a former chief scientific adviser to the UK government:

> The economy is a subset of the ecology; without the services provided by Nature, there can be no economy.[4]

---

i "Industry 4.0 is often used interchangeably with the notion of the fourth industrial revolution. It is characterized by, among others, (1) even more automation than in the third industrial revolution, (2) the bridging of the physical and digital world through cyber-physical systems, enabled by Industrial IoT, (3) a shift from a central industrial control system to one where smart products define the production steps, (4) closed-loop data models and control systems, and (5) personalization/customization of products.

The goal is to enable autonomous decision-making processes, monitor assets and processes in real-time, and enable equally real-time connected value creation networks through early involvement of stakeholders, and vertical and horizontal integration." "Industry 4.0: the fourth industrial revolution explained," *i-Scoop*, https://www.i-scoop.eu/industry-4-0/, accessed on April 27, 2021.

https://doi.org/10.1515/9783110712155-005

Although the six components of the PESTLE framework do not operate independently, we explore them separately for the sake of clarity.

Political Environment

Political considerations limit the freedom of all, criminal or otherwise. Chapter 2 showed that when the state is strong and effective, there is little room for OC to flourish; and when the state is weak or failed, the conditions for OC are good. Corrupt, weak, or failed states create conditions of uncertainty that legitimate businesses find difficult to manage, whereas OC flourishes in such conditions.

Machiavelli in *The Discourses on Livy,* described six modes of governmental operation, three effective and three ineffective:

> Others – and with better judgment many think – say that there are six types of government, of which three are very bad, and three good in themselves but easily become corrupt, so that they too must be classed as pernicious. . . . For Principality easily becomes Tyranny. From Aristocracy the transition to Oligarchy is an easy one. Democracy is without difficulty converted into Anarchy. So that if anyone who is organizing a commonwealth sets up one of the first three forms of government, he sets up what will last but for a while[5]

Machiavelli's "Principality" is an absolute monarchy. The difference between Principality and Tyranny is the benevolence of the ruler. Like Polybius before him,[6] Machiavelli saw long, inevitable, cycles of political change. Princes become tyrants because of the corrupting effect of absolute power. When the nobles can no longer stand the arbitrary and cruel behavior of tyrants, they replace them, and share powers between themselves and the king creating a hereditary aristocracy. With the passage of time, the aristocracy become rent-seekers, controlling resources, and become oligarchs – the few who exploit the many. In due course, political pressures force oligarchs to democratize.

Polybius suggested that democracies inevitably decay into mob rule, and anarchy; and that the ensuing chaos leads to the rise of a new autocrat.[7] The experiences of the United States after 1776, and the UK after the Great Reform Act of 1832[8] present a more optimistic picture. The experience of France after 1789 of the Jacobin Terror leading to Napoleon's rise to imperial power, or that of Russia in 1917 leading to the totalitarian Leninist state, support Polybius' argument, as discussed in our previous book *The Principles and Practice of Effective Leadership.*[9]

From a business strategy point of view, legitimate and illegal businesses have to appreciate (1) that different types of government have different priorities and values, (2) that societies transition from one mode of government to the next, (3) that interactions with the political realm need to adapt accordingly, and (4) that the rise and fall of vested interests *within* government requires them to anticipate the consequences of change and take timely corrective action.

Chapter 2 showed how the Mafia, Triads, and Yakuza responded to their governments and were, at times, symbiotic supporters when the governments were weak, in return being allowed to operate and reap monetary rewards. In Italy, before its reunification, Mafia precursors were subcontractors enforcing law and order on landowners' agricultural estates in the southern Kingdom of Naples,[10] and for the northern Piedmontese government establishing its authority in Sicily after reunification,[11] and later for the Christian Democrat governments (based in Rome) after World War II. In pre-communist China[12] and Taiwan,[13] Triads did the "dirty work"[14] for governments.[15] Far from being secret societies, the Yakuza have always been regulated by the Japanese state.

Sometimes the boundary between political movements and criminal organizations is fluid. For example, the I.R.A.[16] and the Protestant loyalist paramilitaries[17] in Northern Ireland, the FARC in Colombia,[18] Hezbollah in Lebanon,[19] the Taliban in Afghanistan, or Al Shabab in Somalia[20] all began as political movements, only to become OC organizations to finance their activities.[21]

The common aim of OC, and legitimate organizations, when dealing with the political realm, is to (1) maximize their access to resources within their niches of operation, (2) minimize competition, and (3) maximize profit from such actions.

OC uses direct methods of influence such as illegal intimidation, extortion, and murder to achieve their objectives, whereas legitimate organizations cannot, when such actions are outside the law. Instead, legitimate organizations lobby key stakeholders within government, and influencers outside it,[ii] and donate money to political parties to maximize the likelihood of favorable responses to their requests;[22] sometimes this crosses over into bribery and corruption to achieve their ends (discussed in Chapter 3) and in extreme cases they can; resorting to intimidation, extortion, and murder through the use of OC. Occasionally, they have participated in undemocratic regime change, backed by their governments: for example, the coup in Iran in 1953 when democratically elected President Mossadeq was overthrown by the United States to strengthen the rule of the Shah and undo Mossadeq's nationalization of the Anglo-Iranian Oil Company (later to become British Petroleum);[23] and President Allende of Chile was overthrown by the United States at the instigation of Harold Geneen, Chairman and CEO of the American ITT Corporation.[24]

---

ii "A broader definition [of lobbying] is provided by the American Association of Government Relations Professionals (AGRP) which observes that lobbying goes beyond communicating with officials and includes analysing and researching legislative proposals in addition to working with other groups and educating government officials, employees and corporate officers about the implications of various changes. Indeed, some observers have argued that lobbying enhances the legislative process as outside groups can provide legislators with important information and expertise, particularly on topics of a more technical and complex nature, which can in turn improve the quality of legislation." Chambers, A. (2016), "The Lobbying of the EU: How to Achieve Greater Transparency," *Civitas: Institute for the Study of Civil Society*, February 2016, p. 5, https://www.civitas.org.uk/content/files/Anthony-Chambers-EU-lobbying.pdf, accessed on April 23, 2021.

Changes of regime can lead to changes of ownership through expropriation or nationalization. Such changes lead to changes in priorities, and leadership of enterprises, as with Alibaba in China.[25]

Economic Environment

All organizations, including organized crime, need to understand the impact of political policy on the domestic economy, the effects of globalization, and nature of regional and local economies.

It is sometimes assumed that the health of the economy has a direct relationship with the levels of crime. It is suggested that when the economy does well, unemployment drops and therefore people find it easier to get jobs rather than commit crimes to sustain their lives, and that when there are recessions that create increased unemployment, the unemployed turn to crime as a result. The evidence shows a more complicated picture. Research in the US over the period 1960–2009 did not support this presumption applying to *violent* crime, but did find a small but statistically significant relationship with the incidence of *property* crime. Consumer *sentiment* about the economy was found to be more important. However, given the variations in findings between studies of different duration and in different cities in the US, where other factors such as approaches to local policing contributed to outcomes, it is difficult to assert with confidence that changes in short-term macroeconomic factors have a big impact on levels of opportunistic crime.[26] OC is only peripherally interested in opportunistic crime, but an increase in the supply of young potential criminals may be something from which it benefits.

1 Macroeconomic Considerations
OC is a major economic player estimated in 2009 to have invested US$ 1.6 trillion of its US$ 2.1 trillion proceeds in the legal economy.[27] Governmental goals of macroeconomic policy are a high and growing level of national output (GDP), high levels of employment with as low a level of unemployment as is consistent with stable, or gently rising prices.[28] Governments use fiscal policy[iii] and monetary policy[iv] to achieve these objectives.

---

iii Fiscal policy consists of government expenditure and taxation. Government expenditure influences the size of collective as opposed to private consumption. Taxation reduces private spending and affects private saving, as well as investment and production. It is used to influence long-term growth in GDP through its impact on savings levels and on incentives to work and save. Samuelson, P. A., and Nordhaus, W. D. (2002), *Economics, International Edition, Seventeenth Edition* (New York: McGraw-Hill Irwin), pp. 421–422.
iv Monetary policy is undertaken by the central bank fixing the supply of money. Changes in money supply move interest rates, affecting business investment rates of return, mortgages and the

GDP, the usual measure of a country's economic performance, reflects the inter-action of domestic aggregate supply and demand. Aggregate supply is calculated using four factors (capital, labor, land, and technology), their price level, and costs. Aggregate demand is calculated by the levels of public and private consumption and savings or debt. These interactions determine levels and trends in GDP, em-ployment, prices, and inflation, exchange rates, and the balance of payments. These factors interact to create the business cycle with its booms and recessions.[29]

Keynesian (demand side) economic policies aim to stimulate the economy and in the short-to-medium term, can be successful (as was the case in the US in the 1960s) but they may create unwelcome inflation or stagflation (a period when there is falling output and rising prices, and ultimately higher unemployment, as hap-pened from 1973 onward). Fiscal policies are then adopted by governments to re-strain and reduce inflation (as when Paul Volcker of the US Federal Reserve raised interest rates and adopted a tight monetary policy).[30] Some economists worry that the unprecedented expansionary fiscal and monetary policies adopted by govern-ments of developed economies in response to the supply shock caused by the Covid-19 pandemic could trigger a repeat of the 1970s, rating the chance of US stag-flation at 33% in the coming years.[31] Given the high levels of inflation globally not seen since the 1980s, it looks as though they were correct.[v]

2 Microeconomic Considerations

OC organizations need to worry just as much as legitimate businesses about the im-pact of macroeconomic policies globally, nationally, and locally on microeconomic considerations: on the demand for their existing goods and services, on the prices they can charge, on the costs of supplying their goods and services, on the availability and costs of the raw materials, energy, labor, and capital they use to create legitimate revenue streams. They need to worry about cash flow, working capital management (debtors, creditors, and inventory policies) and associated costs of finance, the pay-ment terms they offer to customers and the credit they are offered by suppliers.

OC has potentially three systemic advantages when competing with legitimate businesses: (1) if businesses are a front for money laundering, then profitability is secondary, allowing organizations to continue trading under conditions that would bankrupt legitimate businesses, and capture market share as a result; (2) given the value systems of their investors/sponsors, they are more likely to cut corners, break

ability to buy housing, and the balance of payments through the effect of interest rates on exchange rates. Monetary policy has an important effect on both actual and potential GDP. Ibid., p. 422.
v Isidore, C., (2022), "This is the worst inflation in nearly 40 years. But it was so much worse back then", *CNN*, January 12, 2022, "https://edition.cnn.com/2022/01/11/economy/inflation-history/index.html", accessed on June 25, 2022.

the law, or ignore regulations, allowing them to enjoy the financial benefits of free-riding; and (3) they have fewer competing stakeholder priorities to worry about, making decision-making faster, simpler, and easier, because they do not have to be as concerned about ESG performance assessments by regulators, lenders, and investors. The mix of businesses that OC are typically engaged in (construction, waste management, hospitality, and entertainment) is local in nature, so economic and social policies as they affect local communities, such as state and municipal taxation and investment, and policing and social welfare policies, are important.

3 Globalization

As a result of supply shocks caused by Covid-19's disruption to global supply chains, the pressure to deglobalize supply chains has increased.

Perhaps it is useful to explain how globalization came about and what it is:

> The great economic globalisation only began some ten thousand years ago. Agriculture was invented in quite small areas of the Middle East, China and Mexico and from there spread in a very few thousand years over the whole globe. Again, there were losers; in society after society the hunter-gatherers disappeared or were subdued. Societies of considerable equality, where distinction was personally earned, gave way to taxation and hierarchies. With agriculture came money, writing, armies, kings and priests. These too spread relatively quickly over the globe, though the process was not completed till firearms destroyed almost the last hunter-gatherer societies in the 19th century.[32]

Globalization from an economic perspective includes:

a. *International activities* where borders are crossed involving the sale of goods and services, financial flows, and some movement of people. Typically, a company based in one country exports goods and services without having its own operations established in the countries to which it exports, using third parties to distribute them.

b. *Multinational activities* where companies headquartered in one country establish subsidiaries employing people and investing in fixed assets in the markets that they serve.

c. *Offshore activities* where the primary purpose is to minimize or avoid tax on activities generated by business done in the markets in which they operate. Company subsidiaries based in offshore tax havens are good examples of this.

d. *Global activities* which are integrated and coordinated so that *customers* can be offered a global service, regardless of where they are and where production is located without regard to national frontiers.

Legitimate businesses can choose to operate in any one of the four ways described above. However, OC can only operate using international or offshore activities, as multinational and global activities require regulated/licensed presences in the countries where the business is being done. This does not prevent them from establishing global supply chains comprising independent entities whose activities and ownership cannot be traced back to them. OC can only provide *illicit* products and services to other independent organizations that are at arms-length because they must break the chain of accountability to prevent detection by the authorities. OC organizations operate successfully as money launderers. If they are to benefit from the business opportunities provided by multinational or global modes of operation, they can only achieve this as "hidden" investors in legitimate businesses because such operations require legally transparent reporting lines of authority and accountability.

Most firms do not have real multinational exposure; their primary interest is to serve their local markets, followed by regional markets and then national markets. This is true of OC as well. However, certain major industries are more globalized than others and are important to legitimate businesses but not to OC – notably, physical commodities,[vi] scale-driven goods and services,[vii] manufactured commodities,[viii] consumer goods,[ix] and professional business services.[x]

Localized industries are important to both legitimate businesses and to OC, notably local unbranded goods and services,[xi] for example, gambling, hospitality, and entertainment. As is the case for most legitimate business, the primary focus of OC tends to be on local markets: loan sharking, extortion, prostitution, infiltrating labor unions and legitimate domestic industries such as construction, waste management, the garment trade, and ice-making. Drug smuggling and human trafficking are global; the sources of supply and the final demand are in different countries, as it is for arms trafficking, and blood diamonds.

Social Environment

The importance of the social environment is often underestimated, yet it is an organization's "license to operate." When society decides it does not like what an organization is trying to do or how it is doing its business, the organization has to

---

vi Petroleum, minerals and timber. Source: World Development Report (World Bank); McGraw-Hill/DRI World Economic Outlook 1996; United Nations, 1995, National Income Accounts; McKinsey analysis.

vii Aerospace engines, construction equipment, semiconductors, airframes, shipping, refineries, machine tools. Ibid.

viii Refined petroleum products, aluminum, specialty steel, bulk pharmaceuticals, pulp, specialty chemicals. Ibid.

ix Consumer electronics, PCs, cameras, automobiles, TVs, soft drinks, shoes, luxury goods, pharmaceuticals, film production. Ibid.

x Investment banking, legal services, consulting services. Ibid.

xi Construction materials, real estate, funeral homes, education, household services, medical care, utilities. Ibid.

either stop, or be prepared to face increased costs reflecting society's disapproval through taxation, regulation, and the higher costs of recruitment and retention.

1 The "License to Operate"

A recent example of a failure to prevail upon the social environment is the defeat of the European Super League (ESL) in football (soccer) in April 2021.[33] It failed to get the "license to operate."

For readers who are not familiar with the pyramid structure of football (soccer) competitions, it differs from the way spectator sports are organized in American football, basketball, and baseball; or outside America, in rugby and cricket. Unlike soccer, they all have super leagues of established clubs/teams that compete against each other year after year. These are commercial enterprises, designed to maximize events and profits for their club/team owners.

The English Premier League (EPL), consisting of twenty clubs competing in any given year, is the most followed of the European domestic leagues globally. The foreign billionaire owners of five of the top six English clubs,[xii] and the local billionaire owners of the top three Italian clubs and top three Spanish clubs, regard football (soccer) as an economic enterprise, based on global TV viewership, and wanted to emulate the US and Indian super leagues in the other sports. Their logic was economically rational, but socially, and politically naive.

As owners of global brands, they wanted to maximize their reach for viewership and share of the TV license fees, fees from sponsorship by players, and sales of memorabilia. To do this, they decided to set up the ESL, consisting of twenty teams, fifteen of which would be permanent members (twelve of which had already signed up[xiii]). But European football is different from sports in the United States.[xiv] Even the most famous clubs can be relegated to inferior divisions where the financial rewards are much less, while upstart clubs can rise from inferior divisions and enter the top divisions, adding unpredictability and excitement that does not exist in the other super leagues, where the same clubs/teams compete with each other year after year. This reflects the local nature of football and its place in society. European clubs have been around for more than a hundred years and have devoted, loyal, local fans. In the case of Germany's Bundesliga clubs, by law, fans own 51% of the shares, so owners cannot ignore the feelings and desires of fans.

---

xii Arsenal (Stan Kroenke, American), Chelsea (Roman Abramovich, Russian-Israeli), Liverpool (John W. Henry, American), Manchester City (Sheikh Mansour bin Zayed Al Nahyan, Emirati royal), Manchester United (The Glazer family, American); only Tottenham have an English owner (Daniel Levy).

xiii From England's EPL: Arsenal, Chelsea, Liverpool, Manchester City, Manchester United, and Tottenham Hotspur; from Italy's Serie A: AC Milan, Inter Milan and Juventus; and from Spain's La Liga: Atletico Madrid, Barcelona, and Real Madrid.

xiv England's EPL, Spain's La Liga, Italy's Serie A, Germany's Bundesliga, and France's Ligue 1.

Within 24 hours of the surprise announcement of the formation of the ESL on April 18, 2021, the six English clubs were forced to withdraw by the anger and outrage of the fans, of the managers, of the players of the clubs (none of whom had been consulted), and of all the political parties in England – the government then threatened to introduce legislation to prevent the clubs from playing in the ESL.[34] The world governing body of football (FIFA) and the governing body of European football (UEFA) threatened that any players who played in the ESL would not be allowed to play in the World Cup or the European Cup. Within 48 hours, the ESL was dead; without the six English clubs, it was a non-starter; and the Chief Executive of Manchester United, one of the key protagonists of the proposal, who was much hated by the fans, was forced to resign.[35]

From a financial perspective, the owners proposing the formation of the ESL would have improved the financial outcomes for their clubs and created stronger global brand franchises in which to invest without fearing the consequences of relegation. What the owners failed to realize is that the social license for football clubs to operate in Europe and Latin America involves providing identity, and community to its fans in the cities where the clubs are; but also, to its global supporters. It would be inconceivable to move a club from one city to another in Europe, whereas in the US, 11 NFL teams,[36] 13 major league baseball teams,[37] and 13 NBA teams[38] have been moved from one city to another. It is unsurprising that American owners did not understand the importance of local fans. It is surprising, however, that the Spanish, and Italian owners misread the situation. The owners never gained the social "license to operate" for their scheme.

Misjudging the social and political environment is a serious strategic error that does not just apply to legitimate businesses. It applies to OC as well. The socio-political "license to operate" for OC is well illustrated by the relationship between the mafia and Italian society:

> However, as mafias are a cultural and social phenomenon before being a legal/criminal issue, institutional responses have to be calibrated on social impacts. As noticed:
>
> *Political institutions, in Italy, from time to time, have fixed a threshold of tolerability of mafia interference in the public and social life, upon which they have based legislative, political, cultural interventions.*
>
> The ruling class – and it is agreed among all interviewees – is often complacent with the presence of mafia money and mafia connections in certain aspects of public life, especially in the regions of traditional mafia birth and presence. *Fixing the tolerability threshold is a way to "absorb mafia influence into the power system" because of that convergence of interests between mafia and politics*[39]   [Emphases ours]

In 1992, the Cosa Nostra in Sicily, feeling threatened by the successes of two anti-mafia magistrates, Giovanni Falcone and Paolo Borsellino, assassinated them and their escorts in separate incidents, violating the "tolerability threshold." In the first incident, Falcone, his wife, and three members of his police escort died when their cars were blown up on their way to Palermo airport. In the second incident, two months later, Borsellino and five members of his escort were killed by a car bomb outside his mother's house. The Cosa Nostra celebrated their deaths, believing that the death of the judges removed the threat to their business.[40]

Five days after Borsellino's death, the Italian state responded to what it realized was an existential threat by sending 5,000 soldiers to declare all-out war on the Cosa Nostra. As a result of an effective anti-mafia campaign of relentless arrests by the Italian state, the Cosa Nostra no longer had the capacity to intimidate, or to manufacture heroin imported into the US. They lost that business to the Calabrian 'Ndrangheta who treat them as distributors. Mafiosi are no longer respected or feared by the citizens of Palermo, and shops and restaurants no longer pay for protection:[41]

> On the windows of dozens of storefronts and restaurants in Via Maqueda, the lively street that runs through the city's historic centre, is the "Addiopizzo" (Goodbye extortion) sticker, which is a pledge that the business owners have refused to pay protection money to Mafia bosses. It's just one of the many signs that today Cosa Nostra is the one on its knees.[42]

This was achieved by 4,000 arrests since the murders of Falcone and Borsellino and most crucially the arrest in 1993 and death in prison in 2017 of Toto "the Beast" Riina who ordered the assassinations. There has not been a "boss" capable of replacing him. The harsh prison sentences and denial of access to the outside world made it impossible to continue with "business as usual"; and mafiosi began to break "Omerta" – the vow of silence – to become "pentiti," and informed on their former associates. By 2019, 300 mafiosi were collaborating with the authorities.[43]

The Cosa Nostra has been seriously weakened and its prestige has been damaged and it has lost the fearful respect of Sicilians. As a result of relentless arrests, and the economic crisis following the Global Financial Crisis (GFC), it has been short of cash and foot soldiers to do its dirty work. It is no longer able to attack and defeat the state. In the words of Falcone's sister:

> In comparison to yesterday's bosses, who waged war against the Italian state, the new generation are chicken thieves.[44]

The mafiosi themselves recognize their loss of status and respect and it is obvious to outsiders as well:

> "What kind of bloody mafia are we?" asked Alfredo Giordano, a former mafioso from Palermo caught on wiretap. "The mafia of lost causes." He wasn't even able to recover objects that were stolen from his daughter.

> The mafiosi who speak today used to drive Mercedes down the streets of Palermo in the 1980s. Men who held in their hands the life or death of police officers and journalists have lost their power to intimidate.[45]

Falcone and Borsellino are commemorated in Palermo with obelisks and murals; mafia killings which used to be in the hundreds were reduced to so few that when two hitmen in 2017 killed Mafia boss, Giuseppe Dainotti, as he was riding his bicycle to the grocery, people did not know what to make of it. They mistook the sound of the two shots for fireworks.[46] In short, the Cosa Nostra's social "license to operate" has been seriously damaged:

> Not only has law enforcement become hugely effective against Cosa Nostra, but its income stream from protection rackets has diminished. A campaign of civil resistance against paying the mafia tax has been widely successful. On the streets of Palermo, which was once held hostage under the reign of Riina and his *capos, Cosa Nostra no longer exerts the terror it did. If a mafioso approaches a small businessman and demands payment, he is likely to get beaten up.*
>
> Among anti-mafia investigators, there is no complacency. Federico Cafiero De Raho, the chief anti-mafia prosecutor, told la Repubblica: "Criminal organisations have penetrated politics and the economy without anyone seeing, without being noticed. *The clans have abandoned their strategy of violence and intimidation and now attain their goals not with guns but sitting behind desks, by means of corruption, collusion. Our next task is to find and root out the mafia's accomplices in the professional classes."*
>
> The old-school image of the powerful and intimidating boss who could freeze blood with a look or have someone killed with a word no longer applies. *The mafia's economy is now run through legitimate companies: in Sicily, windfarms and supermarkets, road transport and real estate. Money is laundered via international property deals and banks.*
>
> Roberto Scarpinato, another anti-mafia prosecutor, has denounced the "obscene power," the corrupt businesses and politicians that allow criminal organisations to operate. *He says the mafia no longer needs to force its way into the institutions of state.* "There's less violence: they don't need to kill you if they can buy you."[47]   [Emphases ours]

Something similar happened to the Yakuza in Japan in 1991 after they diversified into real estate accompanied by gang wars in the 1980s. They may have achieved increases in revenue from a new line of business, but they crossed a "tolerability threshold" because the Japanese government introduced new legislation – the *Bōt-aihō* law[48] – that led to Yakuza organizations being officially designated as *bōryo-kudan* or "violent groups," irreversibly altering Yakuza interactions with police, politicians, and the social regard they were held in:

> The AntiBoryokudan Law's primary effect has been to organize public opinion against the Ya-kuza. However, the legislation relies too heavily on individuals and communities to shoulder the burden in the battle against the Yakuza.[49]

This weakened their "license to operate," and led to the loss of three quarters of their official members.[50] The Japanese authorities did not go as far as the Italians who had made it a crime to be a member or associated with the mafia, allowing Yakuza members to remain highly visible and still command some respect:

> Until legislation is enacted that provides prosecutors with the tools necessary to attach criminal liability to Yakuza membership, the Yakuza will remain an influential presence in Japanese society.[51]

Aware of the adverse change in the way society viewed them, the Yakuza made strenuous efforts to present themselves as socially responsible organizations by being visibly the first responders with help for the victims of the Great Hanshin Earthquake in 1995, and helping the police to restore law and order, and again to help the victims of the Great Tōhoku Earthquake and Tsunami in 2011.[52]

2 Costs of Social Disapproval

The costs of social disapproval do not appear in an organization's profit and loss statement. Usually they reflect externalities – the costs of doing business that are paid for by the community and not the company; environmental damage caused by depletion of scarce biodiverse resources, pollution, and waste; public health costs resulting from dangerous working practices and conditions; health and safety costs caused by production processes and products that are not fit for purpose; economic harm caused by financial practices; corruption, and violations of human rights and harassment in the workplace or supply chain.

Social disapproval takes time to materialize because the evidence of what caused the harms and associated costs is incomplete, and can be plausibly denied for many years by the perpetrators of such costs, for example, in the cases of smoking and cancer,[53] diabetes,[54] and cardiovascular disease (CVD);[55] sugar and obesity with its related diseases of diabetes[56] and CVD mortality;[57] fossil fuels and climate change;[58] refineries and pollution.[59]

Sometimes social disapproval occurs because people's perceptions of what is regarded as acceptable changes, as in the cases of child labor and sweatshop working conditions. In 1800 it was regarded as acceptable for an eight-year-old child to work underground in an English coal mine. It no longer is. Child labor is the norm in agrarian societies; today it is regarded as being morally wrong[xv] and companies

---

xv *"Child labour is defined as work that is inappropriate for a child's age, affects children's education, or is likely to harm their health, safety or morals.* It should be emphasized that not all work carried out by children is considered child labour. Some activities may help children acquire important livelihood skills and contribute to their survival and food security. However, much of the work children do in agriculture is not age-appropriate, is likely to be hazardous or interferes with children's education. For instance, *a child under the minimum age for employment who is hired to herd cattle, a child applying pesticides, and a child who works all night on a fishing boat and is too tired to go to school the next day would all be considered child labour.*

Child labour perpetuates a cycle of poverty for the children involved, their families and communities. Without education, these boys and girls are likely to remain poor. The prevalence of child labour in agriculture violates the principles of decent work. By perpetuating poverty, it undermines efforts to reach sustainable food security and end hunger.

Worldwide, the majority of child labour is found in the agriculture sector (71%). Today, 108 million boys and girls are engaged in child labour in crop production, livestock, forestry, fisheries or aquaculture, often working long hours and facing occupational hazards. Child labour

that are accused of employing child labor, even indirectly in their supply chains, suffer severe consequences to their market capitalization. For example, when Gap faced protests over a factory in El Salvador in December of 1995, its stock price fell more than 12%. Wal-Mart's stock fell 3.75% when it was exposed for using child labor in Bangladesh in late 1992.[60] Nike lost 15% in its market capitalization in 2001 when it was revealed that sexual favors were exchanged for jobs and that women had been abused in its suppliers' factories in Indonesia,[61] and Oshkosh B'gosh's fell 9.66% when it was charged with complicity in labor abuses in Saipan.[62] Despite the apparent best efforts in the cocoa industry, problems persist:

> Nestlé, Cargill, Barry Callebaut, Mars, Olam, Hershey and Mondelēz have been named as defendants in a lawsuit filed in Washington DC by the human rights firm International Rights Advocates (IRA), on behalf of eight former child slaves who say they were forced to work without pay on cocoa plantations in the west African country.[63]

In the 1950s and '60s, role models smoked; films and TV showed people smoking. However, as the steady drip-drip of medically-respected science gradually overcame the denials of tobacco companies in developed markets, smoking lost its social cachet. It was banned on flights[64] and public transportation more generally,[65] self-censored out of films and TV,[66] forbidden by companies in offices,[67] then in restaurants,[68] and finally in pubs and bars.[69] Advertising and promotion aimed at young people was prohibited;[70] and the advertising that was allowed became generic, with gruesome pictures of the health consequences of smoking on cigarette packs.[71] To be a smoker was no longer a matter of admiration, it became more likely the subject of a concerned conversation by friends and acquaintances on why the smoker should quit the habit or adverse comments when smoking, given the revelation that secondary smoking was harmful to the health of others.[72] Consequently, tobacco companies found it harder to recruit the best talent,[73] have to pay above market rate to hire and retain them,[74] and senior executives in the tobacco companies are not regarded as role models to be emulated.

Financial services were a highly regarded sector in society before the Global Financial Crisis (2007–2009);[75] those who work in the sector may still be highly paid, but they are no longer as well-regarded or trusted.[76] This is the result of the financial crisis that caused the Great Recession resulting from:

> The shoddy conduct of mortgage brokers in pushing clients into dodgy subprime loans, the massive securitization of mortgages and other loans into overly complex bond investments

---

violates the rights of children. By endangering the health and education of the young, it also forms an obstacle to sustainable agriculture development and food security." [Emphases ours]

Food and Agriculture Organization of the United Nations (2021), "Child Labour in Agriculture," *Food and Agriculture Organization,* http://www.fao.org/childlabouragriculture/en/, accessed on April 28, 2021.

acquired by financial firms around the globe, the failure of regulatory agencies to correct the slapdash lending practices and excessive leverage of financial institutions, the disgraceful work of bond rating firms in evaluating the complex, multi-tranched investments churned out by the banks, the abysmal risk management system employed by AIG, and the massive operations of the shadow banking and over-the-counter derivatives markets.[77]

Those responsible, however, did not go to jail because their behavior was not illegal at the time.[78]

When legitimate businesses grow large enough to present a systemic risk to society as a result of bad decisions, they are protected by the TBTF "Too Big To Fail" argument that the costs to society are too great to bear, regardless of the ensuing social disapproval. OC does not have this protection. It is not usually allowed to grow to the point where its continued existence becomes integral to the functioning of society – a lesson that the Cosa Nostra in Sicily learned to its cost and that the 'Ndrangheta is now learning in the "maxi-trials" that are taking place in Italy that are expected to last another couple of years.[79]

As long as the 'Ndrangheta was localized to Calabria and small, the Italian state left it to its own devices. However, once it replaced the Cosa Nostra and expanded into the north of Italy and then into the Netherlands, Australia, and the UK, it became too large to ignore:

> The 'Ndrangheta mafia from southern Italy made more money last year than Deutsche Bank and McDonald's put together with a turnover of €53bn (£44bn), a study has claimed.
>
> The study by the Demoskopika research institute detailed the international crime syndicate's sources of revenue, including drug trafficking – which brought in an estimated €24.2bn – and illegal garbage disposal, which earned it €19.6bn.
>
> *The southern Italian mafia earned the equivalent of 3.5% of Italy's gross domestic product (GDP) last year,* said the report based on analysis of documents from Italy's interior ministry and police, parliament's anti-mafia commission and the national anti-mafia task force.
>
> *The 'Ndrangheta is thought to have about 400 key "operatives" in 30 countries, but its activities are believed to involve as many as 60,000 people worldwide,* the report said.
>
> Extortion and usury last year brought in a substantial €2.9bn, while embezzlement earned the mafia €2.4bn and gambling €1.3bn. Arms sales, prostitution, counterfeiting goods and people-smuggling were less lucrative, bringing in less than €1bn together.[80]   [Emphases ours]

Social disapproval manifests in the form of "sin taxes" levied on alcohol, tobacco, gambling, and pornography.[81] As early as 1776, Adam Smith wrote that taxes on tobacco, sugar, and rum were appropriate as they were not necessities. Although sin taxes are effective in reducing the consumption of socially undesirable products and services, help offset the social and health costs incurred, and are popular with the voters, they are not high enough to stop the behavior they tax, nor do they completely pay for the social costs incurred.[82] "Sin" taxes are arbitrary: other harmful social or economic behaviors are not taxed in the same way. Lawmakers decide, arbitrarily, that some consequences require the behavior leading to them to be taxed, as in the cases of alcohol and tobacco, but others not, as in the cases of hard drugs which are completely prohibited.[83]

Drug prohibition has had a number of unintended consequences. It can create substance replacement to using "legal" but more hazardous drugs (for instance, opioids), with corresponding increased danger to users; higher hard drug prices leading to injecting unsafe adulterated product in unsanitary environments, leaving users with less disposable income for food, healthcare, and housing; social stigmatization discouraging users to seek help and support, negative attitudes toward users in health care providers, and lower self-esteem in users and increased psychological problems with their associates.[84]

Appreciating these drawbacks and the change in social attitudes toward recreational marijuana has caused some jurisdictions to change their attitudes to marijuana, leading them liberalize and regulate its production and distribution, benefiting users through better quality product and greater safety, benefiting law-abiding producers through increased revenues and lower distribution costs, increasing taxes at the expense of OC, but in the US also incurring higher borrowing costs to reflect the fear that states liberalizing marijuana face greater risks.[85]

We would do well to remember what happens when socially acceptable behavior is prohibited. Prohibition in the US (1920–1933) is a warning to all legislators. It does not stop the prohibited behavior. *Instead, it makes crime socially acceptable*, providing both cover for the criminals who satisfy the forbidden demand and sharply increased profits, allowing OC to grow and flourish, and benefiting mobsters like Al Capone:

> Although consumption of alcohol fell at the beginning of Prohibition, it subsequently increased. *Alcohol became more dangerous to consume; crime increased and became "organized"; the court and prison systems were stretched to the breaking point; and corruption of public officials was rampant.* No measurable gains were made in productivity or reduced absenteeism. *Prohibition removed a significant source of tax revenue and greatly increased government spending.* It led many drinkers to switch to opium, marijuana, patent medicines, cocaine, and other dangerous substances that they would have been unlikely to encounter in the absence of Prohibition.[86]   [Emphases ours]

Pigouvian taxes[xvi] are another way of registering social disapproval of activities being undertaken by legitimate organizations. These are taxes that are high enough to pay for all the externality-based costs to society, without being so high that they create a black market. Carbon taxes are an example. The UK imposed a carbon tax

---

xvi A Pigouvian tax is a government fee on any activity that creates socially harmful externalities. An externality is an activity that creates a negative effect on others in a society but not necessarily the person who carries out that activity.

that was high enough to encourage utility companies to switch from fossil fuels to generate electricity to natural gas which releases less greenhouse gases. As a result, the UK has been able to cut its greenhouse gas emissions to 19th century levels. A "sin" tax would not have been high enough to drive the utilities to use natural gas.[87]

Taxation is not an effective way of dealing with OC unless accompanied by legalizing their product or services, or when it concerns their investments in legitimate fronts used for laundering their illegally gained money.

Both OC and legitimate businesses are affected by the social environment when it comes to changes in demographics (available population, segmented by age, education, lifestage, gender, and ethnicity), in disposable income, in taste, fashion, and the desirability of competing brands that are themselves affected by technological innovation. Both OC and legitimate businesses attempt to maximize their share of available market margin by choosing where and how to compete.

Technological Environment

Schumpeter's "creative destruction"[88] is an integral part of capitalism leading to uncertainty and complexity. Technological impacts arise in two ways.[xvii] The first is disruptive technology where legitimate businesses must consider whether what is happening could render the organization obsolete. The second is operational in nature, where businesses need to concern themselves with answering three questions: (1) "Will what is being proposed work or not?" (2) "How far have we pushed the technology envelope?" and (3) "What is preventing us from doing it?"

1 Disruptive Technological Uncertainty

Disruptive technologies do not just improve performance; they change the game. They pose an existential threat to organizations. Established organizations have much to fear from disrupters, who threaten their dominance by introducing new products and business models. As Jack Welch, one-time CEO of GE put it:

> If the rate of change on the outside exceeds the rate of change on the inside, the end is near.[89]

Yet incumbents find it very difficult to follow this advice. Effective evolution even in organizations with a track record of past success in innovation is often blocked by the "Innovator's Dilemma."[90] Internal vested interests will fight such changes

---

xvii For a detailed discussion of technological uncertainty, see Zinkin, J. (2020), *The Challenge of Sustainability: Corporate Governance in a Complicated World* (Berlin/Boston: Walter de Gruyter Gmbh), pp. 176–182.

when it is not immediately obvious that change is required. And when it becomes obvious that change is required, it may be too late to do anything about it.

The key difference in the behavior of disrupters is their willingness to tolerate levels of uncertainty that incumbents are not. There are two conditions where delaying adopting disruptive technologies developed by competitors makes sense: (1) when the technology is "bleeding edge," in which case it is often better to be second to market and learn from the mistakes of the organization that is first to market; and (2) when rates of adoption take longer than expected, as a result of teething problems causing the new technology to underperform in its introductory phase, or of it being too expensive initially. For example, it took eight years before PCs posed an existential threat to minis and mainframe computers – time enough for IBM to join in and make it happen.[xviii] It took online retailing 15 years to become a threat to brick-and-mortar retailers.[xix]

2 Operational Technological Uncertainty

When faced with operational technological uncertainty, organizations need to consider: (1) "Will what is being proposed work?" (2) "How far have we pushed the technology envelope?" and (3) "What is preventing us from doing it?"

a. *Pushing the technology envelope beyond its known limits* where "unknown unknowns" affect the safety of the offer. In these circumstances, it is often better to be second to market.

b. *Lacking internal processes to ensure success* requires being sure that the right ideas are being selected for further investment. Surprisingly, most organizations have too many creative ideas to choose from rather than too few when it comes to new product ideas.[91] Typically, organizations fail to select well in one of three ways: (1) they seek to minimize uncertainty, filling product development pipelines with relatively riskless projects, which then yield only incremental improvements; (2) they spread their resources too thin, instead of concentrating on those projects with the best returns; or (3) they fail to allocate/reallocate sufficient resources each year because of uncertainty, with the resulting stagnation in innovation and its adverse impact on growth compared with companies that actively reallocate resources.[92]

---

xviii Xerox introduced the Alto in 1973. Only 2,000 were made. IBM introduced the IBM PC using Intel's 8088 chip and Microsoft's MS-DOS in 1981 and created the mass market for personal computers and the so-called "Wintel" monopoly that lasted until 2012.

xix Amazon was launched on July 5, 1994. Online sales overtook general merchandise brick-and-mortar retailing in the US on April 2, 2019. Rooney, K. (2019), "Online shopping overtakes a major part of retail for the first time ever," *CNBC*, April 2, 2019, https://www.cnbc.com/2019/04/02/online-shopping-officially-overtakes-brick-and-mortar-retail-for-the-first-time-ever.html, accessed on December 4, 2019.

While the threat of technology rendering products and services obsolete or uncompetitive applies to legitimate businesses that have major technological components in either the way they produce their goods and services or in the ways they communicate and distribute their offers, they do not really apply to OC because the technology components in the businesses they operate are relatively insignificant and they usually require face-to-face human interaction to be effective. Loan sharking, extortion, prostitution, and trafficking of people cannot be done remotely or by robots. That is not to say that OC will not have to consider trends in technology; they will for the legitimate businesses in which they invest their ill-gotten gains, just as legitimate businesses must, and in online distribution for their gambling, drugs, and pornography interests.

OC may have to consider new technologies in waste management, cement, and construction. They will be affected by the productivity improvements offered by computerization and changes in transportation in how they do their business; and they will have to recognize that automated computerization of customs and shipping documents will reduce opportunities to use bribery and corruption to smuggle legitimate goods like cigarettes across borders. They will, however, benefit from technology developments in the "dark web," raising cybercrime to industrial levels with targeted "ransomware" demands,[93] and moving money around without a trace using cryptocurrencies like Bitcoin.[94]

Legal Environment

Legal certainty is the foundation of the rule of law:

> It is the idea that the law must be sufficiently clear to provide those subject to legal norms with the means to regulate their own conduct and to protect against the arbitrary exercise of public power – has operated as a foundational rule of law value. As such, legal certainty has played a vital role in determining the space of individual freedom and the scope of state power. In this way, the ideal of legal certainty has been central in stabilizing normative expectations and in providing a framework for social interaction, as well as defining individual freedom and political power in modern societies.[95]

To achieve legal certainty, five conditions must apply: (1) laws and decisions must be made public; (2) laws and decisions must be definite and clear; (3) the decisions of the courts must be enforceable; (4) the retroactivity of the laws and decisions must be limited; and (5) legitimate interests and expectations must be protected.[96] Absent these conditions, legal uncertainty[xx] is the result and that makes investing difficult for legitimate businesses.

---

xx For further discussion of legal uncertainty, see Zinkin, *The Challenge of Sustainability*, pp. 182–185.

Legitimate businesses must consider carefully whether they should do business with or have subsidiaries in jurisdictions where these five preconditions for legal certainty do not exist. The short-term benefits of privileged access could well be outweighed by the long-term economic costs and reputational damage[xxi] of having been involved in such jurisdictions.

The law reflects what society thinks – and that changes over time. For example, through the 1950s people were persuaded that smoking was cool and good for the nerves, even though tobacco companies already knew it was harmful. Something similar has been happening over opioids and companies need to decide whether they should settle as Johnson & Johnson[97] and Purdue Pharma[98] did, or fight. Exxon Mobil faced a class action lawsuit in New York over the impact of fossil fuel usage on climate change on the basis that their climate change denial deceived shareholders.[99]

People often assume that obeying the law is a must and legitimate businesses often insist in their governance statements that obeying the law is a minimum standard they set for their employees and operations. Yet many of the same companies choose to break the law by disregarding environmental, health and safety, and consumer protection regulations and pay fines instead. There are several reasons for this behavior. In countries with weak enforcement, they may calculate it is worth running the risk of prosecution and fines because the likelihood of getting caught is low. In the event of getting caught, they can buy their way out of trouble. They may feel they can justify this behavior on the grounds that fines are "just the cost of doing business" and that as long as the bribe or the penalty is less than the bottom-line impact of breaking the law, it is worth doing. The reputational damage caused by prosecution may not feature in their thinking.

Sometimes multinational companies are caught in a jurisdictional crossfire. They face the agonizing dilemma of deciding which set of laws to obey – those of the host country or those of the country where they are headquartered. Sanctions can also present serious problems if there is a political disagreement about the appropriateness of sanctions between countries. For example, BNP Paribas in 2015[100] – a leading French bank – was fined US$ 8.9 billion by the US Department of Justice for doing business in Iran. This was perfectly legal in France when the US sanctioned the Iranian government – forbidding any company to trade with the country, using its extraterritorial reach because the trade was done in dollars and therefore came under US jurisdiction. BNP sought the support of the French government in

---

xxi Unforeseen economic costs could be caused by the arbitrary arrest of key personnel, expropriation of assets, unilateral increases in licensing fees or in the cost of necessary resources supplied by the government or its favored cronies, mandated changes in share ownership or partners with whom work must be done, or politically motivated application of retroactive legislation. Reputational damage could be caused by any of these *and* by scandals involving environmental degradation, human rights abuses, poor safety and working conditions, bribery, corruption, civil war, and ethnic cleansing.

defending its position. This only made matters worse and BNP was fined much more than HSBC – a British bank – which paid US$ 1.9 billion[xxii] without involving the British government.[101]

The law provides a framework that constrains operations of legitimate business and imposes regulatory costs of doing business on them. In the case of OC, the law does the opposite. Because they are outlaws by design, the law creates illicit markets for them in which they can flourish, without having to compete with legitimate organizations that may well be more efficient and capable of providing better products and services at lower cost. In some less developed and more corrupt countries, new legislation is seen as a negotiating opportunity for bribery and corruption to create workarounds.

OC can enter forbidden markets; it can also undercut legitimate businesses in legitimate markets by breaking the law and ignoring environmental and occupational health and safety regulatory requirements, without having to worry about reputational damage to brands or market capitalization. If things go wrong, OC can just shut down the existing operation and set up a new one, forcing regulators to play an unending game of "whack-a-mole."

The legal environment that all businesses face (including OC) is determined by national jurisdictions. Different countries respond according to the specific local threats raised by the criminal groups they have to deal with. Despite the fact that policies against OC vary according to the goals that they pursue (prevention or crime control), three issues in particular reflect the current approach to dealing with OC.[102]

1. Making it an offense[xxiii] to belong to a mafia type association that uses a mafia-type method. Its effect is to find members guilty regardless of whether they

---

xxii The HSBC fine covered Mexican drug money laundering as well as sanction violations in Iran, which represented less than half of the total fine.
xxiii Italian criminal code, article 416*bis* (Mafia-type unlawful association):

"Any person participating in a Mafia-type unlawful association including three or more persons shall be liable to imprisonment for 3 to 6 years. Those persons promoting, directing or organizing the said association shall be liable, for this sole offense, to imprisonment for 4 to 9 years. Mafia-type unlawful association is said to exist when the participants take advantage of the intimidating power of the association and of the resulting condition of submission and silence to commit criminal offenses, to manage, at all levels, control, either directly or indirectly, of economic activities, concessions, authorizations, public contracts and services, or to obtain unlawful profits or advantages for themselves or for others, or with a view to preventing or limiting the freedom to vote, or to get votes for themselves or for others on the occasion of an election.

Should the association be of the armed type, the punishment shall be imprisonment for 4 to 10 years pursuant to paragraph 1 and imprisonment for 5 to 15 years pursuant to paragraph 2. An association is said to be of the armed type when the participants have firearms or

intend to commit a crime. The result has been to weaken OC wherever it has been applied. RICO provisions in the US have a similar effect.[xxiv]

> To think of organized crime as a collective criminal effort that can be targeted through an all-inclusive offence, is indeed the distinctive approach of Italian authorities, mainly made it necessary by the disruptive power of mafias in the past 30–40 years. *The offence of membership in mafia-type associations is now an established weapon in the fight against mafias and it is considered the real turn of the screw of the system; the focus of the offence today is proving that an association uses the "mafia method."* The idea that there is the need to prove the existence of an association, its structures, its modus operandi, before being able to contest the criminal activity, is indeed the revolution of both membership offences in the Criminal Code.[103]
>
> [Emphasis ours]

The current 'Ndrangheta "maxi-trial" prosecutions in Italy would not have been possible had it not been specifically named under 416*bis* of the Italian criminal code in 2014;

2. Allowing the forfeiture and confiscation of illicitly acquired assets;
3. Authorizing special means of investigation including undercover agents, wire-taps, and witness protection programs designed to get associates to break their vows of secrecy and name others in return for lighter sentences. Each country has its own ways of implementing these policies.[xxv]

Environment

Climate change will have a major impact on businesses (both OC and legitimate) in three ways: (1) increasingly frequent and costly extreme weather events, (2) rising sea levels caused by melting ice, and (3) the need for humanity to change how it manages land.

---

explosives at their disposal, even if hidden or deposited elsewhere, to achieve the objectives of the said association. If the economic activities of which the participants in the said association aim to achieve or maintain the control are funded, totally or partially, by the price, the product or the proceeds of criminal offenses, the punishments referred to in the above paragraphs shall be increased by one-third to one-half. The offender shall always be liable to confiscation of the items that were used or meant to be used to commit the offense and of the items that represent the price, the product or the proceeds of such offense or the use thereof.

The provisions of this article shall also apply to the Camorra and to any other association, whatever its local title, seeking to achieve objectives that correspond to those of Mafia-type unlawful association by taking advantage of the intimidating power of the association."

Quoted in Adamoli, S. et al. (1998), "Organised Crime Around the World," *European Institute for Crime Prevention and Control Affiliated with the United Nations*, Publication Series, No. 31, p. 133.
xxiv For details, see ibid., p. 135.
xxv For details see ibid., pp. 135–172.

1 Extreme Weather Events

It seems that climate change is linked to increasingly severe and costly extreme weather events: hotter heat waves, drier droughts, bigger storm surges, and greater snowfall.[104]

2 Rising Sea Levels

If glaciers continue to melt at the current rates around the world, severe problems will result. The rise in sea levels will displace people as coastal climate refugees increase competition for ever scarcer land and food, leading to greater economic hardship and maybe to unforeseen conflicts. Melting ice does not just contribute to the rise in sea levels (estimated at least a half meter in the next eighty years), it puts billions of people at risk in Asia and South America as a result of their dependence on glaciers to store water for them, acting as "water towers in the clouds." Climate change makes things worse in low-lying, coastal areas, river deltas, drylands, and in permafrost areas. Over the period 1961–2013, the annual area of drylands in drought has increased, on average, by more than 1% per year, with large variations in given years. Storm surges could make matters worse, as Hurricane Sandy did in New York in 2012.[105]

3 Changing Land Management

Land management will need to change so that less CO_2 is released and so that agricultural soil erosion is reduced. Where there is no tillage, erosion is 10 to 20 times greater than the rate at which soil is formed. *Where there is conventional tillage, it is eroding 100 times faster than it is being formed.* Peat lands will have to be restored by halting drainage schemes so they continue to act as long-term sinks for CO_2 sequestration. Deforestation to create grazing land for livestock will have to cease.[106] Changing land use is far more difficult than we imagine because land cannot multitask, and yet some of the proposed solutions, such as planting 1.2 trillion trees across 2.2 billion acres, ignores the fact that those acres are already in use as some of the world's most productive farmlands.[107]

These changes are expected over time to lead to mass migration and increased instability in vulnerable countries,[108] providing human trafficking opportunities for OC.

The introduction of tougher environmental policies may have the unintended consequence of excluding legitimate businesses from activities they previously engaged in, leaving those activities open to OC, creating a barrier to entry, eliminating legitimate competition, and increasing the profitability of illicit activities.

"Closed loop thinking" will be required to minimize use of scarce natural resources (minerals and timber in particular), to eliminate sources of pollution and waste in supply chains serving end-users, and to ensure that when products and services have been consumed, the remaining materials are recycled, reused, and remanufactured.[xxvi] Success in achieving a circular economy may hurt OC investments in waste management by reducing demand for illegal waste disposal in landfills[109] and the sea.[110] Legitimate businesses may solve the problem of owning dirty business activities by selling them off to other less environmentally conscious legitimate businesses or to fronts for OC:

> Today, like it or not, every company is responsible for its full life cycle impacts.
>
> A company's responsibility does not end at the factory gate. Coca-Cola and Pepsi are not only responsible for the energy and water used to make their products; they are also responsible – in a growing way – for the obesity epidemic and the litter of used soda cans and bottles that end up on roadsides or in the Great Pacific garbage patch. . . . Over the past several decades, a growing number of companies have sold off their "dirty businesses" perhaps as part of their transformation to becoming more sustainable companies. But selling off your dirty businesses, especially to owners in countries that are not strictly regulated, does not help the global ecosystem. Responsibility for legacy businesses can have a long tail, as U.S. companies have found with their former contaminated ("Superfund") sites.[111]

OC has become increasingly involved in the illegal wildlife trafficking chain of poaching, trafficking, and consumption. This current involvement does not just threaten endangered species, but security, rule of law, sustainable development, and economic wellbeing of local communities in poorer parts of the world.[112]

> "Wildlife trafficking breeds corruption, empowers criminals, and generates tens of billions of dollars a year for transnational organized criminal networks," said Dawson. "Wildlife trafficking can [also] be an indicator of weak state presence or governance," that allows organized criminal networks and armed militia groups to undermine economic prosperity and "destroy the social fabric of communities, whose youth are conscripted as poachers and often paid in drugs."[113]

The "Five Forces" Framework

The key insight in Michael Porter's framework is that companies need to respond to more sources of competition than just their head-to-head competitors. The model looks at the market margin available in a given industry. The amount of money both businesses (OC and legitimate) can make from operating in a given product market is determined by five forces all competing for the market margin available. The interactions between organizations and their head-head competitors, suppliers, and customers determines the attractiveness of the product market. If it is too

---

xxvi For a detailed discussion of the operational challenge posed by "closed loop thinking" to achieve a circular economy, see Zinkin, *The Challenge of Sustainability*, pp. 65–76.

profitable because there is too much market margin, then other longer term competitive forces come into play.

Head-to-Head Competitors

Their strength and numbers determine how much market share both OC and legitimate organizations can capture. This lays the foundation for the amount of profit a company can make in a given product market. Head-to-head competitors in legitimate markets are other companies offering the same type of products and services either as commodities or as brands. In the case of OC, the situation is somewhat different. OC organizations do not just compete with other OC organizations, they also compete with the state in the provision of security of the person and property, and in taxation to pay for it (called taxation when imposed by the state and extortion when performed by OC) demonstrated by the fact that when the state is strong, OC is weak, and vice versa. In addition, products and services offered by OC cannot benefit from comprehensive marketing strategies, other than by word of mouth and advertising on the dark web, as they cannot do visible advertising and selling, since this would lead to immediate prosecution by the authorities.

Supplier Power

The relative bargaining power of suppliers is affected by how many suppliers there are and how strongly they compete with each other to get their customers' business. This will decide how much margin they cede to the company and how much money it can make from them.

Buyer Power

The relative bargaining power of customers or clients is determined by how important they are as a percentage of the suppliers' business and therefore how much the loss of any single one can hurt the bottom line.

New Entrants

The ability to enter a product market to capture some of the extra market margin will be determined by the ease/difficulty of entering the market – the so-called "barriers to entry." Low barriers to entry allow new entrants; high barriers to entry discourage them. New entrants will drive down prices and margins either as a result of their extra capacity fighting for the same business or, worse still, if they introduce dramatically superior and disruptive technology providing better value at much lower prices, putting an incumbent company's existence at risk. If there are too many players in a market and the barriers to exit are high, making leaving the market too expensive, it can become a bloodbath. This applies to both OC and to legitimate businesses. Ironically, when products and services are prohibited by law, this creates an insuperable barrier to entry for legitimate businesses, removing competition and making the product market more profitable for OC, who by definition remain as the only players.

Alternatives and Substitutes

The attractiveness of alternatives or substitutes to customers will depend on relative price and performance when compared with the original product or service. Alternatives replace the demand for a company's product with something different, satisfying the underlying need in a different way. Substitutes are alternative solutions that become attractive when the original becomes too expensive. Both place a ceiling on the amount of market margin any product market can command.

The "Five Forces" Framework does not give due weight to the evolutionary dynamics of growth. Organisms (including all organizations) seek to maximize their use of resources by dominating niches and then ultimately decline. The decline of organisms, and organizations, is caused by one of three changes in their environments: (1) they exhaust the ability of their chosen niche to support them or they become inefficient and lose their evolutionary advantage; blinded by success, they lose their ability to respond to threats posed by new competition; (2) a new competitor arises with better adaptive mechanisms to respond to the changing conditions of the niche; or (3) their entry into another niche to continue growing because they have exhausted resources of their own threatens an incumbent that responds effectively to the new threat.

OC and legitimate businesses need to remember the perils of market dominance, namely excessive visibility and a resulting lowering of the "tolerability threshold" of society or of the state. Just as OC either gets crushed by the state or defeats it when they are engaged in an existential struggle, so companies that become too dominant in a given sector get broken up by states that decide to break up monopoly power, such as Standard Oil Company (New Jersey) in 1911[114] and AT&T in 1984[115] in the US and Alibaba's Ant Alipay in 2021[116] in China, and maybe Meta Platforms Inc. (Facebook) and Alphabet (Google) in the future in the US.

References

1 *What is Political Economy* (Princeton University Press), p. 4, http://assets.press.princeton.edu/chapters/s6819.pdf, accessed on April 26, 2021.

2 Ibid.

3 CFI (2021), "Political Economy," *Corporate Finance Institute,* 2015–2021, https://corporatefinanceinstitute.com/resources/knowledge/economics/political-economy/, accessed on April 26, 2021.

4 Tickell, C. (2005), International Media Environment Summit, Kuching, Sarawak, November 30, 2005.

5 Machiavelli, N. (1531), *The Discourses on Livy* (Harmondsworth: Pelican Classics, 1970), Book 1, Discourse 2, p. 106.

6 Polybius (1472), *The Rise of The Roman Empire* (London: Penguin Classics), 1979.

7 Paspaliaris, P. (2021). "China in Polybius' trap," *Academia Letters, Article 1060,* June 2021, https://doi.org/10.20935/AL1060, accessed on December 10, 2021.

8 "The Great Reform Act 1832," *UK Parliament,* https://www.parliament.uk/about/living-heritage/evolutionofparliament/houseofcommons/reformacts/overview/reformact1832/, accessed on April 23, 2021.

9 Zinkin, J., and Bennett, C. (2021), *The Principles and Practice of Effective Leadership* (Berlin/Boston: Walter De Gruyter).

10 History.com Editors (2019), "Origins of the Mafia," *A&E Television Networks,* May 28, 2019, https://www.history.com/topics/crime/origins-of-the-mafia accessed on January 22, 2021.

11 Ibid.

12 Purbrick, M. (2019), "Patriotic Chinese Triads and Secret Societies: From the Imperial Dynasties, To Nationalism, and Communism," *Asian Affairs,* August 15, 2019, https://www.scienceopen.com/document?vid=a61f8c1b-d473-4032-9a6c-af2d655bb80a, accessed on March 5, 2021.

13 Maguire, K. (1997) "Modernisation and Clean Government: Tackling Crime, Corruption and Organised Crime in Modern Taiwan," *Crime, Law and Social Change,* 28, p. 75, https://link.springer.com/article/10.1023%2FA%3A1008204328221, accessed on March 11, 2021.

14 Yang, S. (2020), "Declassified Secret Documents Show Close Ties between Taiwan KMT, Bamboo Union before 1984," www.taiwannews.com.tw, June 25, 2020, https://www.taiwannews.com.tw/en/news/3953426, accessed on March 10, 2021.

15 Shelley, L. I. (1994), "Review: Mafia and the Italian State: The Historical Roots of the Current Crisis," *Sociological Forum,* December 1994, 9, No. 4, Special Issue: Multiculturalism and Diversity (December 1994), pp. 662, 669, https://www.jstor.org/stable/685007, accessed on January 22, 2021.

16 Alvarez, L. (2005), "Police Fear I.R.A. Is Turning Expertise to Organized Crime," *The New York Times,* January 19, 2005, https://www.nytimes.com/2005/01/19/world/europe/police-fear-ira-is-turning-expertise-to-organized-crime.html, accessed April 23, 2021.

17 "Some Loyalists 'Just Crime Gangs' Says Chief Constable," *BBC News,* April 10, 2018, https://www.bbc.com/news/uk-northern-ireland-43711229, accessed on April 23, 2021.

18 Saab, B. Y., and Taylor, A. W. (2009), "Criminality and Armed Groups: A Comparative Study of FARC and Paramilitary Groups in Colombia," *Brookings,* May 22, 2009, https://www.brookings.edu/articles/criminality-and-armed-groups-a-comparative-study-of-farc-and-paramilitary-groups-in-colombia/, accessed on April 23, 2021.

19 Leuprecht, C. et al. (2017), "Hezbollah's Global Tentacles: A Relational Approach to Convergence with Transnational Organized Crime," *Terrorism and Political Violence,* 29, No., pp. 902–921, https://www.tandfonline.com/doi/full/10.1080/09546553.2015.1089863, accessed on April 23, 2021.

20 "View on Africa: how organised crime sustains al-Shabaab," *Institute for Security Studies,* https://issafrica.org/amp/events/view-on-africa-how-organised-crime-sustains-al-shabaab, accessed on April 23, 2021.

21 "Transnational Organized Crime: A Growing Threat to National and International Security," *National Security Council,* https://obamawhitehouse.archives.gov/administration/eop/nsc/transnational-crime/threat, accessed on April 23, 2021.

22 Chambers, A. (2016), "The Lobbying of the EU: How to Achieve Greater Transparency," *Civitas: Institute for the Study of Civil Society,* February 2016, https://www.civitas.org.uk/content/files/Anthony-Chambers-EU-lobbying.pdf, accessed on April 23, 2021.

23 New World Encyclopedia Contributors (2019), "Anglo-Iranian Oil Company," *New World Encyclopedia,* May 29, 2019, https://www.newworldencyclopedia.org/entry/Anglo-Iranian_Oil_Company, accessed on November 15, 2021.

24 "Papers Show I.T.T. Urged US to Help Oust Allende," *The New York Times,* July 3, 1972, p. 3, https://www.nytimes.com/1972/07/03/archives/papers-show-itt-urged-us-to-help-oust-allende-suggestions-for.html, accessed on November 15, 2021.

25 McMorrow, R., and Yu, S. (2021), "The Vanishing Billionaire: How Jack Ma Fell Foul of Xi Jinping," *The Financial Times Magazine,* April 15, 2021, https://www.ft.com/content/1fe0559f-de6d-490e-b312-abba0181da1f, accessed on April 25, 2021.

26 Finklea, K. M. (2011), "Economic Downturns and Crime," *CSR Report for Congress,* December 19, 2011, https://digital.library.unt.edu/ark:/67531/metadc821092/m2/1/high_res_d/R40726_2011Dec19.pdf, accessed on May 1, 2021.

27 Le Moglie, M., and Sorrenti, G. (2020), "When Godfathers become Entrepreneurs: On Organized Crime's Infiltration in Legal Economy," *Vox^EU CEPR,* August 1, 2020, https://voxeu.org/article/organized-crime-s-infiltration-legal-economy, accessed on May 1, 2021.

28 Samuelson, P. A., and Nordhaus, W. D. (2002), *Economics, International Edition, Seventeenth Edition* (New York: McGraw-Hill Irwin), p. 419.

29 Ibid., pp. 422–429.

30 Ibid., pp. 426–427.

31 Davis, A. (2021), "Summers Sees 'Least Responsible' Fiscal Policy in 40 Years," *Bloomberg,* March 20, 2021, https://www.bloomberg.com/news/articles/2021-03-20/summers-says-u-s-facing-worst-macroeconomic-policy-in-40-years, accessed on May 2, 2021.

32 Zinkin, M. (2001), "Not New and Never Costless: Globalisation," *International Relations,* 15, No. 5, p. 27 (London/Thousand Oaks/New Delhi: Sage Publications), quoted in Zinkin, J. (2020), *The Challenge of Sustainability: Corporate Governance in a Complicated World* (Boston/Berlin: Walter de Gruyter GmbH), pp. 83–84.

33 Wilson, J. (2021), "ESL Plotters Overlooked Paradox that 'Global Fans' Like Football As It Is," *The Guardian,* April 24, 2021, https://www.theguardian.com/football/blog/2021/apr/24/esl-plotters-overlooked-paradox-that-global-fans-like-football-as-it-is, accessed on April 26, 2021.

34 Crace, J. (2021), "ESL Achieves What Few Thought Possible by Uniting MPs and Country," *The Guardian,* April 19, 2021, https://www.theguardian.com/politics/2021/apr/19/esl-achieves-what-few-thought-possible-by-uniting-mps-and-country, accessed on April 26, 2021.

35 "Europe's Super League scores a spectacular own goal," *The Economist,* April 24, 2021, https://www.economist.com/business/2021/04/22/europes-super-league-scores-a-spectacular-own-goal, accessed on April 26, 2021.

36 Marvez, A. (2016), "The Long Goodbye: 11 Most Painful NFL Relocations," *Fox Sports,* October 20, 2016, https://www.foxsports.com/stories/nfl/the-long-goodbye-11-most-painful-nfl-relocations, accessed on April 26, 2021.

37 Hayes, M. (2017), "13 Major League Baseball Teams That Have Relocated," *World Atlas,* November 29, 2017, https://www.worldatlas.com/articles/13-major-league-baseball-teams-that-have-relocated.html, accessed on April 26, 2021.

38 Smith, T. (2010), "How Did I Get Here? A History of Franchise Movement In The NBA," *Bleacher Report,* October 12, 2010, https://bleacherreport.com/articles/488118-how-did-i-get-here-a-history-of-franchise-movement-in-the-nba, accessed on April 26, 2021.

39 Sergi, A. (2015), "The Italian Anti-Mafia System Between Practice and Symbolism: Evaluating Contemporary Views on the Italian Structure Model Against Organized Crime," *Policing,* August 18, 2015, p. 5, https://www.academia.edu/15032458/The_Italian_Anti_Mafia_System_between_Practice_and_Symbolism_Evaluating_Contemporary_Views_on_the_Italian_Structure_Model_against_Organized_Crime?email_work_card=abstract-read-more, accessed on April 28, 2021.

40 Tondo, L. (2019), "Sicilians Dare to Believe the Mafia's Cruel Reign is Over," *The Guardian,* September 22, 2019, https://www.theguardian.com/world/2019/sep/22/mafia-godfathers-sicily-palermo-italy, accessed on April 26, 2021.

41 Ibid.

42 Ibid.

43 Ibid.

44 Ibid.

45 Ibid.

46 Ibid.

47 Longrigg, C. (2017),"How Totò Riina's War on the Italian State Almost Destroyed the Cosa Nostra," *The Guardian,* November 18, 2017, https://www.theguardian.com/world/2017/nov/18/how-toto-riinas-war-on-the-italian-state-almost-destroyed-cosa-nostra, accessed on November 7, 2021.

48 Hill, P. B. E. (2003), *The Japanese Mafia, the Law and the State* (Oxford: Oxford University Press), cited in *Themis: Research Journal of Justice Studies and Forensic Science*, 2, Art 12, 2014, p. 10.

49 Reilly, E. F. (2014), "Criminalizing Yakuza Membership: A Comparative Study of the Anti-Boryokudan Law," *Washington University Global Studies Law Review*, 13, No. 4, 2014, p. 802, https://openscholarship.wustl.edu/law_globalstudies/vol13/iss4/9, accessed on April 28, 2021.

50 Power News (2017), "Fragmented Yamaguchi-gumi a Sign of Changing Yakuza Times," *Society*, September 4, 2017, https://www.nippon.com/en/features/c04201/, accessed on March 4, 2021.

51 Reilly, "Criminalizing Yakuza Membership," p. 802.

52 Ibid., pp. 803–804.

53 CDC (2010), *How Tobacco Smoke Causes Disease: The Biology and Behavioral Basis for Smoking-Attributable Disease: A Report of the Surgeon General* (Atlanta: Center for Disease Control), https://www.ncbi.nlm.nih.gov/books/NBK53010/, accessed on April 27, 2021.

54 CDC (2014), Smoking and Diabetes," *Surgeon General's Report on Smoking and Health 50th Anniversary*, 2014, https://www.cdc.gov/tobacco/data_statistics/sgr/50th-anniversary/pdfs/fs_smoking_CVD_508.pdf, accessed on April 27, 2021.

55 CDC (2014), "Smoking and Cardiovascular Disease," *Surgeon General's Report on Smoking and Health 50th Anniversary*, https://www.cdc.gov/tobacco/data_statistics/sgr/50th-anniversary/pdfs/fs_smoking_CVD_508.pdf, accessed on April 27, 2021.

56 Orenstein, B. W. (2017), "Can Eating Too Much Sugar Cause Type 2 Diabetes?" *Everyday Health,* September 26, 2017, https://www.everydayhealth.com/type-2-diabetes/diet/can-eating-too-much-sugar-cause-diabetes/, accessed on April 27, 2021.

57 Carbone, S. et al. (2019), "The Effects of Dietary Sugars on Cardiovascular Disease-Related Mortality: Finding the Sweet Spot," *Mayo Clinic Proceedings*, 94, No. 12, December 1, 2019, pp. 2, 375–2, 377, https://www.mayoclinicproceedings.org/article/S0025-6196(19)30911-5/fulltext, accessed on April 27, 2021.

58 Hall, S. (2015), "Exxon Knew about Climate Change almost 40 years ago," *Scientific American,* October 26, 2015, https://www.scientificamerican.com/article/exxon-knew-about-climate-change-al most-40-years-ago/, accessed on April 27, 2021.

59 US Environmental Protection Agency (2003), "Environmental Impact of the Petroleum Industry," *Hazardous Substance Research Centers/South and Southwest Outreach Program,* Update #12, June 2003, https://cfpub.epa.gov/ncer_abstracts/index.cfm/fuseaction/display.files/fileID/14522#:~:text=Air% 20pollution%20hazards%3A%20Petroleum%20refineries,%2C%20ethylbenzene%2C%20and%20xy lene).&text=Refineries%20also%20release%20less%20toxic,light%20volatile%20fuels%20and%20oils, accessed on April 27, 2021.

60 Bartley, T., and Child, C. (2011), "Movements, Markets, and Fields: The Effect of Anti-Sweatshop Campaigns on U.S. Firms, 1993–2000," *Social Forces*, 90, No. 2, December 2011, p. 440, https://www.jstor.org/stable/41682661, accessed on April 27, 2021.

61 "Disaster of the Day: Nike," *Forbes,* February 22, 2001, https://www.forbes.com/2001/02/22/ 0222disasternike.html?sh=e3395d85ee9f, accessed on April 27, 2021.

62 Bartley and Child (2011), p. 440.

63 Balch, O. (2021), "Mars, Nestlé, and Hershey to Face Child Slavery Lawsuit in U.S.," *The Guard-ian,* February 12, 2021, https://www.theguardian.com/global-development/2021/feb/12/mars-nestle-and-hershey-to-face-landmark-child-slavery-lawsuit-in-us, accessed on May 3, 2021.

64 Pallini, T. (2020), "It's been 20 Years Since Smoking was Completely Banned on All US Flights. Here's How Smoking Went from Normal to Banned," *Business Insider,* March 8, 2020, https://www. businessinsider.com/when-did-smoking-get-banned-on-planes-in-the-us-2020-2, accessed on April 28, 2021.

65 "Compliance with the Smoking Ban in Urban Public Transport in Chile," *NCBI Resources,* https://www.ncbi.nlm.nih.gov/pmc/articles/PMC7398597/, accessed on April 28, 2021.

66 Lezard, N. (2017), "The Smoking Ban 10 Years On: What's Changed on Page and Screen?" *The Guardian,* July 7, 2017, https://www.theguardian.com/books/2017/jul/07/smoking-ban-movie-ciga rettes-legislation-work-public-tobacco, accessed on April 28, 2021.

67 West, R. (2002), "Banning Smoking in the Workplace," *NCBI Resources,* July 27, 2002, https:// www.ncbi.nlm.nih.gov/pmc/articles/PMC1123708/, accessed on April 28, 2021.

68 "The Background of Smoking Bans," *NCBI,* 2010, https://www.ncbi.nlm.nih.gov/books/ NBK219563/, accessed on April 28, 2021.

69 WHO (2013), "Compliance of Ban on Smoking in PUBS AND BARS," *World Health Data Plat-form,* 2021, *World Health Organization,* https://www.who.int/data/gho/data/indicators/indicator-de tails/GHO/compliance-of-ban-on-smoking-in-pubs-and-bars, accessed on April 28, 2021.

70 "Ban Tobacco Advertising to Protect Young People," https://www.who.int/mediacentre/news/ releases/2013/who_ban_tobacco/en/, accessed on April 28, 2021.

71 USFDA (2021), "Cigarette Labeling and Health Warning Requirements," March 9, 2021, https:// www.fda.gov/tobacco-products/labeling-and-warning-statements-tobacco-products/cigarette-label ing-and-health-warning-requirements, accessed on April 28, 2021.

72 National Academy of Sciences (2010), "Secondhand Smoke Exposure and Cardiovascular Ef-fects: Making Sense of the Evidence," *NCBI Resources,* https://www.ncbi.nlm.nih.gov/books/ NBK219563/, accessed on April 28, 2021.

73 Daube, M., and Chapman, S. (2016), "The Problem with Selling a Lethal Product: You Just Can't Get the Staff," *The Guardian,* July 12, 2016, https://www.theguardian.com/commentisfree/2016/jul/ 13/the-problem-with-selling-a-lethal-product-you-just-cant-get-the-staff, accessed on April 29, 2021.

74 Bilinski, P., and Novak, J. (2014), "The Compensation Premium in the 'Sin Industries' of To-bacco, Alcohol, and Gambling," *Cass Business School,* December 22, 2014, https://www.cass.city.ac. uk/faculties-and-research/research/cass-knowledge/2014/december/the-compensation-premium-in-the-sin-industries-of-tobacco-alcohol-and-gambling, accessed on April 29, 2021.

75 Zinkin, J. (2014), *Rebuilding Trust in Banks: The Role of Leadership and Governance* (Singapore: John Wiley and Sons).

76 Lautenschläger, S. (2015), "Reintegrating the Banking Sector into Society: Earning and Re-establishing Trust," speech given at 7th *International Banking Conference "Tomorrow's Bank Business Model – How Far Are We from the New Equilibrium,"* Bocconi University, Milan, September 28, 2015, https://www.ecb.europa.eu/press/key/date/2015/html/sp150928.en.html, accessed on April 29, 2015.

77 Schein, E. J. (2016), "The 2007–2009 Financial Crisis: An Erosion of Ethics: A Case Study," *Journal of Business Ethics*, 146, pp. 805–830 (2017), https://doi.org/10.1007/s10551-016-3052-7, accessed on April 29, 2021.

78 Holder, E. H. (2013), quoted in Douglas, D. (2013), "Holder Concerned Megabanks Too Big to Jail," *The Washington Post*, March 6, 2013, https://www.washingtonpost.com/business/economy/holder-concerned-megabanks-too-big-to-jail/2013/03/06/6fa2b07a-869e-11e2-999e-5f8e0410cb9d_story.html, accessed on April 29, 2021.

79 Agence France Presse (2021), "Italian 'Maxi Trial' Results in Conviction of 70 'Ndrangheta Suspects," *The Guardian*, November 6, 2021, https://www.theguardian.com/world/2021/nov/06/italian-maxi-trial-results-in-conviction-of-70-ndrangheta-suspects, accessed on November 7, 2021.

80 Agence France Press (2014), "'Ndrangheta Mafia 'Made More Money Last Year than McDonald's and Deutsche Bank," *The Guardian*, March 26, 2021, https://www.theguardian.com/world/2014/mar/26/ndrangheta-mafia-mcdonalds-deutsche-bank-study, accessed on November 16, 2021.

81 Amadeo, K., and Kelly, R. C. (2021), "Sin Taxes, Their Pros and Cons, and Whether They Work," *The Balance*, January 30, 2021, https://www.thebalance.com/sin-tax-definition-examples-4157476, accessed on April 29, 2021.

82 Ibid.

83 Ibid.

84 Bretteville-Jensen, A. L. et al. (2017), "Costs and Unintended Consequences of Drug Control Policies," *Council of Europe*, November 2017, p. 27, https://rm.coe.int/costs-and-unitended-consequences-of-drug-control-policies/16807701a9, accessed on April 29, 2021.

85 Yilla, K., and Wessel, D. (2020), "Liberalizing marijuana will incur substantial costs for state borrowing," *Brookings Institution*, July 14, 2020, https://www.brookings.edu/blog/up-front/2020/07/13/liberalizing-marijuana-will-incur-substantial-costs-for-state-borrowing/, accessed on April 29, 2021.

86 Thornton, M. (1991), "Alcohol Prohibition Was a Failure," *Cato Institute*, July 17, 1991, https://www.cato.org/policy-analysis/alcohol-prohibition-was-failure, accessed on April 30, 2021.

87 Amadeo and Kelly (2021).

88 Schumpeter, J.A. (1950), *Capitalism, Socialism and Democracy, Third Edition* (New York: HarperCollins).

89 Welch, J., https://www.goodreads.com/quotes/185636-if-the-rate-of-change-on-the-outside-exceeds-the, accessed on September 27, 2018.

90 Christensen, C. (1997), *The Innovator's Dilemma* (Boston, MA: Harvard Business Review Press).

91 Ibid.

92 Zinkin (2020), p. 181.

93 Greenberg, A. (2021), "The Colonial Pipeline Hack Is a New Extreme for Ransomware," *Wired*, May 8, 2021, https://www.wired.com/story/colonial-pipeline-ransomware-attack/, accessed on May 10, 2021.

94 "New Technology Has Enabled Cybercrime on an Industrial Scale," *The Economist*, May 6, 2021, https://www.economist.com/international/2021/05/06/new-technology-has-enabled-cybercrime-on-an-industrial-scale, accessed on May 8, 2021.

95 Fenwick, M., and Wrbka, S. (2016), "The Shifting Meaning of Legal Certainty," Fenwick, M., Wrbka, S. (eds.), *Legal Certainty in a Contemporary Context* (Singapore: Springer), https://link.springer.com/chapter/10.1007/978-981-10-0114-7_1, accessed on December 6, 2019.

96 Maxeiner, J.R. (2008), "Some Realism About Legal Certainty in Globalization of the Rule of Law," Houston Journal of International Law 31, No. 1 (2008), pp. 27–46.

97 Helmore, E. (2019), "Lawsuits, Payouts, Opioids Crisis: What Happened to Johnson & Johnson?" *The Guardian,* October 18, 2019, https://www.theguardian.com/business/2019/oct/18/johnson-and-johnson-opioids-lawsuits-product-recalls, accessed on December 6, 2019.

98 Williams Walsh, M. (2019), "Judge Orders Pause in Opioid Litigation Against Purdue Pharma and Sacklers," *The New York Times,* October 11, 2019, https://www.nytimes.com/2019/10/11/health/purdue-bankruptcy-opioids.html, accessed on December 6, 2019.

99 "New York Sues Exxon Mobil, saying it Deceived Shareholders on Climate Change," *The New York Times*, October 24, 2018, https://www.nytimes.com/2018/10/24/climate/exxon-lawsuit-climate-change.html, accessed on December 6, 2019.

100 Reuters (2015), "BNP Paribas Sentenced in $8.9 billion Accord Over Sanctions Violations," Reuters, May 1, 2015, https://www.reuters.com/article/us-bnp-paribas-settlement-sentencing/bnp-paribas-sentenced-in-8-9-billion-accord-over-sanctions-violations-idUSKBN0NM41K20150501, accessed on October 6, 2019.

101 Reuters (2012), "HSBC to Pay $1.9 billion U.S. Fine in Money-laundering Case," Reuters, December 11, 2012, https://www.reuters.com/article/us-hsbc-probe/hsbc-to-pay-1-9-billion-u-s-fine-in-money-laundering-case-idUSBRE8BA05M20121211, accessed on October 6, 2019.

102 Adamoli, S. et al. (1998), "Organised Crime Around the World," *European Institute for Crime Prevention and Control affiliated with the United Nations,* Publication Series, No. 31, 1998.

103 Sergi (2015), p. 5.

104 EDF (2021), "Extreme Weather Gets a Boost from Climate Change," *Environmental Defense Fund,* 2021https://www.edf.org/climate/climate-change-and-extreme-weather, accessed on May 7, 2021.

105 Intergovernmental Panel on Climate Change, (2019), *Climate Change and Land: Summary for Policymakers*, https://www.ipcc.ch/2019/08/08/land-is-a-critical-resource_srccl/, accessed on August 12, 2019.

106 Meyer, R. (2019), "This Land Is the Only Land There Is," *The Atlantic,* August 8, 2019, https://www.theatlantic.com/science/archive/2019/08/how-think-about-dire-new-ipcc-climate-report/595705/, accessed on August 19, 2019.

107 Ibid.

108 Chalzanoël, M. T., and Puscas, S. (2019), "Climate Change and Migration in Vulnerable Countries," *UN Sustainable Development Goals,* September 3, 2019, https://www.un.org/sustainabledevelopment/blog/2019/09/climate-change-and-migration-in-vulnerable-countries/, accessed on May 8, 2021.

109 D'Amato, A. et al. (2015), "Waste and Organized Crime in Regional Environments: How Waste Tariffs and the Mafia Affect Waste Management and Disposal," *Resource and Energy Economics,* 41, August 2015, pp. 185–201, https://www.sciencedirect.com/science/article/abs/pii/S0928765515000299, accessed on May 5, 2021.

110 Sergi, A., and South, N. (2016), "'Earth, Water, Air, and Fire', Environmental Crimes, Mafia Power and Political Negligence in Calabria," in Antonopolous, G., *Illegal Entrepreneurship, Organised Crime and Social Control: Essays in Honour of Prof. Dick Hobbs* (New York: Springer).

111 Sergi (2015), p. 5.

112 WWF (2020), "Wildlife Crime Initiative," *Wildlife Crime Initiative News,* https://wwf.panda.org/discover/our_focus/wildlife_practice/wildlife_trade/wildlife_crime_initiative/, accessed on May 5, 2021.

113 Dawson, C. (2018), "Criminal Elements: Illegal Wildlife Trafficking, Organized Crime, and National Security," *NEWSSECURITYBEAT,* January 19, 2018, https://www.newsecuritybeat.org/2018/01/criminal-elements-illegal-wildlife-trafficking-organized-crime-national-security/, accessed on May 5, 2021.
114 The Editors of Encyclopaedia (2020), "Standard Oil," *Encyclopedia Britannica,* 24 March, 2020, https://www.britannica.com/topic/Standard-Oil, accessed 17 November 2021.
115 Beattie, A. (2021), "AT&T's Successful Spinoffs," *Investopedia,* May 7, 2021, https://www.investopedia.com/ask/answers/09/att-breakup-spinoff.asp, accessed on November 17, 2021.
116 Ray, S. (2021), "Alibaba Shares Drop As China Reportedly Seeks To Break Up Jack Ma's Alipay," *Forbes,* September 13, 2021, https://www.forbes.com/sites/siladityaray/2021/09/13/alibaba-shares-drop-as-china-reportedly-seeks-to-break-up-jack-mas-alipay/?sh=7ff629e12bc8, accessed on November 17, 2021.

Chapter 6
The Criminal Strategy Internal Continuum

The strategic factors that organized crime and legitimate organizations must consider are the same. Their strategic decisions are constrained by their external and internal environments. They need to refresh mission, vision, and values as a result of changes in the environment discussed in Chapter 5 and how these will affect their purpose, principles, power, people, and processes.

Mission, Vision, and Values

Today's business leaders need the ability to see through the chaos to have a clear vision for their organizations. They must define the True North of their organization: its mission, values, and strategy. *They should create clarity around this True North and refuse to let external events pull them off course or cause them to neglect or abandon their mission, which must be their guiding light.*[1]   [Emphasis mine]

Mission and Vision

Clear definition of mission is essential. A clear mission enables an organization to develop a vision and set of values which become the basis of its code of conduct. The mission answers the general questions, "Who does the organization serve?" "What products or services does the organization offer to serve its beneficiaries?" and "How does the organization provide its products and services?" It also answers the following seven specific questions:[2]

1. Is there a clear business focus and is it understood by everybody within it?
2. Is there a compelling, differentiated mission setting the organization apart from the competition?
3. Who are its competitors for market margin (discussed in Chapter 5)?
4. What are its ambitions: to be a technology leader or follower; and which segment of the customer universe is it targeting in the product/category life cycle – early adopter, growth, maturity, or decline?
5. Which market segment does it want to serve: prestige, premium, value for money, low-cost mass market; and what psychographics is it seeking to satisfy?

https://doi.org/10.1515/9783110712155-006

6. Can the mission adapt to changes in the external environment or does it run the risk of "stuckness"?[i]
7. Does the mission ensure the organization's long-term "license to operate"?

All organizations (legitimate or criminal, for-profit or not, privately held or publicly listed) must have answers to the first six questions. However, when answering the seventh question, there is a difference between OC and legitimate businesses – the part played by ethical considerations.

Defining *a sustainable mission and vision* protects both the organization's financial viability and its social "license to operate." The organization has to: (1) choose what the senior people do, ensuring their personal purpose and values align with those of the organization; (2) ensure the society within which the organization operates will accept its activities and allow it to continue long-term; (3) evaluate whether the identified opportunities have the scale to make good business sense; and (4) assess whether the organization has the necessary competencies to make a success of opportunities.

Modern OC is not concerned with the ethical dimensions of the mission, its primary aim has become enrichment, regardless of the social and ethical issues involved. This was not true of the Cosa Nostra, Triads, and Yakuza when they were founded; they had political and social objectives in protecting alienated sections of society from hostile governments (discussed in Chapter 2). The Yakuza philosophy of *Ninkyodo* was an ethical code and way of life that placed importance on helping the weak and recognizing the importance of self-sacrifice:

> The old-school yakuza, while still being essentially criminals, but mostly professional gamblers or street merchants – also maintained a code of honor which forbid theft, robbery, sexual assault, fraud and dealing in drugs. (Of course, racketeering, extortion, and other money-making ventures were not off-limits. Even a noble semi-samurai has to earn a living.)[3]

Once the mission has been agreed it must be translated into a vision that is compelling both emotionally and rationally. It must be communicated so that:

> *Everybody understands "what's in it for them" in achieving the Vision*, and equally what are the consequences for them and the organization as whole for failing. It is the responsibility of the CEO to operationalize the Vision, by ensuring it is broken down into milestones and targets with due dates. *Perhaps the most important and often neglected part in this is to ensure that every employee has a clear "line of sight" between achieving the Vision and their own job.*
>
> *CEOs who are not wholehearted in their support of the Vision have no business being in the company, as they can do tremendous damage to what makes it unique.*[4]   [Emphases ours]

---

i "Stuckness" occurs when an organization allocates strategic resources that cannot be reallocated once they have been committed. It preserves excess capacity, creating expensive barriers to exit, and explains why some industries yield low ROI, regardless of how well the companies in those industries are managed.

Two examples of founders who answered all these questions, are Henry Ford, and Michael Marks and Thomas Spencer, the founders of Marks and Spencer, one of the most successful department stores of the 20th century:

Henry Ford

> I will build a motor car for the great multitude . . . it will be so low in price that no man making a good salary will be unable to own one – and enjoy with his family the blessing of hours of pleasure in God's great open spaces. When I'm through everybody will be able to afford one, and everyone will have one. The horse will have disappeared from our highways, the automobile will be taken for granted and we will give a large number of men employment at good wages.

Henry Ford was explicit about his mission and vision. He defined the beneficiaries of his endeavors: "the great multitude"; he defined the difference in their lives he would make: "enjoying God's great open spaces with their families"; he even defined his measures of success: everyone would own a car and the horse would have "disappeared from the highways," solving an apparently insoluble environmental problem of horse manure in cities[5] and a "large number of men would be employed at good wages." He succeeded beyond his wildest dreams and, as a result, replaced one environmental problem with another. He instituted a new way of assembling cars, thereby answering the fourth question about the necessary competencies without which he would not have been able to mass produce cars.[6]

Marks and Spencer

> The business of Marks and Spencer, they decided, was not retailing. It was social revolution . . . to subvert the class structure of nineteenth-century England by making available to working class and lower middle-class customers upper-class goods in superior quality but at a price the customers could afford. . . . This then yielded specific marketing and innovation objectives, and also objectives in respect to productivity, to people and social responsibilities.[7]

Marks and Spencer (M&S) was incredibly successful in the 20th century: customers loved its value for money; employees loved working for it. It was innovative, introducing ready-to-eat quality meals, copied by all its rivals. It achieved its mission of breaking down the visible class barriers in England; people were no longer immediately identifiable by the clothes they wore or the food they ate. Recently, like NASA after putting a man on the moon, M&S has been struggling to redefine its purpose and find a new long-term mission.

Henry Ford, Michael Marks, and Thomas Spencer are not unique in having had a purpose that was not solely profit maximization. Robert Owen (textiles) founded New Lanark near Glasgow in 1816; Sir Titus Salt (textiles) founded Saltaire outside Bradford in 1851, George Cadbury (chocolate) founded Bourneville near Birmingham in 1879, and William Hesketh Lever (soap) founded Port Sunlight near Liverpool in

1888.[8] In the US, George Pullman did likewise on the outskirts of Chicago, where his township was described as "the most perfect city in the world."[9]

What is illuminating is the range and breadth of services provided in these townships. For example, in Saltaire, Sir Titus Salt built 850 houses, each with its own fresh water from the Saltaire reservoir, a park, church, school, and library. He believed he had a moral duty to improve the physical, material, and moral conditions of his workers in Bradford that had been polluted, unhealthy, and immoral.[10] In so doing, he was following the revolutionary example set by Robert Owen, who, in addition, invented the idea of the cooperative store, buying in bulk and selling quality products to his workers and sharing the profits with them. He also kept them on with full pay during a trade dispute with the US in 1806 – when his transition to enlightened employer began.[11] William Hesketh Lever adopted a philosophy of "prosperity sharing":

> Lever built Port Sunlight to house the workers at his soap factory, Lever Brothers, which eventually became the global giant, Unilever. The village represents one man's vision to provide industrial workers with decent, sanitary housing in a considered architectural and picturesque form.

> However, rather than a philanthropic venture, Lever claimed it was all part of a business model he termed "prosperity-sharing." *Rather than sharing the profits of the company directly with his employees, Lever provided them with decent and affordable houses, amenities and welfare provisions that made their lives secure and comfortable and enabled them to flourish as people. It was also intended to inspire loyalty and commitment.*[12]   [Emphasis ours]

Port Sunlight had no workingman's pub, reflecting the founder's abhorrence of alcohol. Even more intriguingly, the workers' homes, laid out in a garden village, were built to designs by architects who entered an annual competition for the best homes, so that Port Sunlight still boasts 300 Grade II listed buildings, an art gallery, and a theatre.[13] Quality of life mattered, as did the promotion of virtue for their workers. The desire of these philanthropist-entrepreneurs to do good was reinforced by the recognition their workers would be more productive if they had improved working and living conditions and if their health was better as a result of reduced pollution. Titus Salt also realized that there would be less militancy and unrest: strikes were rare in Saltaire though not in neighboring Bradford. The same was true of Port Sunlight and Birkenhead.

Was this paternalism merely a device for "securing a compliant, captive workforce which could be indoctrinated into disciplined behavior that ensured continued profits?"[14] The same question could be asked of the company towns built in the US or Japan. The answer is probably the same as Salt's – namely that both objectives applied because investing beyond the narrowly defined needs of the company in the social capital of the community within which it operated, "fulfilled the obligations he believed he owed his workers."[15] These entrepreneurs invested money in improving their community and environment *before* they made their money – unlike the great robber-baron philanthropists of the late 19th century US, who "gave back to the community" some of the economic surplus they had extracted through their economic power (Andrew Carnegie and John D. Rockefeller being the best known), and who were the precursors of the "corporate philanthropy" model so prevalent in the US.[ii]

Values

The values statements adopted by most organizations often fail to be distinctive. They fail to differentiate the behavior that can be expected from one legitimate organization to another. They have no impact unless they are translated into observable and measurable behavior.

All too often, organizational values are totemically inscribed on mousepads, company mugs, and posters in reception areas and on office walls. Yet employees have difficulty remembering what they are, or how they make their organization different from and better than its competitors, and what they mean in practice. Abstract concepts like accountability, belonging, boldness, care, commitment, courage, creativity, customer focus, diversity, fun, inclusivity, integrity, keeping promises, loyalty, reliability, respect, results, pride, and teamwork appear in most organizations' lists.[16]

Often little thought is given to how the values in the chosen list of desired behaviors interact with each other, for example, maintaining that "get it right first time" – a cardinal principle of total quality – is a core value, while at the same time emphasizing taking risks by breaking things and learning fast from failure is also a core value, without recognizing that this may seem confusingly contradictory to junior front-line personnel.

If values are to be more than cliché statements on mugs, mouse pads, and wall posters in reception areas, they must be translated into measurable and observable behavior and discussed in employee reviews and personal development plans. This requires the values to be *translated from abstract nouns into action statements* describing desired behavior and performance expectations.

How Different are Organized Crime and Legitimate Business Values?

We tend to think of values statements as being morally positive in and of themselves. This is not correct. What gives the value statements their moral weight is the superordinate goal the behaviors and outcomes the value statements are designed to create.

[ii] Chambers, J. (2005), "Cisco: Giving Back is "Good Business," *BusinessWeek Online*, August 11, 2005, where John Chambers, then CEO of Cisco argued that strong corporate citizenship is not just charity, it is also "a critical element of a company's brand and reputation."

Corporate value statements are in vogue now. Everyone has one and they include just about every superlative the English language can muster: *Teamwork, respect, accountability, loyalty, relationships, results, integrity, entrepreneurial, dependable and pride are just a few of the many words that festoon corporate codes of conduct and websites.*

These virtues, it is thought, will proclaim to the world what the firm stands for and inspire employees to engage in ethical conduct. The irony is that these same values are embraced by organized crime.

The Mafia's "core values" are loyalty, obedience and honor. Their so-called "Ten Commandments" mandate respect, truthfulness, and a type of moral value system.

Russian organized crime syndicates have a "Thieves' Code" that includes such laudable requirements as maintaining confidentiality, teaching the trade to the young, and keeping promises. Los Angeles street gangs have "honor codes" grounded in the values of respect, reputation, pride, self-respect and dignity

The key to ensuring that your corporate values pass the "Mafia test" is to clearly define your organization's purpose as one that promotes human flourishing – a claim that criminal enterprises cannot reasonably make. For law-abiding corporations, this is a fairly straightforward exercise[17]   [Emphases ours]

When you define your corporation's purpose be sure to avoid falling into the trap of stating that your primary end is to maximize profits or shareholder value. *Firms that make this mistake unwittingly align their value statements with criminal enterprises that are focused entirely on satisfying their selfish need for personal enrichment.*

The risks associated with making this error are real. *There are countless examples of firms that lost their way by either deliberately or inadvertently establishing their sole purpose as maximizing profit and ultimately engaging in criminal conduct to "make the numbers."*[18]   [Emphasis ours]

A singular focus on bottom-line results is the gateway to cutting regulatory corners, breaking the law and paying fines as part of the "costs of doing business," bribery and corruption to get business done, violating codes of conduct, bringing forward sales. It works to blur the boundary between legitimate business behavior and OC. The apology offered by Darkside, the "ransomware" hackers who attacked the Colonial pipeline in the US causing President Biden to declare a state of emergency, suggests that they really understand the importance of not breaching the state's "threshold of toleration" (discussed in Chapter 4):

"Our goal is to make money, and not creating problems for society," DarkSide said, adding that it would *"check each company that our partners want to encrypt to avoid social consequences in the future. . . . We only attack companies that can pay the requested amount. . . . We do not want to kill your business"*

The DarkSide hackers also try to reassure their victims that they will play by their own rules, saying: "We value our reputation. If we do not do our work and liabilities, nobody will pay us." It even offers to provide technical support, "in case of problems" using the decryption tool that their victims receive when they pay up.[19]   [Emphasis ours]

In an ironic, but accurate, comment on DarkSide's May 2021 "ransomware" attack on the Colonial pipeline company,[20] Bloomberg's Matt Levine highlights the convergence of values of OC and legitimate businesses:

> *If you run an investment bank and you want aggressive rainmakers to pursue hard-won business in distant parts of the world, some of them might do some bribes, and if you cut the level of bribes to zero it might lead to unacceptable losses of legitimate business* . . . [and] *in a large enough company your enforcement will necessarily be somewhat statistical, and absolutely zero crime might be hard to achieve and not worth it.*
>
> What if your company's business is crime? What if you are a Mafia family, or a ransomware hacking group? If your business is crime, you have to do crime to get revenue. But *the optimal level of crime is also not infinite: If you do too many crimes, or crimes that are too bad, you will get in too much trouble. Doing more and bigger crimes should increase your crime-based revenue, but it also increases the resources that officials will expend on trying to shut you down, and thus your risks of being stopped and punished.* At some point the lines cross, and you should forego some criminal revenue in order to keep your legal risk manageable.
>
> This is more or less the same calculation that regular businesses often make – "we don't want this piece of business, even though it's very lucrative, because it has too much legal risk" – *just with a different baseline. An ordinary business wants to commit very few felonies, perhaps zero; a crime business wants to commit many. But they both have to make decisions at the margin, about whether to commit one more felony.*[21]　　　　　　　　　　　　　　[Emphases ours]

Too much crime committed by a legitimate organization risks destroying its social "license to operate"; too much crime committed by OC risks breaching the state's "threshold of toleration." As Levine points out, this is not a question of difference in kind, but one of degree, or to use his words: "a different baseline." In other words, there really is no difference between OC and legitimate businesses, other than where the boundaries (baselines) are drawn regarding behavior, and the willingness of society and the government to put up with what is being done to maximize profit, regardless of externalities. Moreover, the difference in where the boundaries or baselines are drawn is only a difference of degree and not of kind.

If we compare the values of entrepreneurs like Owen, Salt, Lever, Ford, Marks, and Spencer with those of today's business leaders, we sense there is an important difference in the significance they place on maximizing shareholder value – based on (1) Milton Friedman's 1970 defective, but universally accepted, argument that the purpose of business is to increase profits to maximize shareholder value,[22] and (2) UK Prime Minister Margaret Thatcher's misunderstood 1987 statement that there is no such thing as society – interpreted as justifying a crassly individualist worldview, one that prized selfishness, greed, and the trashing of social obligations:

> I think we have gone through a period when too many children and people have been given to understand "I have a problem, it is the Government's job to cope with it!" or "I have a problem, I will go and get a grant to cope with it!" "I am homeless, the Government must house me!" and so *they are casting their problems on society and who is society? There is no such*

thing! There are individual men and women and there are families and no government can do anything except through people and people look to themselves first. It is our duty to look after ourselves and then also to help look after our neighbour and life is a reciprocal business and people have got the entitlements too much in mind without the obligations, because there is no such thing as an entitlement unless someone has first met an obligation. . . . *There is no such thing as society. There is a living tapestry of men and women and people and the beauty of that tapestry and the quality of our lives will depend upon how much each of us is prepared to take responsibility for ourselves* and . . . to turn round and help by our own efforts those who are unfortunate.[23]   [Emphases ours]

Maybe one of the lessons we are learning as a result of the Covid-19 pandemic is that there is such a thing as society, as UK Prime Minister Boris Johnson emphasized in a video on March 30, 2020, appearing to repudiate Margaret Thatcher.[24]

Introducing the "Five P" Performance Framework

Once an organization has decided on its mission and vision, it must ensure its "purpose" reflects them – in other words, decide with whom it will do business and with whom it will not. Next, it must articulate its values or "principles," defining how it will do business and what it stands for. It must then choose the organizational design or structure needed to allocate resources effectively with appropriate reporting relationships and job descriptions – that is, its "power" structure. The "power" structure then needs to be staffed with suitable "people" and the whole entity needs "processes" to hold it together.

Aligning the "Five Ps" properly with the mission and vision is essential if mission and vision are to be achieved (see Figure 6.1). If any one of the Five Ps is misaligned with the mission and vision, they will not be achieved. Working independently, they may create inconsistent behavior and undermine the values of the organization. Working synergistically, the Five Ps determine and reinforce acceptable behavior and values (shown by the dotted arrows). The resulting Five P performance framework[iii] defines "purpose," "principles," "power," "people," and "processes"; providing five lenses through which performance can be reviewed, establishing where things are going according to plan, and where more investment or corrective actions are needed.

---

iii For a more detailed discussion of the "Five P" performance framework, see, Zinkin, J. (2019), *Better Governance Across the Board: Creating Value Through Reputation, People and Processes* (Boston/Berlin: Walter de Gruyter Inc.), pp. 125–138.

Aligning the organization to achieve the mission and vision

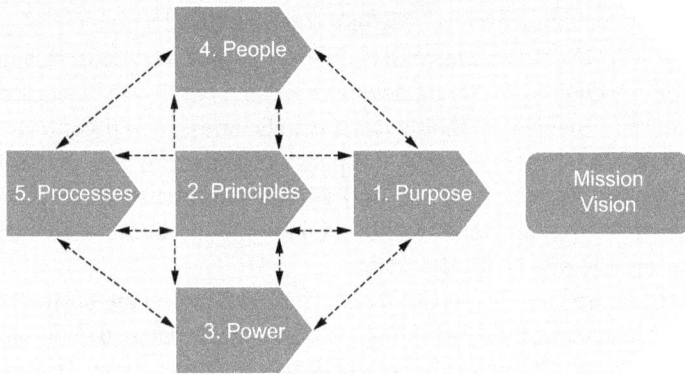

Source: Zinkin, J., (2014), *Corporate Directors Onboarding Program*, Kuala Lumpur, April 16, 2014

Figure 6.1: The "Five Ps": five lenses to track performance.

Purpose

A good way to ensure an enterprise's "purpose" aligns with its mission and vision is to ask six questions:

1. Who are the intended beneficiaries of the organization?[iv]
2. What difference in their lives is it hoping to make?
3. What value will they place on that difference? Consider Peter Drucker's answer:

> It is the customer who determines what a business is. It is the customer alone whose willingness to pay for a good or service converts economic resources into wealth, things into goods. What the business thinks it produces is not of first importance – especially not to the future of the business and to its success. . . . What the customer thinks he/she is buying, what he/she considers value, is decisive – it determines what a business is, what it produces and whether it will prosper.[25]   [Emphases ours]

4. How will it make that difference? Both OC and legitimate businesses have to choose:[v]
   a. Between differentiation, low-cost leadership, and focus strategies;[vi,26]
   b. Between making an irreversible commitment from which there is no exit when conditions change, and keeping flexible options open for as long as possible;[27]

---

iv For a more detailed discussion, see ibid., pp. 126–127.
v For further discussion, see ibid., pp. 128–129.
vi For further detailed discussion, see ibid., pp. 127–128.

    c.   Between being first-to-market or a follower, learning from the mistakes of others;[vii]

    d.   Between developing brands or selling commodities.[viii]

5.   How much will it cost to achieve that difference? The answer to this question depends on the choices regarding how both OC and legitimate businesses make the difference in the lives of their chosen beneficiaries: their organizational design; staffing levels; remuneration and pension policies; where they choose to locate production; cost of capital; and whether and when they can capture economies of scale, scope, and learning, taking into account the lifetime of investments and the rate of obsolescence.

6.   What rate of return can it expect as a result? OC and legitimate businesses need to think not just about the operational ratios involved, but also about matching the risk appetite of the investors/shareholders they answer to. It also means thinking about transfer pricing policies and where to pay taxes to optimize shareholder returns. OC organizations have much greater freedom to maneuver than legitimate businesses particularly in the areas of transfer pricing and money laundering.

Principles

These are the values at the heart of the way the organization functions. They determine what kind of business it does and with whom it will do business. The "principles" determine:

1. What the organization stands for and its culture.

> *Firms whose managers act on the principle that employees are self-interested opportunists who must be forced to do their job will tend to create just that.* Conversely a company that functions on the basis of trust and co-operation creates a system in which honest, co-operative people flourish. Self-fulfilling prophecy makes every company a force for either good or ill.

> Since the 1980s, the assumptions baked into the management model are the pessimistic ones. In the crash of 2008, we can see where the template based on them (incentives, compliance with letter rather than spirit, rejection of ethical considerations) leads. If the 21st century that management makes possible is to end happily, managers will have to absorb its most important lesson from the 20th: *what matters most in management is not what you make but what you believe.*[28]   [Emphases ours]

---

vii For further discussion, see ibid., p. 128.
viii For further discussion, see ibid., p. 129.

Companies get what they expect: if they do not believe employees will work based on trust, collaboration, and values, but only based on greed and self-seeking, they will develop reward and recognition systems that reinforce such behavior. The reverse is also true:

> How we do business – and what business does to us – has everything to do with how we think about business, talk about business, conceive of business, practice business. *If we think, talk, conceive, and practice business as a ruthless, cutthroat, dog-eat-dog activity, then that, of course, is what it will become. And so, too, it is what we will become, no matter how often (in our off hours and personal lives) we insist otherwise.* If, on the other hand, business is conceived – as it often has been conceived – as an enterprise based on trust and mutual benefits, an enterprise for civilized, virtuous people, then that in turn, will be equally self-fulfilling. It will also be much more amiable, secure, enjoyable, and last, but not least, profitable.[29]　　　　　[Emphasis ours]

2. *The "tone at the top" and the "tone in the middle."* Given that "a fish rots from the head," it is important for the leaders of organizations to model the right behaviors, setting the "tone at the top"; failure of the organization will be attributed to failures of leadership. This is true of both OC and legitimate businesses. Codes of conduct exist to ensure that people lower down the organization know what they can and cannot do, setting the "tone in the middle."

3. *Careers of employees and how they are treated.* Talent management must reflect the needs of the business strategy. However, management must also ensure that the people who are recruited and promoted share the same values as those of the company. This is essential if the "tone at the top" is to be preserved. This is where there is an important difference between OC and legitimate businesses.

　　This weakening of lifelong, exclusive economic commitment both ways, by the clan to its members and the members to the clan, is the result of changes in the economic environment. It reflects the same economic pressures as the disappearance of guaranteed lifetime employment and lifelong loyalty to legitimate businesses that was common before Milton Friedman's 1970 article.

4. *Being a responsible citizen.* This recognizes that if legitimate businesses are to maintain their social "license to operate," they must consider the needs of the community, and of the impact they have on the environment in terms of degradation, pollution, and congestion – including what happens in their supply chains wherever they are – as far as working conditions and corruption are concerned. OC organizations, however, do not concern themselves with such issues, as their competitive advantage against legitimate competitors comes from their willingness to break or work around laws designed to protect communities from bad actors and damaging externalities. As a result, it is easier for OC leadership to make their members focus single-mindedly on the cardinal values of loyalty and obedience regardless of the impact of such behavior outside their organizations.

　　There may be another reason why legitimate business is beginning to behave more like OC – the erosion of the three pillars of Protestant capitalism developed in

Geneva in the 17th century, for which financial services sector have been responsible. The three pillars were deferred gratification, mutuality, and trust.

Credit cards and securitization mean that we no longer defer gratification, the mainspring for investing. Investments were designed to create a better future and people lived according to the maxim that "anything worth having is worth waiting for." However, when NatWest Bank launched its Access credit card in the UK in the mid-1960s, its tagline was: "We take the waiting out of wanting!" Securitization had much the same effect for businesses. Immediate gratification became acceptable. The world of 24/7 news and finance made it all seem so natural that nobody questioned a fundamental shift in social values.[30]

Mutuality underpins all long-term relationships. It is essential if systemic integrity is to be preserved. Yet, as the 2007 subprime mortgage crisis demonstrated, there was no mutuality in the way organizations in the supply chain behaved. They were not in the slightest bit interested in the problems they were creating for others down the supply/value chain. It was the "Greater Fool Theory" of finance in action with a vengeance.

When we were growing up in the UK, bank managers were among the most trusted members of the community. They were like honorary uncles, invited to children's birthday parties; they gave advice; and they often took the view that what their client wanted to do was unwise, and exercised their discretion to refuse to do business on the grounds it would not be sensible for the client to undertake the transaction. Yet by 2011, five out six people in the UK and three out of four in the US no longer trusted banks "to do the right thing," according to the Edelman Global Trust Barometer's findings.

Perhaps another reason for the increasing convergence in social values between OC and legitimate business that underpin being a responsible citizen, is the unintended consequence of consumerism and mass marketing. Mass marketing techniques legitimizing conspicuous consumption use six of the "Seven Deadly Sins" to promote consumer-based economies: pride (showing off what one has that others do not), envy (wanting to "keep up with the Joneses"), greed (reinforcing the natural desire to want more than what one has), gluttony (eating out and consuming ever more fancy and expensive meals), sloth ("pamper yourself"), and lust (the tourism, hospitality, and entertainment industries promote it surreptitiously). Only wrath does not feature in the techniques used by the millions of people and dollars invested in creating and maintaining satisfied customers. The credit card is perhaps the most dangerous tool used by legitimate businesses, offering people instant gratification, downplaying the need to be responsible for one's finances, increasing credit limits whenever possible to tempt people into spending still more to buy things and experiences they do not really need, creating an addiction to materialism, hiding the consequences in the fine print of legalese that most customers do not read or understand; all in order to satisfy six of the seven deadly sins. The dangers of excessive addiction to credit for luxuries as opposed to necessities are not just moral and financial, but ecological as well. The relentless focus on increasing consumption made possible by credit threatens the sustainability of the planet.

Power

"Power" covers organizational design, job descriptions, roles and responsibilities, and reporting relationships, as well as how people are treated by their superiors – hence the term "power."

Fons Trompenaars and Christopher Hampden-Turner identified four types of organization: "Incubator," "Family Firm," "Guided Missile," and "Eiffel Tower." The differences in their operating philosophies are shown in Table 6.1.

Table 6.1: Characteristics of the Four Organizational Cultures.

Behavioral Characteristics	"Incubator"	"Family Firm"	"Guided Missile"	"Eiffel Tower"
Employee relationships	*Diffuse,* spontaneous relations arising from shared creative processes	*Diffuse,* intuitive, holistic, lateral, and error correcting	*Specific,* problem-centered, professional, practical, cross-disciplinary	*Specific,* logical, analytical, vertical, and rationally efficient
Attitude toward authority	Status *achieved* by individuals exemplifying creativity and growth	Status *ascribed* to parent figures who are close and powerful	Status *achieved* by project group members who contribute to targeted goal	Status *ascribed* to "superior" roles who are distant yet powerful
Ways of thinking and learning	*Diffuse,* process-oriented, creative, ad-hoc, inspirational	*Diffuse,* intuitive, holistic, lateral, and error correcting	*Specific,* problem-centered, professional, practical, cross-disciplinary	*Specific,* logical, analytical, vertical, and rationally efficient
Attitudes toward people	*Diffuse,* co-creators	*Diffuse,* family members	*Specific,* specialists and experts	*Specific,* human resources
Ways of changing	Improvise and attune	"Parent" changes course	Shift aim as target moves	Change rules and procedures

Table 6.1 (continued)

Behavioral Characteristics	"Incubator"	"Family Firm"	"Guided Missile"	"Eiffel Tower"
Ways of motivating/ rewarding	*Management by enthusiasm* Participating in the process of creating new realities	*Management by subjectives* Intrinsic satisfaction in being loved and respected	*Management by objectives* Pay or credit for performance and problems solved	*Management by job description* Promotion to greater position, larger role
Criticism and conflict resolution	Must improve the idea, not negate it	Turn other cheek, save others' faces; do not lose power game	Constructive, task-related only, then admit error and correct fast	Criticism is accusation of irrationality, unless there are procedures to arbitrate conflicts

Source: Based on Trompenaars, F., and Hampden-Turner, C. (2006), *Riding the Waves of Culture: Understanding Cultural Diversity in Business,* 2nd Edition (London: Nicholas Brealey Publishing), p. 178.

Depending on whether the organization is an "Incubator," "Family Firm," "Guided Missile," or "Eiffel Tower,"[ix] the four life-stages of organizations will also determine what kind of power relationships are likely to be most effective:

1. *Start-Ups* share many of the characteristics of an "Incubator." The mental models about the importance of vision, of testing new ideas, of "moving fast and breaking things" and learning from the breakages, the types of relationships, and how to measure performance only apply to start-ups. This is likely to be true of OC when it is still in its gang stage of development where lines of business and territorial boundaries have yet to be finalized.

Relationships between people tend to be *diffuse*. It is too early in start-ups to talk of careers and, as a result, management style is "management by enthusiasm." Those accustomed to *specificity* in thought processes, measuring performance, in relationships and predictability, will find it difficult to adjust to the context of a start-up or a gang. Those accustomed to *diffuseness* in thought processes, performance measurement, personal relationships, and unpredictable outcomes will flourish.

The challenge in a start-up is to turn ideas into practice.

---

ix For a more detailed discussion of the four organizational archetypes, see Zinkin, J., and Bennett, C. (2021), *The Principles and Practice of Effective Leadership* (Berlin/Boston: Walter de Gruyter), pp. 177–179.

2. *Growth stage* shares many features with the start-up. As time passes and predictability begins to matter, organizations (other than "Family Firms" and owner-managed businesses) will begin focusing on processes, procedures, and predictability of outcomes. Vision still matters, as does management by enthusiasm, but less than in start-ups.

In the case of "Family Firms," what will matter most is the temperamental and social fit with the founder and family. In "Family Firms," individuals need to be comfortable with a philosophy of "management by subjectives" where goals and objectives can change on the whims of the owner of the firm. Those uncomfortable with these contextual requirements will be forced out of the organization (or killed in the case of gangs and more developed OC organizations).

The primary focus in the growth stage is to create scalable value and start accumulating value for later extraction and distribution to shareholders and members in the case of OC.

3. *Maturity stage* is when organizations reach full development, and it hardly matters whether they started out as "Incubators" or "Family Firms." What matters is stability, order, and predictability. Most organizations choose between becoming a "Guided Missile" or an "Eiffel Tower." Instead of the *diffuse* approach to relationships, tasks, and performance measurement, those employed find themselves working in cultures where *specificity* replaces *diffuseness*. The key difference between the "Guided Missile" and the "Eiffel Tower" is the flexibility with which objectives and tasks change. "Guided Missiles" respond to changing contexts and situations more rapidly than "Eiffel Towers" because their environments are subject to greater competition, customer choice, and, in the case of multinationals, national cultural variations. A premium is placed on adaptability and "helicopter vision."[31]

The key challenges in mature, process-driven organizations remain the same: mastering the politics, how to "tell truth to power," and how to "think out of the box," lest they become trapped in an ossified culture because of the legacy effect.

The challenge in mature organizations is how to best reconcile the need to create value, extract value, and distribute it sustainably.

4. *Decline stage* requires a short-term focus on optimizing the bottom-line, ruthlessly cutting costs and eliminating people who have done nothing wrong other than being in the wrong place at the wrong time. Most people are temperamentally ill-suited to doing this, letting the organization drift gradually downward, at first slowly, and then rapidly as it approaches bankruptcy. *The main business priority is extracting the maximum value in the shortest time, focusing on cash.*

Both OC and legitimate organizations must ensure that whichever of the four types of organizational design they choose, it will be sufficiently flexible to avoid the problem of so-called "stuckness" if the business strategy requires a change of direction. Perhaps the most obvious questions in this regard are the following:

1. *To make or buy?* By choosing to outsource do organizations risk losing control of key intellectual property or a core competency leaving them exposed later when the unexpected happens, because although the lost competency was not core, it was, however, mission-critical. Global supply chains have grown up as organizations have chosen to outsource manufacturing across the globe to those places and companies that have a track record of being able to supply goods and services to specification, reliably, and cheaper than if they were made domestically by their own organizations. OC organizations that are involved in drug, human, arms, and wildlife trafficking have come to depend on coordinated, but arms-length, supply chains with independent players, so that they can switch sources when the authorities arrest suppliers in the supply chain.

2. *To carry out research and development or license?* Organizations doing their own R&D have to invest a great deal of time, effort, and money with no guarantee the investment will bear fruit. If they have deep pockets and can survive the likelihood that for every success, they may have to finance up to twenty failed projects,[x] then choosing to do their own R&D makes sense. However, if time is of the essence, or if the company does not have the financial or human resources to execute the R&D, then licensing may be a sensible solution, as has happened with vaccinations to deal with the Covid-19 pandemic.

3. *To own fixed assets or rent/lease them?* This choice will determine the breakeven point and profitability, as well as affect the asset intensity of the business, maybe yielding a return on assets that is higher than if the assets were fully owned – depending on the tax treatment of leases. It might also affect the "stuckness" of the business by removing a barrier to exit – depending on the length of the rental or lease agreement. These issues apply to both OC and legitimate businesses.

4. *To go direct, through distributors, franchisees, or via the Internet?* The answer to this question has a huge impact on the size of the sales force and on the physical assets (bricks and mortar) organizations need to have. The acceleration to online distribution caused by the Covid-19 pandemic makes decisions regarding the role of the Internet even more fundamental, not just for legitimate business with their investments in bricks and mortar under threat, but for OC as well, particularly in their transnational lines of business.

---

x "According to the Professor Clayton Christensen [of Harvard Business School], there are over 30,000 new products introduced every year, and 95 percent fail. According to University of Toronto Professor Inez Blackburn, the failure rate of new grocery store products is 70 to 80 percent." Emmer, M. (2018), "95 Percent of New Products Fail. Here Are 6 Steps to Make Sure Yours Don't," *Inc.*, July 6, 2018, https://www.inc.com/marc-emmer/95-percent-of-new-products-fail-here-are-6-steps-to-make-sure-yours-dont.html, accessed on May 25, 2022.

Choice of structure affects the distribution of power and the appropriateness of relationships within and between organizations.

People

OC organizations and legitimate businesses must ensure that the people they employ reflect accurately their chosen business strategies and their priorities in terms of timing and resource rationing. Doing this effectively demands answers to the following four questions:

1. *Does the organization have the right number of people?* In answering this question, organizations must consider their current business strategies and how they expect them to evolve over time and how that will affect the organizational design of the company. This will determine the number of jobs/roles needed to fulfill the agreed mission and vision, and if not, what can be done about it.
2. *Does the organization have the right skills and competencies to do the job properly?* Too often when people are recruited or promoted, the most important criterion is their ability to perform the job based on their past performance,[xi] without paying sufficient attention to whether the nature of the job is changing. Despite the rapid pace of change that renders many competencies obsolete, and the fact that developing competency dictionaries is a backward-looking exercise and therefore not a very good guide to what competencies are likely to be needed in the future, there is an "evergreen" set of core competencies, in particular leadership competencies, that always apply. They are: managing change, developing people, and being creative.

    When organizations do not have the necessary competencies to implement the agreed upon business strategy, they are faced with two choices: (1) either change the strategy recognizing they do not have the people to implement it, or (2) find them, either by recruiting or hiring outsiders who have the necessary skills.
3. *Does an organization's people have the right character to work in line with its "principles"?* Organizations often hire and promote people based on their ability to meet targets they are set; their past track record; or their apparent list of competencies, *without considering enough whether they have the right character to fit with the "principles" espoused by the organization.* Too often organizations excuse people whose behavior does not fit with their values either on the grounds of their seniority or on their ability to make a positive impact on the short-term bottom line.

---

xi This explains the famous "Peter Principle" which states people are promoted to their level of incompetence.

There is a saying that attitude matters more than aptitude because attitude cannot be taught, whereas aptitude can.

4. *Which of four types of leaders does it need?* There are four leadership roles: *"Captain"*, *"Navigator"*, *"Engineer"*, and *"Shipbuilder"*. Large organizations, unlike most smaller firms, can afford to fill the roles with specialists.[32]

a. *"Captains"* (CEOs or OC bosses) establish codes of conduct and inspire subordinates, articulating the mission, defining responsibilities and rewards, setting project timelines, and deciding when corrective action is needed. They are not superheroes but the focus of attention around whom subordinates can rally.

Part of our difficulty with appreciating the role that effective executive leadership can play in learning is that all of us are used to the "captain of the ship" image of traditional hierarchical leaders. However, when executives act as teachers, stewards, and designers, they fill roles that are much more subtle, contextual, and long term than the traditional model of the power-wielding hierarchical leader.[33]

b. *"Navigators"* are found in staff functions, developing and stress-testing key assumptions of plans, examining scenarios. They look at trends and their impact on the business, establish early warning signals, and advise "captains" when conditions change. In mafia organizations they are *consiglieri*. Their role is to help "captains" chart a course for getting their organizations from where they currently are to where they want to go.[34]

c. *"Engineers,"* called "line leaders" by Senge, are the people in the boiler room who keep the organization moving and they are often hard to engage because of their day-to-day focus and skepticism of big new ideas. In mafia-like organizations these are *capo di famiglia*:

As pragmatists, they often find ideas like systems thinking, mental models, and dialogue intangible and "hard to get their hands around"

Again, and again, we have found that healthy, open-minded skeptics can become the most effective leaders and, eventually, champions of this work. They keep the horse in front of the cart by focusing first and foremost on business results. *Such people invariably have more staying power than the "fans" who get excited about new ideas but whose excitement wanes once the newness wears off.*[35]   [Emphasis ours]

d. *"Ship-builders"* are planners, enterprise risk managers, and auditors who ensure appropriate processes and procedures, creating an appropriate organizational infrastructure.

Having these four different types of leaders within an organization has three important benefits. The first is that they each bring different points of view to any discussion involving changes in strategy and process, reflecting their different approaches to their responsibilities. The second is that it helps create an atmosphere where "speaking truth to power" is encouraged. The third is that, as a result, it creates what Machiavelli termed "friction"[36] that reduces the risk of groupthink, making it easier for the organization to respond more effectively to changing conditions.

Processes

Processes are the glue that binds the organization together: strategic planning, budgeting and financial reporting, approved policies and procedures – regularly inspected for lapses and loopholes and taking corrective action. Processes include all forms of internal formal and informal feedback mechanisms. Measurement and remuneration processes should align with the mission and vision.

The most important process problems both OC and legitimate businesses face are: setting the appropriate KPIs and ensuring that they employ and retain the right people.

1. *Setting appropriate KPIs:* The appropriateness of KPIs (key performance indicators) determines whether the mission and vision can be achieved. To deliver what is required, KPIs must be divided into outcome, output, and input KPIs. Outcome KPIs answer the six "purpose" questions: "Who are the beneficiaries of the organization?" "What difference in their lives will the organization make?" "What value will they place on that difference?" "How much will it cost to deliver that value?" "What return can be expected as a result?" "How will the organization know it has succeeded?" Output KPIs cover the products and services created to deliver the desired outcomes and appear in the elements of the income statement. Input KPIs are the resources needed to ensure that projects are planned and resourced appropriately. There is no difference in setting KPIs between OC and legitimate business.

2. *Planning succession and managing talent:* Typical ways of planning succession to ensure there is a qualified supply of candidates for key/pivotal positions in legitimate business is to engage in elaborate personnel development planning, including training initiatives, coupled with leadership assessment exercises to decide what might be the best next moves over a one-, three-, and five-year timetable.[xii] These can be divided into "traditional" methods of moving existing employees within an organization to new positions as and when required, and "alternative" approaches such as job rotations (employees filling various positions for short periods to help them gain experience), talent pools (spreading roles by appointing many employees across more positions), and outsourcing.[37] Managing talent requires four steps: (1) developing a talent strategy based on the business strategy and defining "talent," (2) identifying pivotal positions in

---

xii For a more detailed discussion of succession planning and talent management, see Zinkin and Bennett, *The Principles and Practice of Effective Leadership*, pp. 173–175.

the organization and what competencies are required *currently and in future,* (3) identifying and developing people to fill the talent pipeline, and (4) monitoring and evaluating progress and its cost effectiveness. Regardless of whether they are OC organizations or legitimate businesses, they should check whether their business strategies are vulnerable to failures in closing gaps between current and future organization design and current and future talent.

3. *Retaining recruits:* Unlike legitimate businesses, OC organizations adopt complicated and quasi-religious initiation rites of passage to impress on new recruits that they are leaving the normal world to enter into an exclusive and secret membership and that there is no return to the legitimate world (see Chapter 7).

References

1 George, B. (2017), "VUCA 2.0: A Strategy For Steady Leadership In An Unsteady World," *HBS Working Knowledge,* featured in *Forbes,* February 17, 2017, https://www.forbes.com/sites/hbswor kingknowledge/2017/02/17/vuca-2-0-a-strategy-for-steady-leadership-in-an-unsteady-world/ #7d64970d13d8, accessed on December 19, 2019.
2 Zinkin, J. (2020), *The Challenge of Sustainability: Corporate Governance in a Complicated World* (Berlin/Boston: Walter de Gruyter GmbH), pp. 224–225.
3 Adelstein, J. (2014), "Ninkyodo, dude! Even the Yakuza Are Speaking English Now!," *Japan Subculture Research Center,* July 21, 2014, http://www.japansubculture.com/ninkyodo-dude-even-the-yakuza-are-speaking-english-now/, accessed on May 12, 2021.
4 Ibid., p. 226.
5 Johnson, B. (2022), "The Great Horse Manure Crisis of 1894," *Historic UK,* https://www.historic-uk.com/HistoryUK/HistoryofBritain/Great-Horse-Manure-Crisis-of-1894/, accessed on May 6, 2022.
6 Zinkin, J. (2019), *Better Governance Across the Board: Creating Value Through Reputation, People and Processes* (Boston/Berlin: Walter de Gruyter, Inc), pp. 50–52.
7 Drucker, P. F. (2007), *Management Challenges for the 21st Century* (Oxford: Butterworth Heinemann), pp. 86, 93–94, quoted in ibid., pp. 51–52.
8 Smith, N. C. (2003), "Corporate Social Responsibility: Whether or How?," *California Management Review,* 45, No. 4, pp. 52–76, https://doi.org/10.2307/41166188, accessed on May 12, 2021.
9 *Economist* (1995), "The Strange Death of Corporationville," December 23, 1995, p. 73, cited in ibid.
10 Styles, J. (1994), *Titus Salt and Saltaire: Industry and Virtue* (Salt Estates Ltd., Shipley, England), pp. 12–13.
11 "Early History and Robert Owen," *Undiscovered Scotland,* https://www.undiscoveredscotland. co.uk/lanark/newlanark/history1.html, accessed on May 12, 2021.
12 "History and Heritage" *Port Sunlight Village Trust,* https://www.portsunlightvillage.com/about-port-sunlight/history-and-heritage/, accessed on May 12, 2021.
13 "Do You Want to Live in a Beautiful Conservation Area in a Grade II Listed Property?," *Port Sunlight Village Trust,* https://www.portsunlightvillage.com/properties/, accessed on May 12, 2021.
14 Styles (1994), p. 38.
15 Ibid., p. 39.

16 "Company Values Glossary," *HubSpot*, 2021, https://offers.hubspot.com/company-values-glos
sary?hubs_post-cta=anchor&hsCtaTracking=0d54c232-f3a1-4708-bd21-f534c5131a8a%7Cca85cddf-
0d5a-47b8-b497-94305537e844, accessed on May 10, 2021.

17 Nortz, J. (2014), "Do Your Corporate Values Pass the Mafia Test?" *The Business Journals*,
June 23, 2014, https://www.bizjournals.com/bizjournals/how-to/growth-strategies/2014/06/do-
your-corporate-values-pass-the-mafia-test.html, accessed on May 10, 2021.

18 Ibid.

19 Bradshaw, T., and Murphy, H. (2021), "We Regret 'Creating Problems', Say Colonial Petroleum
Pipeline Hackers," *Financial Times*, May 10, 2021, https://www.ft.com/content/0afb53f0-f382-442a-
9a32-02824ce8bb70?accessToken=zwAAAXlZGY-wkc8K-1Pw84JEKtOaMgKCTOi7cA.MEQCIExP-
kyFlWWTS_sPC_bVB_eHSiO1fSR2foyf46rspCEdLAiBH-7M5Q5E13gfMuXvpVaM-
OfgeR6KcAszODJFjL9nMLw&sharetype=gift?token=bbcbfa82-128d-4ee3-97a1-5feff0ab78ad, accessed
on May 11, 2021.

20 Ibid.

21 Levine, M. (2021), "Money Stuff: Crypto Markets Are Where the Fun Is," *Bloomberg Opinion*,
May 12, 2021, https://www.bloomberg.com/news/newsletters/2021-05-11/money-stuff-crypto-markets-
are-where-the-fun-is, accessed on May 12, 2021.

22 *New York Times* (1970), "A Friedman Doctrine – The Social Responsibility of Business Is to Increase its Profits," *New York Times*, September 13, 1970, https://www.nytimes.com/1970/09/13/ar-
chives/a-friedman-doctrine-the-social-responsibility-of-business-is-to.html, accessed on May 13,
2021.

23 Thatcher, M. (1987) "Interview for *Woman's Own* ('No Such Thing as Society')," September 23,
1987, https://www.margaretthatcher.org/document/106689, accessed on May 13, 2021.

24 Saunders, R. (2020), "'There is Such a Thing as Society.' Has Boris Johnson Repudiated Thatch-
erism?" *New Statesman*, March 31, 2021, https://www.newstatesman.com/politics/uk/2020/03/
boris-johnson-thatcher-society-no-such-thing-policies, accessed on May 13, 2021.

25 Drucker, P. (1955), *The Practice of Management* (Oxford: Butterworth Heinemann), p. 35, quoted
in Zinkin (2014), p. 127.

26 Porter, M. (1985), *Competitive Advantage: Creating and Sustaining Superior Performance*
(New York: The Free Press), pp. 41–42.

27 Bruner, B. (2012), "Stuck in the Middle? Take the Flexible Approach," January 16, 2012,
https://blogs.darden.virginia.edu/brunerblog/2012/01/stuck-in-the-middle/, a guest post quoted by
Symonds, M., *Forbes*, February 24, 2012, https://www.forbes.com/sites/mattsymonds/2012/02/24/
stuck-in-the-middle-take-the-flexible-approach/#4d1184142ebd, accessed on July 5, 2018.

28 Caulkin, S. (2012), "The Wrong Direction: Management Has Lost its Way – and its Power Has
Sent Business Down a Dangerous Road," *FT Business Education*, December 3, 2012, p. 12.

29 Solomon, R.C. (1999), *A Better Way to Think About Business: How Personal Integrity Leads to
Corporate Success* (New York: Oxford University Press, 1999), p. xxii.

30 Zinkin (2014), p. 77.

31 Bridges, W. (1991), *Managing Transitions*, cited in "Bridges' Transition Model: Guiding People
Through Change," *MindTools*, Emerald Works, https://www.mindtools.com/pages/article/bridges-
transition-model.htm, accessed on April 20, 2020.

32 This section is based on Zinkin, J., and Bennett, C. (2021), *The Principles and Practice of Effective
Leadership* (Berlin/Boston: Walter de Gruyter GmbH).

33 Senge, P. (1995), "Rethinking Leadership in The Learning Organization," *The Systems Thinker*,
https://thesystemsthinker.com/rethinking-leadership-in-the-learning-organization/, accessed on
September 5, 2018, quoted in Zinkin (2014), pp. 324–325.

34 Wohl, R. A., and Wohl, L. (2011), *Navigating Organizations Through the 21st Century: A Metaphor for Leadership* (Bloomington: Indiana: Xlibris), pp. 24–25, quoted in ibid., p. 325.

35 Senge (1995), quoted in ibid., p. 325.

36 Zinkin and Bennett (2021), p. 11.

37 Ip, B., and Jacobs, G. (2006), "Business Succession Planning: A Review of the Evidence," *Journal of Small Business and Enterprise Development*, 13, No. 3, 2006, p. 339.

Chapter 7
Differences between OC and Legitimate Enterprises

An organization must ensure its purpose reflects its mission and vision – in other words, decide with whom it will do business and with whom it will not. Using the "Five P" performance framework (introduced in Chapter 6) helps identify where differences in behavior arise between OC and legitimate enterprises.

Purpose

Legitimate businesses have always had Peter Drucker's "the purpose of business is to create and maintain satisfied customers"[1] and/or Milton Friedman's "the social responsibility of business is to maximize shareholder value"[2] to guide them. Reconciling the two has not always been easy and the context in which businesses operate has changed from managerial capitalism (ca. 1950–1960) to shareholder capitalism (ca. 1970–2009) and now to stakeholder capitalism (ca. 2010 onward). Legitimate businesses have a relatively straightforward relationship with the state, where it usually acts as their rule-setter and regulator; except in sectors where there are state-owned or linked enterprises where it is a competitor.

For OC, things are more complicated. The original purposes of Mafias, Yakuzas, and Triads was to protect their communities when political elites failed to provide adequate protection for their communities. They also provided an alternative to untrustworthy judges in settling disputes in the community. Over time, these two purposes morphed into three which reflect and inform their competitive relationship with the state:[3]

1. *Predation* where OC organizations seek to expand their monopoly of territory at the expense of the state and potential territorial rivals, often resorting to violence;
2. *Parasitism* where OC organizations appropriate the resources of the state, through a mix of covert violence, blackmail, bribery, and corruption;
3. *Symbiosis* where OC organizations work with the state to achieve common objectives when the state itself does not have a monopoly on violence, is regarded as illegitimate by a significant section of the community, or is engaged in a civil war where OC can do the states' "dirty work."

Legitimate businesses cannot adopt the same level of predatory competition as OC because: (1) the state will not tolerate an existential challenge from a legitimate business and will use the law to take it over or shut it down; (2) when it comes to head-to-head competition, there are regulatory limits to the amount of market share businesses can aim for before they hit regulatory barriers and, unlike OC, they cannot resort to open force to achieve their growth objectives. However, they

https://doi.org/10.1515/9783110712155-007

can adopt strategies of parasitism, or symbiosis through crony capitalism and associated rent-seeking, and do so successfully in countries that are corrupt. State-owned enterprises are a clear example of symbiosis that often leads to unfair competition or monopolies.

Six Questions

A good way to ensure an organization's purpose aligns with its mission and vision is to ask six questions:

1 Who are the Intended Beneficiaries of the Organization?[i]

The first class of beneficiaries of OC are people who are looking for security where there is none provided by the state and for products and services denied them because they are illegal. OC organizations can therefore claim that they provide two fundamental services: providing protection where there is no legitimate or acceptable governing authority and, more contentiously, providing the goods and services that people want but that are not offered by legitimate organizations because they are illegal. Combining these two points, Diego Gambetta explains how OC emerged to protect commercial transactions that are the basis of the economy,[4] and they do this by creating trust:

> Rather than producing cars, beer, nuts and bolts, or books, they produce and sell trust.[5]

> In essence, mafiosi operate in those economic transactions and agreements where trust, while of paramount importance, is nevertheless fragile, and where it is either inefficiently supplied or cannot be supplied at all by the state: typically, in illegal transactions in otherwise legal goods, or in all transactions in illegal goods.[6]

While there is some truth in this idea, there are two important differences between what OC organizations and legitimate businesses with established brands offer. The first is that the essence of branded goods is that the trust their users have is earned as a result of reliability and consistent quality and performance, whereas this is not always the case with OC products like hard drugs that are adulterated to improve margins. Moreover, given the lack of consumer protection regarding illicit (contraband and counterfeit) products, OC does not have to take responsibility for any harms their products may do. The second is that the violence used by OC when providing "protection" suggests that those who are being "protected" may not always choose the service of their own free will. However, customers of protection provided

---

i For a more detailed discussion, see Zinkin, J. (2019), *Better Governance Across the Board: Creating Value Through Reputation, People and Processes* (Boston/Berlin: Walter Gruyter, Inc), pp. 126–127.

by the state also have little choice in the matter – they pay taxes and get protection in return. The only choice they have is whether to look to the state or to OC to provide it depending on which is more present and effective, unlike customers and clients of legitimate businesses who have a wide range of choices, including not to buy.

The second class of beneficiaries are political elites coexisting with OC organizations to create a triangular relationship of needs between themselves, OC and businessmen, that culminates in corruption shown in Figure 7.1.

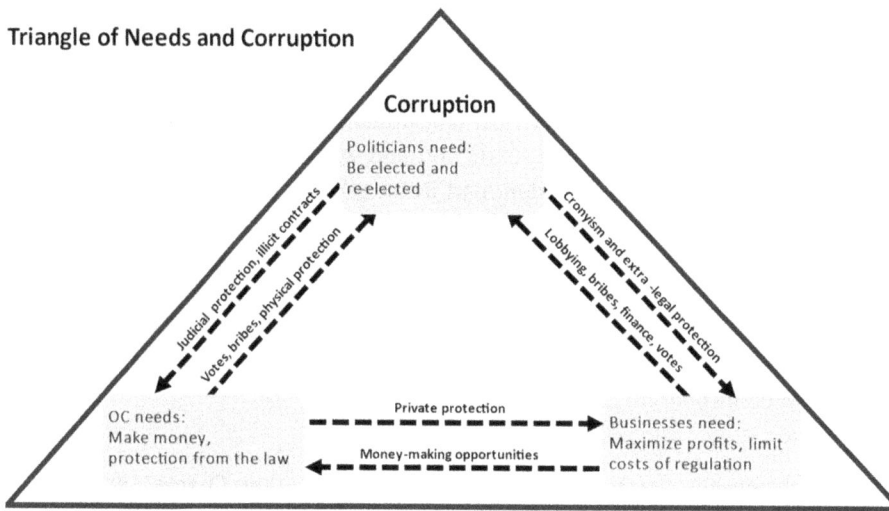

Triangle of Needs and Corruption

Corruption

Politicians need:
Be elected and
re-elected

Judicial protection, illicit contracts
Votes, bribes, physical protection

Cronyism and extra-legal protection
Lobbying, bribes, finance, votes

OC needs:
Make money,
protection from the law

Private protection

Money-making opportunities

Businesses need:
Maximize profits, limit
costs of regulation

Figure 7.1: Triangle of Needs and Corruption.

Figure 7.1 shows the needs of the political elite: politicians need to get elected, stay in power, and get re-elected. To that end, OC organizations benefit politicians by marshalling votes directly to help them at election time, finance them through bribes, and in some countries offer physical protection. In return, they expect to make money (their primary purpose) and to get protection from law enforcement through the offices of corrupted (usually local) politicians.

Legitimate businesses also benefit political parties and politicians by helping them win votes at elections through their support of issues through lobbying, funding advertising during elections, and providing them with briefs and talking points through their lobbyists. Lobbying, however, should not be seen as a benevolent exercise. It is often used to weaken elected representatives and to make them afraid of the power of the organization, best summed up in these words by an Amazon lobbyist:

> We want policymakers and press to fear us.[7]

Sometimes lobbyists pay bribes and give kickbacks in return for winning contracts on an uneven playing field. They may even pay elected representatives to ask questions in Congress that are designed to put their offers in a favorable light.[8] In return, they hope to become members of the "chumocracy" with expedited access to decision-makers and to contracts that the government hands out – as happened with the UK government during the early stages of the coronavirus pandemic – preferably without having to go through the tedious and costly business of open tendering.[9] In rare cases, they may seek extra-legal protection or pardons for their past malpractices (for example, the exiled oil trader, Marc Rich, when President Clinton completed his term of office[10]).

OC and legitimate businesses often have arms-length relationships to mutual benefit, in the area of financial crime, in four operations: (1) money laundering where the transactions are intermediated by a host of legitimate and not-so-legitimate accountants, lawyers, and bankers; (2) construction and waste management where OC in many jurisdictions plays an important part in the sectors; (3) when companies want to offload activities that are no longer regarded as reflecting good ESG behavior; and (4) in the hospitality and entertainment industry which is a sector OC has penetrated in many countries. OC offers protection from violence and protection from monetary and tax authorities tracking financial malpractice. In return, it looks for opportunities to make money through blackmail and extortion or else through a privileged seat at the table when it comes to money laundering.

2 What Difference is the Organization Hoping to Make in their Clients' Lives?

The answer to this question depends on whether the clients are OC clients and on which type they are. If they are politicians, it is to help get them into power, stay in power, deliver their manifestos, and get re-elected. This is only true, however, if their clients are members of a political elite with whom they can co-exist, either by following a parasitic or symbiotic strategy. Should the political elites, however, be hostile to their interests, then, if they are powerful enough, OC organizations may adopt a predatory strategy where they seek to expel the state from the territories they wish to monopolize; and in some cases, they succeed, as in Mexico,[11] Colombia,[12] and the Central American "Northern Triangle,"[13] and in others they fail, as in the case of the Cosa Nostra in Sicily.[14]

If the clients are citizens in areas where the state has lost its right to rule, OC organizations will justify their behavior by claiming that only *they* can provide the trust and protection that is necessary for life and livelihoods to continue normally. While this may be partially true, their beneficiaries are likely to feel that they are reluctant clients rather than beneficiaries of OC, just waiting for the time when they can throw off the yoke of OC, as happened in Palermo once the Cosa Nostra were cut down to size.[15]

If the clients are legitimate businesses, OC organizations can work in two ways to provide better value for money than the legitimate competition: using their money-laundering front operations, they can operate like any legitimate business serving its clients, but with the advantage of being able to offer cheaper products and services because as money-laundering fronts they do not expect to make money; or they can offer better value because they do not adhere to ESG laws and regulations in parts of their supply chains (discussed in more detail later), making it less costly for them to do business.

3 What Value will Beneficiaries Place on that Difference?

Consider Peter Drucker's answer, as it applies to legitimate businesses:

> *It is the customer who determines what a business is. It is the customer alone whose willingness to pay for a good or service converts economic resources into wealth, things into goods.* What the business thinks it produces is not of first importance – especially not to the future of the business and to its success . . . *What the customer thinks he/she is buying, what he/she considers value, is decisive – it determines what a business is, what it produces and whether it will prosper.*[16]   [Emphases ours]

This is correct, but only under certain conditions. It is not valid:

a. *If the business is a monopoly* and customers have no choice but are forced to use it, then what the monopolist considers value is what matters. This explains why, even in legitimate business conditions, citizens are often so badly served by government bureaucracies and by utilities that operate local monopolies. Wherever OC organizations operate territorial monopolies, they will determine what is value and not their clients, hence the protection they offer is often only extortion and their clients have no choice but to put up with it, as there is nowhere else to go.

b. *If the business is providing illicit products and services,* customers have no legitimate avenues of redress if the product is not delivered, not "fit for purpose," or harmful because there are no regulatory bodies or legal channels to which they can appeal, given that they would incriminate themselves in so doing. This explains why human and sex traffickers can promise a wonderful new life to desperate refugees and migrants, provide appalling conditions and routes that cost the trafficked a fortune and maybe even their lives, without any guarantees that what they are promising is reality – and still get away with it. Illegal immigrants are not going to go to the police when they discover upon arrival in their desired destination that what they were promised fails to materialize. The same applies to OC organizations that specialize in smuggling contraband and counterfeit branded goods. Disappointed customers are not going to report them to the police or to the media.

c. *If customers are "captive,"* they can no longer decide whether they will continue to have a transactional relationship with the organization when it does not provide good value, because they are involved in illegal activities. There are three types of "captives" who no longer have agency:

The first are people who are trafficked. People smugglers, human and sex traffickers, keep their clients under guard during their journeys to their destinations, taking and keeping all their money, travel documents and IDs, so that they cannot get away from them until they find employers who also take away their ability to be independent and underpay them for their services or treat them as bonded slaves. Illegal immigrants are unwilling to go to the authorities to get justice because of their status. Only OC operates in this area; legitimate businesses and individuals are, however, complicit if they employ such people.

The second are professional business people who have become entangled in white collar crime, either as launderers of money or as advisers to money launderers and the OC organizations that facilitate financial crime. They become vulnerable to blackmail and lose their ability to ensure that the services they receive are 'fit for purpose,' because seeking redress will expose them as criminals.

The third are addicts who need to feed their addiction regardless of value and product quality and who will not care whether the drugs they use are harmful, adulterated, or fake.

As a result, if any of the three conditions above apply, OC can make additional profit by ignoring Drucker's warning, whereas legitimate businesses cannot.

4 How will the Organization Make That Difference?

Both OC and legitimate businesses have to choose between: Michael Porter's differentiation, low-cost leadership, and focus strategies;[ii,17] making an irreversible commitment from which there is no exit when conditions change and keeping flexible options open for as long as possible;[18] being first-to-market or a follower, learning from the mistakes of others;[iii] and developing brands or selling commodities.[iv]

5 How Much will it Cost to Achieve that Difference?

The answer to this question depends on the choices regarding how both OC and legitimate businesses make the difference in the lives of their chosen beneficiaries: their organizational design; staffing levels; remuneration and pension policies; where they choose to locate production; cost of capital; and whether and when they can capture economies of scale, scope, and learning, taking into account the lifetime of investments and the rate of obsolescence.

---

ii For further detailed discussion, see ibid., pp. 127–128.
iii For further discussion, see ibid., p. 128.
iv For further discussion, see ibid., p. 129.

6 What Rate of Return Can it Expect as a Result?

OC and legitimate businesses need to think not just about the operational ratios involved, but also about matching the risk appetite of the investors/shareholders they answer to. It also means thinking about transfer pricing policies and where to pay taxes to optimize shareholder returns. OC organizations have much greater freedom to maneuver than legitimate businesses particularly in the areas of transfer pricing and money laundering.

Principles

These are the values at the heart of the way an organization functions. They determine what kind of business it does and with whom it will do business. The principles determine:

What the Organization Stands for and its Culture

> *Firms whose managers act on the principle that employees are self-interested opportunists who must be forced to do their job will tend to create just that.* Conversely a company that functions on the basis of trust and co-operation creates a system in which honest, co-operative people flourish. Self-fulfilling prophecy makes every company a force for either good or ill.
>
> Since the 1980s, the assumptions baked into the management model are the pessimistic ones. In the crash of 2008, we can see where the template based on them (incentives, compliance with letter rather than spirit, rejection of ethical considerations) leads. If the 21st century that management makes possible is to end happily, managers will have to absorb its most important lesson from the 20th: *what matters most in management is not what you make but what you believe.*[19]   [Emphases ours]

Companies get what they expect: if they do not believe employees will work based on trust, collaboration, and values, but only based on greed and self-seeking, they will develop reward and recognition systems that reinforce such behavior. The reverse is also true:

> How we do business – and what business does to us – has everything to do with how we think about business, talk about business, conceive of business, practice business. *If we think, talk, conceive, and practice business as a ruthless, cutthroat, dog-eat-dog activity, then that, of course, is what it will become. And so, too, it is what we will become, no matter how often (in our off hours and personal lives) we insist otherwise.* If, on the other hand, business is conceived – as it often has been conceived – as an enterprise based on trust and mutual benefits, an enterprise for civilized, virtuous people, then that in turn, will be equally self-fulfilling. It will also be much more amiable, secure, enjoyable, and last, but not least, profitable.[20]   [Emphasis ours]

Perhaps there is an important difference here between how OC and legitimate businesses operate. OC organizations think and talk about business as being ruthless, cutthroat "dog-eat-dog" activity, not just in the ways they choose to compete, but also in the ways they treat their members; and so that is how they are. Unfortunately, this difference is not as marked as one might hope, because there are many legitimate businesses with toxic leadership that behave in the same way and become unpleasant places to work. However, there are also many legitimate businesses that conceive of themselves as enterprises for civilized, virtuous people, whereas no OC organization can claim to do so.

The "Tone at the Top" and the "Tone in the Middle"

Given that "a fish rots from the head," it is important for the leaders of organizations to model the right behaviors, setting the "tone at the top"; failure of the organization will be attributed to failures of leadership. This is true of both OC and legitimate businesses. Codes of conduct exist to ensure that people lower down in the organization know what they can and cannot do, setting the "tone in the middle."

Careers of Employees and How They are Treated

How OC recruits, retains, and promotes people differs from legitimate businesses, not in terms of objectives, but in terms of modalities. Both OC and legitimate businesses need employees whose personal values and purpose align with those of their employers to maximize their productivity at minimum cost. However, the ways OC goes about recruiting and retaining employees (members of their organizations) differ from legitimate businesses.

Consider recruitment: It is fashionable for large legitimate organizations to hire from diverse pools of talent, based on the purported benefits of diversity,[21] but OC tends to do the opposite. The 'Ndrangheta, Yakuza, and Taiwanese Triads recruit their members from the same ethnic group, region, clans, and often literally from the same families; the exception now being the Hong Kong Triads who have allowed non-Cantonese members to join (see Chapter 2).

Core OC organization membership is exclusive[v] in order to minimize the risk of infiltration by the police, but also because being invited to join an exclusive organization

---

[v] OC works with people from diverse backgrounds in their affiliated relationships, such as lawyers, accountants, underground investment bankers, and tax experts in order to get access to skills and connections they lack. The same applies when they are involved in international criminal activities.

confers status and respect on initiates among their peer groups.[22] It reinforces the importance of loyalty and obedience as bonds are greater because of heightened trust and shared values with members from the same subculture. It made it easier for Mafias and Yakuza to create emotional and economic dependency and replace the biological family, binding members for life once they joined:

> The *family* is to be understood here as a human organization, not always coinciding with the natural family – which has the additional tasks of instilling values and world views, establishing codes of conduct and rules of coexistence, and strictly enforcing them. This bond, due of its high level of idealization and fusion, makes it impossible for a member to change from a 'familial' to a 'political' belonging. The non-recognition of the latter is reduced to the point of becoming synonymous with belonging to the family clan – the only recognized social group.

> *This means the possibility of psychic growth (their subjectivity) for a member of Cosa Nostra is psychologically obstructed, because their existence depends, without their awareness, on the choices and desires of the group. The mafia, in other words, is a deeply enslaving and dogmatic culture demanding obedience, loyalty and an extreme sense of belonging from its affiliates.*

> Interesting in this regard was the study of statements made by *pentiti* (police collaborators) in the courts. *They affirmed that within their Cosa Nostra clan, the emotional value of their sense of belonging was greater than that felt in their real, genetic families. Suffice to say, most emotional ties are substantially aimed at the strengthening of alliances or to the conservation of power structures, and therefore have no relation to personal needs, which are, on the contrary, "sacrificed" or deleted.*

> All this only helps to emphasize feelings of brotherhood and belonging to the organization, but these . . . are entirely false and unauthentic, despite their necessity in feeding the mechanisms of social consensus and interest of *Cosa Nostra family* for its members.[23]   [Emphases ours]

Joining the Yakuza meant more than joining a gang. It was a home for the new member and his boss became his new father. Loyalty required him in some gangs to cut ties with his biological family. This cutting of ties was part of the appeal, finding a family with members who could be brothers.[24]

> Members are meant to observe strict codes of loyalty, silence, obedience, and the like.

> With these codes in place, the Yakuza were like family. It was more than just a gang. When a new member came in, he accepted his boss as his new father. Over a ceremonial glass of sake, he would formally accept the Yakuza as his new home.

> Loyalty to the Yakuza had to be complete. In some gangs, a new recruit would even be expected to completely cut ties with his biological family.

However, the core membership, the DNA of OC organizations, is ethnically, culturally, and geographically homogeneous.

> To the men who joined these gangs, though, this was part of the appeal. They were social out-casts, people who had no connection in any part of society. The Yakuza, to them, meant find-ing a family in the world, finding people you could call your brothers.[25]

> All *tekiya* members were bound by a strict organization, an authoritarian *oyabun* (literally, par-ent role), and the following "Three Commandments of Tekiya: (1) Do not touch the wife of an-other member; (2) Do not reveal the secrets of the organization to the police; and (3) Keep strict loyalty to the *oyabun-kobun* (literally, father-role/child-role) relationship."[26]

This manufactured sense of family allowed OC to enforce the values of obedience, lifelong loyalty, and honor in ways that are impossible for legitimate businesses, reinforced by (1) the fact that violation of the shared values is likely to lead to death as a sanction, and (2) that there are no dilemmas presented by the need to consider the needs of the community or the environment, given OC's single-minded focus on obtaining wealth by fair means or foul. Recently, it has become economically more difficult for the Yakuza and Triads in Hong Kong to demand such lifelong obedience and loyalty as a result of changes in their domestic social and economic standing. Yakuza and Hong Kong Triad members are now allowed to change clans and do side business on their own (see Chapter 2).

This weakening of lifelong, exclusive economic commitment goes both ways: by the clan to its members, and the members to the clan, and is the result of changes in the economic environment.

Being a Responsible Citizen

Figure 7.2 shows what legitimate businesses need to consider across their supply/value chains.

They must consider the needs of the community, and of the impact they have on the environment in terms of degradation, pollution, and congestion, including what happens in their supply chains wherever they are, as far as working condi-tions and corruption are concerned, if they are to maintain their social "license to operate."

OC, however, has no such compunction and so it is able to compete with legiti-mate businesses and undercut them because it does not incur the costs associated with meeting regulatory requirements in raw materials processing, shipping and transport, production, distribution, and marketing and sales as they affect the envi-ronment, society, or the workplace. OC organizations' competitive advantage against legitimate competitors comes from their willingness to break or work around laws de-signed to protect communities from bad actors and damaging externalities.

As a result, it is easier for OC leadership to make their members focus single-mindedly on the cardinal values of loyalty and obedience regardless of the impact of such behavior outside their organizations.

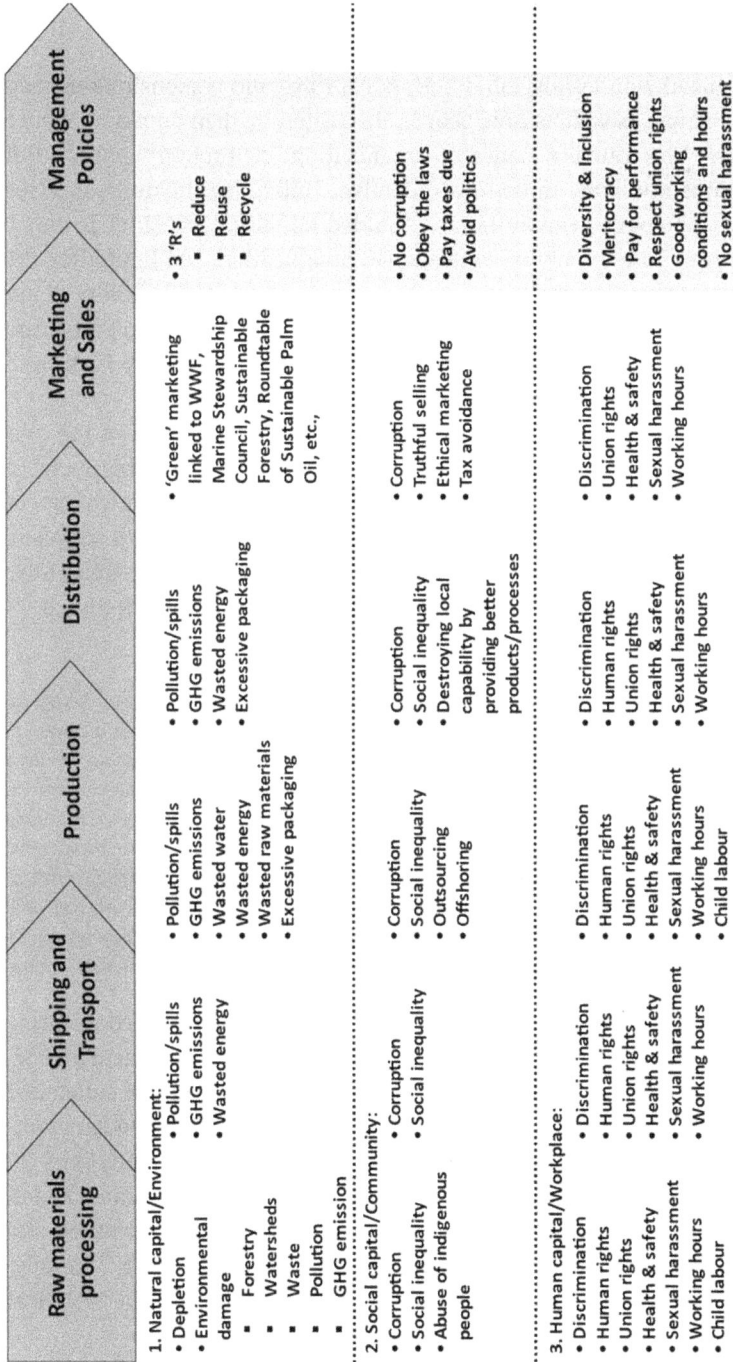

Figure 7.2: Being responsible across the value chain.
Source: Zinkin, J. (2020), *The Challenge of Sustainability: Corporate Governance in a Complicated World* (Berlin/Boston: Walter de Gruyter), p.133.

Power

This covers organizational design, job descriptions, roles and responsibilities, and reporting relationships, as well as how people are treated by their superiors, hence the term "power." The four life-stages of organizations determine what kind of power relationships are likely to be most effective. Unlike legitimate businesses which can be "Incubators", "Family firms," "Guided Missiles," or "Eiffel Towers," because they operate in a variety of contexts, OC organizations are limited by the fact that they operate outside the law, and this requires a greater flexibility of approach. Consequently, OC organizations do not adopt the "Eiffel Tower" structure with its bureaucratic inflexibility, instead opting for a blend of "Family Firm" and "Guided Missile" approaches once they are well-established and mature.

Both OC and legitimate organizations must ensure that whichever of the four types of organizational design they choose, it will be sufficiently flexible to avoid the problem of so-called "stuckness" if the business strategy requires a change of direction. Supply disruption matters less to OC because they can switch suppliers who trade in commodities, as opposed to legitimate businesses that use global supply chains for established brands and where a breakdown in the supply chain could lead to shortages, quality problems, and reputational damage.

> Despite the obvious differences between trafficking heroin, rhino horn, or a human being, all these activities share many common features, being all comparable to commercial businesses; *they are so-called "transit crimes," international illegal trades where criminal groups are involved using the same opportunity structure that facilitates legal economic activities.* In these cases, OC organizations operate as opportunistic economic agents: *they do not care what they trade as long as there is a valuable profit, which entails that in many cases only at the local level – the extreme end of the trafficking chain – there are product specialists, and that the traditional rigid structures are superseded by more decentralised, flexible, and dynamic ones. Business-like groups can obviously be very heterogeneous: they can be long-established criminal networks, looser gangs run by very young leaders, or they might even lack a clear leadership.*[27]   [Emphases ours]

The Internet is changing the way trafficking is done and reducing the need for structured, physically present, criminal organizations. For example, both payment and delivery can now be made from a safe distance through online banking and automated postal services. It is easier and less risky to contact customers and intermediaries virtually, whereas previously it was necessary to meet them face-to-face. In addition, OC organizations no longer need physical representation overseas and they can take full advantage of anonymity of the Internet. Nevertheless, mafia-type organizations still seem reluctant to take full advantage of the benefits the Internet provides.[28] In Italy, it seems that only some *Camorra* groups use the Internet to exploit the technical knowhow (economic, financial, or legal) of outside associates.[29]

The reasons given for this reluctance are, first, that traditional mafia ways of doing business are so efficient they see no reason to change, particularly since the leaders of OC organizations are not "digital natives"; and that this might change as the younger ICT-savvy generations move into positions of power. Already the younger frontline "soldiers" are using Facebook to identify their victims and track their habits.[30] However, the use of the Internet and mobile phones by younger members of the Mafia had its disadvantages in allowing the FBI to track criminal activity:

> Older members complain that the millennials – who grew up in the suburbs instead of city streets – are softer, dumber and not as loyal as mobsters of the past. Plus, they're always texting. "Everything is on the phones with them," said a former made member of the Colombo family who knows some of the men accused in the case.
>
> Trying to talk to a junior employee who won't look up with his phone is annoying in any industry. But for the mob, there are more pragmatic reasons to be wary of iPhone-addicted staffers:
>
> One Colombo associate is accused of sending threatening texts to a union official over extortion collections. "Hey, this is the 2nd text, there isn't going to be a 3rd," the associate wrote, according to court records. "I am sure that is frowned upon in mob circles," former FBI agent and crisis management consultant Richard Frankel said of what appeared to be incriminating texts.[31]

The second and perhaps more powerful reason is that Mafias, Yakuzas, and Triads value face-to-face interactions in order to build trust:

> In this regard, the following case is emblematic: a criminal network linked to a Camorra clan trafficked cocaine between Naples, Northern Italy, and Spain. For money laundering purposes, high-level members of the network had contacts with a broker and legal consultant with ICT expertise based in the UK. This broker (a member of a virtual network committed in carrying out these types of illicit operations) basically operated a sophisticated online banking fraud by proposing false investments to wealthy clients. *In order to obtain a sufficient level of trust regarding the non-member partner, a meeting was organised offline to discuss the details of the illegal operation.*[32] [Emphasis ours]

The Internet is seen as a valuable tool when it comes to gambling because it offers the possibility of increasing profits in a low-risk, high-reward manner without touching the network of social relationships at the core of OC.[33]

Choice of structure affects the distribution of power and the appropriateness of relationships within and between organizations. It is tempting to assume that all mafias are organized/structured in the same way as the Cosa Nostra in Sicily and the US. This is not correct, just as it is not correct to assume that all legitimate businesses are organized/structured in the same way (see Chapter 6).

The 'Ndrangheta and Camorra are organized/structured differently from the Cosa Nostra and each other. Yakuza and Triads, however, are organized/structured in ways that are similar to the Cosa Nostra.

Cosa Nostra

The Cosa Nostra adopted a top-down militarized version of the patriarchal family because its frontliners are foot soldiers who have to face death in certain circumstances. Its roles are male; the maternal aspect of families being provided by the psychological embrace of the organization as a whole.[34] The "family" of soldiers (called "men of honor") is a cell of 50–300 members, headed by a *capo famiglia*. The *capo famiglia* is responsible for the activities of the "family" he leads, and his remit is territorially defined. His role is to maximize the wealth-creating capacity of his "family," and to protect the interests of his men both within the territory for which he is responsible and in relation to the other "families" that make up the Cosa Nostra.[35]

Capo famiglia are elected by and from the "men of honor" in a given "family," usually unanimously since the "men of honor" know enough between them to judge the suitability of prospective candidates. Once elected, the *capo famiglia* appoints a deputy and advisers. Below the *capo famiglia* are *capo decina,* with ten soldiers under their command, and they have access to the *capo famiglia.* The *capo famiglia* from the same province elect provincial representatives to the "regional committee" that is the governing body of the Cosa Nostra.[36]

'Ndrangheta

The 'Ndrangheta is organized differently, reflecting its different business strategy. It is a local and global organization.[37] It began as a local organization focusing primarily on kidnapping and ransom from which it built up capital to invest in the heroin and cocaine trade. Although it worked with Cosa Nostra at the beginning of its diversification, it was soon to replace it. By the end of the 1990s, it had a network of local representatives in residence in Colombia. Although it also established operations in Northern Italy, the ties to Calabria, and to Aspromonte, in particular, bind the members both in terms of policy decisions, emotionally, and morally:

> In the case of the Calabrian 'Ndrangheta the blood tie between the members and the organization finds a *form of celebration also in the possibility for the affiliates to localize the criminal group in a specific and tangible place, that is the Aspromonte heartland, and specifically the Sanctuary of Our Lady of Polsi in San Luca, where once a year, during the celebration of the Feast in September, all the 'Ndrangheta chiefs meet in order to plan new illicit earnings or to restore peace between families . . .* "Calabria is the mom, the cradle, the vertex where the organization was born [. . .] It is like Jerusalem for Christians." In this sense, no one does anything without "Mummy" orders. The imperativeness with which 'Ndrangheta imposes its control over the affiliates also permeates the way how the "blood-brothers" perceive the external outgroup as well as their membership. Just the feeling of "being part of a sect" implies a "double morality" determining the appearance of feelings of exclusiveness and segregation. *In this way, people outside the organization are perceived as dehumanized. The presence of a dehumanization*

mechanism leads the affiliate to develop a radical form of emotional detachment that finds ex-
pression in the normalization of the violence as well as in the removal of the member's sense of
responsibility for the offences committed.[38]   [Emphases ours]

Camorra

The Camorra is not organized in the normal sense of the word, as the following
makes clear:

> The Camorra is not an organization like the Mafia that can be separated from society, disci-
> plined in court, or even quite defined. It is an amorphous grouping in Naples and its hinter-
> lands of more than 100 autonomous clans and perhaps 10,000 immediate associates, along
> with a much larger population of dependents, clients, and friends. It is an understanding, a
> way of justice, a means of creating wealth and spreading it around. It has been a part of life in
> Naples for centuries – far longer than the fragile construct called Italy has even existed. At its
> strongest it has grown in recent years into a complete parallel world and, in many people's
> minds, an alternative to the Italian government, whatever that term may mean. Neapolitans
> call it "the system" with resignation and pride. The Camorra offers them work, lends them
> money, protects them from the government, and even suppresses street crime. The problem is
> that periodically the Camorra also tries to tear itself apart, and when that happens, ordinary
> Neapolitans need to duck.[39]

Even though the Camorra appears to be hydra-headed organization most of the
time, with different clans fighting to control the drug trade in the piazzas of Naples,
it was rigorously organized by one man, Paolo Di Lauro[vi] (from 1982 to 2004), only
to descend into factional fighting when the Italian state was successful in finally
incarcerating him. The problem for the Italian state is the Neapolitans apparently
would prefer to be ruled by the Camorra than the state despite its factional fighting:

> *some of the police – even those who have not been corrupted – would rather not see the govern-*
> *ment prevail, because they fear the even greater disorder that would result.* Another judge
> pointed out to me that the government needs the Camorra for social control. He said, "For a
> political leader, it's easier to speak to a Camorra boss than to 100,000 people to get a message
> across." More than that, he said: *the Camorra sets standards, enforces laws, keeps police power*

---

vi Di Lauro first diversified the business he took over after assassinating his boss, La Monica, who
did not want to get into narcotics from its traditional activities in gambling, extortion, and cigarette
smuggling to establish a successful narcotics empire and trafficking in counterfeit branded goods.
He was careful not get into alliances or alienate any of the powerful Camorra clans. Before his arrest, he had invested in legitimate businesses: textiles, home furnishings, meat and dairy products,
bottled water, cash-and-carry wholesale markets, prepared-food distribution, shopping-mall development, residential real estate, hotels, restaurants, shops of all sorts in Naples, and a clothing store
in Paris in the 12th Arrondissement. Langenwiesche, W. (2012), "The Camorra Never Sleeps," *Vanity
Fair*, May 2012, https://www.vanityfair.com/culture/2012/05/naples-mob-paolo-di-lauro-italy, accessed on March 3, 2021.

itself in check, fends off aggressive tax collectors, employs a huge percentage of the population, creates and distributes wealth more efficiently than any other sector of society, and stands in to keep things going, especially in times like these, when the national economy has failed . . .[40]

[Emphases ours]

Yakuza

The Yakuza were organized feudally, in much the same way as Cosa Nostra, exemplified by the Yamaguchi-gumi:

> At the top of the pyramid is the godfather or *kumicho* (supreme chief) of the syndicate.[41] Under the *kumicho* rule a group of usually four *shatei* (younger brothers). Next follows a group of eight directors called *wakashira-hosa* (assistant young leaders), one of whom will be appointed a *wakashira* (young leader). The *shatei, wakashira,* and *wakashira-hosa* function as a board of directors who meet monthly and decide on syndicate policy . . . A senior consultative group called the *sanro-kai,* dispenses advice on whatever matters are presented it . . . Below this hierarchy lies a series of lesser offices: one *kambuatsu-kai* (executive), and several *wakashu* (young men), who each command their own legions of *kobun* (children) or *kumi-in* (enlisted men)[42]

> In this system, the *oyabun* provide food, clothing, shelter, protection, advice, and help for their *kobun,* who in return, owe labor, unswerving loyalty, and unquestioning obedience to their bosses. For example, an innocent *kobun* would be expected to go to prison for a crime committed by his *oyabun.*[43]

However, in August 2015, the group split for the first time, with the Kobe Yamaguchi-gumi breaking away over a leadership succession dispute. In 2016, there were clashes between the two factions that led to police actions against them. In 2017, the newly formed Kobe Yamaguchi-gumi itself suffered the loss of a splinter group, the Ninkyo Yamaguchi-gumi whose members defected because they were unhappy at the level of fees they had to pay. At the end of 2016, the Yamaguchi-gumi had 5,200 members and Kobe Yamaguchi-gumi had 2,600 before it split in 2017. Relations between the Yamaguchi-gumi, its two breakaway gangs, and other Yakuza gangs in Japan changed as a result, with the original Yamaguchi-gumi becoming friendly with the Tokyo-based Inagawa-Kai, while the two breakaways became closer with other gangs in Western Japan.[44] Tougher legislation in 2016 against the Yakuza has limited their ability to fight for territory and now the frontliners on both sides are much more cautious:

> We go out drinking much less often so we don't run into any problems with the Kobe gang. As there's nowhere else to go, we always just drink canned beer at home, the office, or friends' companies. And when we do go out, it's to somewhere owned by relatives or the younger members' women, so we keep it in the family.

Recently, our drinking and karaoke all take place in the daytime. It's easy to get caught up in trouble at night, so we don't have any choice. But I still have to be ready to deal with any friction that crops up during the nighttime, so I can't enjoy a relaxing sleep. My phone is always by my pillow.[45]

There now is stalemate between the gangs reflecting an East-West alignment that, combined with the fragmentation of the formerly dominant Yamaguchi-gumi, has eroded the traditional ways in which Yakuza were organized:

the rules of yakuza society are changing. Its gangs were formerly characterized by their adherence to the *jikisan* loyalty system . . . it refers to members who have gone through the *sakazuki* drinking ritual with the *oyabun* (gang boss), receiving the cup directly. The ritual is a way of creating symbolic parent-child or fraternal relationships to ensure firm devotion.

Leaving an organization after completing this ritual was taboo in a world where the *oyabun* had ultimate power

Zetsuen and *hamon* (excommunication) punishments effectively drove those who received them out of yakuza society. Associating with these outcasts was regarded as a hostile act against the gang that imposed the discipline. This was an iron rule that contributed to maintaining the yakuza order.

It is now crumbling. "Before, it was the end for gangsters who received these punishments," notes Sakurai. "But now they've lost their power. It doesn't matter if you've been given *hamon* or *zetsuen*. You can still be welcomed at an opposing group. If members aren't scared of getting these punishments, they can do what they like. The rules have changed, and it's making people nervous."[46]

The reason for this breakdown in the power structure is not just the change in the attitude of the police, but also the fact that the membership has fallen dramatically. At the start of the 1990s, Yakuza membership was 70,000 but was down to 18,000 by the end of 2016. In the case of the Yamaguchi-gumi it has been cut by three quarters. The economic hold the *oyabun* have over the members has weakened so much that they are allowed to have side businesses and can change gangs – something previously unheard of.[47]

Triads

Triads have faced similar problems in Hong Kong as the Yakuza with similar results. Members can now have side business and cooperate with other gangs.[48]

People

OC organizations and legitimate businesses must ensure that the people they employ reflect accurately their chosen business strategies and their priorities in terms of timing and resource rationing.

There is a saying that attitude matters more than aptitude because attitude cannot be taught, whereas aptitude can. Character and values determine attitude even more in OC organizations than in legitimate businesses because what is expected of their members is more narrowly defined with more extreme negative behavioral characteristics; in part because once members join they cannot leave, and in part because what they asked to do violates the norms of socially accepted behavior:

> As in other organizations, within *Cosa Nostra* exist rigid criteria for selection, based on careful and long observation of the person seeking to be affiliated. To enter, he must demonstrate *a range of personality characteristics, which must fit closely to the stereotype of the typical Sicilian male. In particular, elevated self-esteem and the ability to kill without questioning and without hesitation or compassion. . . . Behind the ritual, hides affiliation to a new "family" that stands as a guarantee for life of his male identity through that which he is asked of to prove it: contempt for life and feelings.* The values of mafia culture seem supported above all by a rigid ideological skeleton.[49]

Processes

The most important process problems for OC and legitimate businesses are setting the appropriate key performance indicators (KPIs) and ensuring that they employ and retain the right people. There is one key difference in setting KPIs between OC and legitimate businesses. OC KPIs do not have to reconcile competing stakeholder priorities, nor do they have to reflect ESG regulatory requirements. Because OC organizations flourish in weak or failed states, unlike legitimate businesses, the KPIs they set take no account of the damage they do to society and the state. Their KPIs focus on maximizing short-term monetary gain without considering their impact on the socio-political commons. This simpler approach allows OC organizations to delegate financial targets to the frontliners (so-called "made men" in the Cosa Nostra) according to lines of business for which they are responsible day-to-day, making it clear how much they are allowed to keep for themselves and how much they are expected to pass up the line to their captains and bosses.[50] Legitimate businesses, on the other hand, are increasingly constrained by regulations that are designed to protect the socio-political commons by penalizing behavior that harms the environment and human rights. (These implications are discussed further in Chapter 8.)

In OC, the sense of shared values, identity and brotherhood in the "family" made it easier for New York's Mafias, for example, to use the clan structure to delegate power to lower levels in the organization and thus have a pool of aspiring candidates for promotion based on merit:

> Each of the five NYC Mafia families was run by a boss and underboss. Under the bosses were captains who ran teams of "made" men. Each "made" man had a crew of associates, criminals not yet admitted to the family. These crews specialized in a particular vice – gambling, loan sharking, prostitution, union corruption, hijacking, and so forth. Crews usually kept 70 to 80 percent of their ill-gotten gains and passed the balance up to the captain and bosses who provided protection from police using bribes and supported the families of incarcerated made men.
>
> The most successful and loyal "made" men got promoted to captain, and the captains usually appointed one of their own to boss when the current boss died or was jailed. It was a true meritocracy where only successful and loyal "made" men moved up. Associates waited years to become "made" men, and only after his captain sponsors the candidate to the boss. That captain then assumes responsibility for the new "made" man for the rest of that captain's life in the mob.
>
> Contributing to the Mafia's meritocracy succession planning was a highly decentralized decision making model. Each "made" man and his crew decided what heists to commit or whether to loan money to a particular desperate borrower. Often the captain was not consulted. The boss rarely planned crimes. Rather he kept peace in the family and made high level decisions about promoting "made" men to captains. "Made" men who botched their vice were eliminated one way or another, and only those who survived and thrived remained to assume leadership positions.[51]

This may help explain why decapitating any OC that adopts a similar approach does not always lead to the demise of the group, as there are always enough people lower down who have the demonstrated track record to step up and replace the missing bosses.

Unlike legitimate businesses, OC organizations adopt complicated and quasi-religious initiation rites of passage to impress on new recruits that they are leaving the normal world to enter into an exclusive and secret membership. For example, Cosa Nostra trains its recruits using generations of information and myth to transmit the idea of an idealized world, suggesting that once they become accepted *mafiosi*, they will be treated by the community as a source of authority to whom everybody turns for favors or solutions. To achieve this desirable status, the novice must express formal consent to join the mafia world, share its objectives and methods. More important, the novice must accept that since Cosa Nostra does not recognize the importance of feelings, there is no room for sentiment, as that is a sign of weakness. As the *capo famiglia* explains the rules that govern being a "man of honor," it becomes clear that the novice is no longer free to renounce membership because that would mean death. The dependence relationship the new *mafioso* is expected to have toward his mafia "family" is a matter of self-preservation because the "family" has the power of life and death over its members.[52] The 'Ndrangheta used similar processes of initiation and entanglement to recruit and retain its members via its "status contract":

> The status contract is the resultant of the mythological foundation of the origin of the *Honored Society* by three Spanish knights and the recourse to affiliation ceremonies as well. Everything in the mafia world runs around the respect of the rules and the presence of the myth. It is sufficient to say that also the rites of passage, as for example baptism, pre-initiation and affiliation procedures, are ruled by specific norms . . . there are rules about how to live, how to die, how to betray and how to maintain honour. In this sense, *rules are the pillar of this criminal organization because they legitimate the exercise of the power and any other form of violence as well as the spreading of the organized crime syndicate within and beyond their communities of settlements.*[53] [Emphasis ours]

Yakuza and Triads have similar initiation processes (see Chapter 2), but have been finding it harder to retain their recruits as a result of the increasingly difficult domestic environment in which to operate.

References

1 Drucker, P. (1955), *The Practice of Management* (Oxford: Butterworth Heinemann), p. 35.
2 Friedman, M. (1970), "The Social Responsibility of Business is to Increase its Profits," *New York Times Magazine,* September 13, 1970.
3 Dudley, S., "Elites and Organized Crime: Introduction, Methodology, and Conceptual Framework," *Insight Crime,* p. 24, https://idl-bnc-idrc.dspacedirect.org/bitstream/handle/10625/55845/IDL-55845.pdf, accessed on November 17, 2021.
4 Gambetta, D. (1993), *The Sicilian Mafia* (Cambridge, MA, 1993), pp. 19–20.
5 Gambetta, D. (1988), "Fragments of an Economic Theory of the Mafia," *The European Journal of Sociology* (or Archives of European Sociology), 29, pp. 127–145, cited in ibid., pp. 25–26.
6 Ibid., p. 26.
7 Herdener, D. (2021), quoted by Dastin, J., Kirkham, C., and Kalra, A. (2021), "Amazon Wages Secret War on Americans' Privacy, Documents Show," *Reuters,* November 19, 2021,, https://www.reuters.com/investigates/special-report/amazon-privacy-lobbying/, accessed on November 20, 2021.
8 Pogrund, G., and Greenwood, G. (2021), "Owen Paterson Case: Randox Won Test Deal Despite Lack of Equipment," *The Times,* November 7, 2021, https://www.thetimes.co.uk/article/owen-paterson-case-randox-won-test-deal-despite-lack-of-equipment-5wdrc296b, accessed on November 20, 2021.
9 Editorial Board (2021), "The Conservatives and the Whiff of Chumocracy," *The Financial Times,* August 1, 2021, https://www.ft.com/content/9230bc88-9038-40a3-a785-14e78253ecd9, accessed on November 20, 2021.
10 Lichtblau, E, and Maharaj, D. (2001), "Clinton Pardon of Rich a Saga of Power, Money," *Chicago Tribune,* February 18, 2001, https://www.chicagotribune.com/sns-clinton-pardons-analysis-story.html, accessed on November 20, 2021.
11 Gaura, E. (2018), "20 Places in Mexico Foreigners Should Never Set Foot In," *The Travel,* October 4, 2018, https://www.thetravel.com/20-places-in-mexico-foreigners-should-never-set-foot-in/, accessed on November 21, 2021.

12 Friedersdorf, C. (2020), "Why the War on Cocaine Still Isn't Working," *The Atlantic*, June 21, 2020, https://www.theatlantic.com/ideas/archive/2020/06/why-the-war-on-cocaine-still-isnt-working/613297/, accessed on November 21, 2021.

13 "Northern Triangle: Terrifying to Live in, Dangerous to Leave," *World Vision*, November 2, 2020, https://www.worldvision.ca/stories/child-protection/northern-triangle, accessed on November 21, 2021.

14 Longrigg, C. (2017), "How Totò Riina's War on the Italian State Almost Destroyed Cosa Nostra," *The Guardian*, November 18, 2017, https://www.theguardian.com/world/2017/nov/18/how-toto-riinas-war-on-the-italian-state-almost-destroyed-cosa-nostra, accessed on November 7, 2021.

15 Ibid.

16 Drucker (1955), p. 35 quoted in Zinkin, *Better Governance Across the Board: Creating Value Through Reputation, People and Processes* (Boston/Berlin: Walter de Gruyter, Inc), p. 127.

17 Porter, M. (1985), *Competitive Advantage: Creating and Sustaining Superior Performance* (New York: The Free Press), pp. 41–42.

18 Bruner, B. (2012), "Stuck in the Middle? Take the Flexible Approach," January 16, 2012, https://blogs.darden.virginia.edu/brunerblog/2012/01/stuck-in-the-middle/, a guest post quoted by Symonds, M., *Forbes*, February 24, 2012, https://www.forbes.com/sites/mattsymonds/2012/02/24/stuck-in-the-middle-take-the-flexible-approach/#4d1184142ebd, accessed on July 5, 2018.

19 Caulkin, S. (2012) "The Wrong Direction: Management Has Lost Its Way – and Its Power Has Sent Business Down a Dangerous Road," *FT Business Education*, December 3, 2012, p. 12.

20 Solomon, R.C. (1999), *A Better Way to Think About Business: How Personal Integrity Leads to Corporate Success* (New York: Oxford University Press, 1999), p. xxii.

21 Eswaran, V. (2019), "The Business Case for Diversity in the Workplace is Now Overwhelming," *World Economic Forum*, April 29, 2019, https://www.weforum.org/agenda/2019/04/business-case-for-diversity-in-the-workplace/, accessed on May 14, 2021.

22 Huang, H-L. (2007), "From the *Asian Boyz* to the *Zhu Lian Bang* (the Bamboo Union Gang): A Typological Analysis of Delinquent Asian Gangs," *Asian Criminology* 2, pp. 127–143, https://doi.org/10.1007/s11417-007-9033-0, accessed on March 10, 2021.

23 Di Maria, F., and Falgares, G. (2013), "Mafia Organization: Governance Processes and Leadership Function," *Integral Leadership Review*, January 2013, http://integralleadershipreview.com/8287-mafia-organization-governance-processes-and-leadership-function/, accessed on May 14, 2021.

24 Szczepanski, K. (2019), "History of Japanese Organized Crime, the Yakuza," *ThoughtCo*, July 17, p. 2, https://www.thoughtco.com/the-yakuza-organized-crime-195571, accessed on March 4, 2021.

25 Oliver, M. (2020), "Inside the Yakuza, The 400-Year-Old Japanese Criminal Syndicate," https://allthatsinteresting.com/yakuza-history, accessed on January 22, 2021.

26 Gragert, B. A. (1997) "Yakuza: The Warlords of Japanese Organized Crime," *Annual Survey of International & Comparative Law*, 4, No. 1, Article 9, p. 152.

27 Ibid.

28 Lavorgna, A. (2015),"Organised Crime Goes Online: Realities and Challenges," *Journal of Money Laundering Control*, 18, No. 2, March 24, 2015, http://dx.doi.org/10.1108/JMLC-10-2014-0035, accessed on May 17, 2021.

29 Ibid.

30 Ibid.

31 Alex and Alex. (2021), "Succession Lessons from the Mafia and Bill Gross," *Citywire*, October 8, 2021, https://citywireusa.com/professional-buyer/news/succession-lessons-from-the-mafia-and-bill-gross/a1566362, accessed on November 17, 2021.

32 Ibid.

33 Ibid.

34 "Di Maria and Falgares" (2013).

35 Ibid.

36 Ibid.

37 Calandra, F. (2017), "Between Local and Global: the 'Ndrangheta's Drug Trafficking Route," *International Annals of Criminology*, 55, No. 1, May 2017, https://www.cambridge.org/core/journals/international-annals-of-criminology/article/between-local-and-global-the-ndranghetas-drug-trafficking-route/C3996BE6CBABCB974526B2DD9DF8FFC6#ref70, accessed on May 22, 2021.

38 Ibid.

39 Langenwiesche, W. (2912), "The Camorra Never Sleeps," *Vanity Fair*, May 2012, https://www.vanityfair.com/culture/2012/05/naples-mob-paolo-di-lauro-italy, accessed on March 3, 2021.

40 Ibid.

41 "Honorable Mob," *The Economist*, January 27, 1990, available at LEXIS/NEXIS, cited in Gragert, "Yakuza," p. 165.

42 Kaplan D. E., and Dubro, A. (1986), *Yakuza: The Explosive Account of Japan's Criminal Underworld* (Macdonald Queen Anne Press), p. 132, cited in Gragert, "Yakuza," p. 165.

43 Gragert (1997), p. 168.

44 "Fragmented Yamaguchi-gumi a Sign of Changing Yakuza Times," *Society*, Oct. 4, 2017, https://www.nippon.com/en/features/c04201/ accessed on March 4, 2021.

45 Ibid.

46 Ibid.

47 Ibid.

48 Chu, Y. K. (2005), "Hong Kong Triads after 1997," *Trends in Organized Crime*, 8, No. 3, Spring 2005, p. 5, https://doi.org/10.1007/s12117-005-1033-9, accessed on March 8, 2021.

49 "Di Maria and Falgares" (2013).

50 Wolinsky, J. (2021), "What Mobsters Can Teach Elon Musk About Succession Planning," *Entrepreneur Asia Pacific*, January 12, 2021 https://www.entrepreneur.com/article/363211, accessed on November 17, 2021.

51 Ibid.

52 "Di Maria and Falgares" (2013).

53 Calandra (2017).

Chapter 8
Business Strategy Implications

Our research, when writing Chapters 1–4, led us to the sad conclusion that even though there ought to be, there is no ethical "bright line" differentiating the business strategies of legitimate businesses and organized crime. There are only differences of degree.

Our conclusions were unsurprising:

1. *Breaking societal rules where there are sufficient incentives, or a lack of serious consequences is natural.*
2. *We have **all** been guilty of criminal behavior.* When speeding on the highway or receiving a parking ticket, do you feel you have committed crime? Do directors and senior managers consider they are criminals if their companies pay fines; or do they regard it as "the cost of doing business," as long as the fines cost less than the cost of following rules. The CEO of P&O Ferries admitted that the company chose to break the law and pay any resulting fines rather than following due processes laid by the UK's employment act.[1] Do organizations that pay fines without admitting wrongdoing, feel they have committed crimes? The answer is "No."
3. *If investors, shareholders, boards, and management believe that the sole purpose of business is to maximize shareholder value* regardless of other considerations, the temptation will be to indulge in criminal practices.
4. *As long as the punishment does not fit the crime, individuals will succumb to temptation.*

To establish how these factors affect the business strategies of organizations, we consider the impact of politics, economics, social conditions, and legislation. (see Chapter 5) The impact of technology and environment is moderated by the other four factors.

Politics

States often co-opt legitimate businesses and OC to achieve their objectives; only to turn on them when ruling elites feel threatened. The most important political determinant of any business strategy is competition between ruling elites and their challengers. How competition manifests is determined whether the state chooses an extractive or an inclusive approach to power:[2]

> Politics is the process by which a society choose the rules that will govern it. Politics surrounds institutions for the simple reason that while inclusive institutions may be good for economic

https://doi.org/10.1515/9783110712155-008

prosperity of a nation, some people or groups . . . will be much better off by setting up institutions that are extractive . . . who wins depends on the distribution of political power in
society.[3]

Political institutions determine who has power and to what ends it can be used. *If the distribution of power is narrow and unconstrained, then . . . those who can wield this power will be able
to set up economic institutions to enrich themselves and augment their power at the expense of
society.*[4]   [Emphasis ours]

Those controlling political power . . . find it more beneficial to use their power to limit competition, to increase their share of the pie, or even to steal and loot for others rather than support
economic progress.[5]

Ruling elites have two advantages when faced by disruptive competition from legitimate businesses or OC. They determine what is legal and what is not; actions that
are devastating in their impact on legitimate organizations and open up opportunities for OC. The second is that they offer or withhold respectability for leaders in
both legitimate businesses and OC, inviting them to join the establishment or reject-
ing them by closing the doors on "new men". History has many examples of ruling
elites using political and social exclusion to prevent disruption of the established
order through innovation.[6]

The rise, stagnation, and decline of Venice is illustrative. In 12th century Venice, a revolutionary trading contract was introduced, the *commenda*. It lasted for
the duration of a single trading journey. There were two partners – the "sedentary"
partner (who put his capital into the venture and remained in Venice), and the
"traveling" partner who accompanied the goods. The *commenda* allowed young ad-
venturers with little capital to participate in the expansion of trade. The sedentary
partner put in the lion's share of the financial investment and losses were shared
according to each partner's level of investment.

This economic inclusiveness allowed new families to rise and opened the political system, weakening the powers of the Doge as more people became qualified
through their trading wealth to vote. The pressures for political reform accelerated
after the Doge's murder in 1171.[7] There were changes in the law and the judiciary,
with new private contract and bankruptcy laws that led to modern banking, Venice's expansion looked secure. However, the innovations led to reduced profits and
rents for ruling elites and the rise of enterprising "new men" challenged their political power.

The ruling elites responded by seeking to restrict access of the new elites to the
system, leading to the gradual "Closure" (*La Serrata*) of Venice. In February 1297,
the rules for being a member of the Great Council changed: applicants were auto-
matically approved if they had been members in the previous four years. New nom-
inations now were approved by the Council of Forty (Venice's Exco), needing only
twelve votes. After September 11, 1298, current members and families no longer required to be confirmed, making the incumbents a hereditary aristocracy – a change

in status that was officially recognized in 1315 with the release of the "Gold Book" (*Libro d'Oro*) – the official registry of Venice's nobility.[8] Then the use of the *commenda* contracts was banned; reserving profitable long-distance trade with Asia for the nobility. Venice's economic dynamism stagnated, population fell and,[9] with the discovery of the sea routes to Asia, the role of Venice as a trading post was challenged. The inflexibility resulting from the *Serrata* meant Venice was unable to respond; "Venice went from economic powerhouse to museum."[10]

It is important to remember the four elites that interact politically (see Chapter 1). Political elites seek to achieve hegemony over communities; economic elites seek to control the means of production; social elites determine the acceptability of behavior of political and economic elites; bureaucratic elites control the effectiveness of implementation of the state's policies.

Chapter 1 discussed the jealous nature of the state: (which claims to "own" its citizens); how it is often hostile to international non-state actors (on grounds of sovereignty); and how it is suspicious of powerful independent institutions, lest they become a "state within the state." This is because of competition between the elites each fearful of losing out in what they see as a zero-sum world. Legitimate businesses should beware becoming too important, too visible, or too influential. The current crackdown on the tech giants in China[11] (Alibaba, Tencent, Didi Chuxing) and the new attitude of the US government towards Alphabet[12] (parent of Google) and Meta[13] (parent of Facebook) are reminders that getting too big, too visible, and too influential can be dangerous – the same issues that drove the Italian state's crackdown on the Sicilian Cosa Nostra in the 1990s. As long as legitimate business strategies and OC present no significant threat to the interests of ruling elites, the state is likely to largely ignore them.

As long as subjects or citizens, who help the ruling elite, remember not to become viewed as overmighty, they can flourish; if they are perceived as overmighty, they are doomed. We saw in Chapter 1, that many criminals have been able to gain social acceptance because of their value to the state in its time of need. In American history the colonies had many pirates selling contraband because of the high taxes on goods sourced from England – taxes which led to the struggle for Independence. The system during the colonial period was described as:

> This system of cooperation between criminals, government officials, merchants and the citizens who purchased illegal goods constitutes the basic ingredients for one of the prominent forms of American organized crime, which we have come to call syndicated organized.[14]

The state's demand for exclusive control over its subjects is justified as being to "achieve the common good" when it may be no such thing; it may be the behavior of ruling elites defending their interests to continue extractive rent-seeking instead, with disastrous economic and social results[15].

Economics

Chapter 3 discussed the global economic costs resulting from OC and the pervasiveness of OC, illustrated by the testimony of Senator William Roth to the US Senate in 1983:

> Organized crime in Chicago touches practically everyone's life or livelihood. And the evidence shows that the tentacles of mob activity in this city reach into government, law enforcement, unions, and other legitimate political, social, and economic functions.[16]

Chicago Police Superintendent Brzeczek's testimony supported Senator Roth's claim:

> Where do we buy our goods? Who does our dry cleaning or collects the garbage from our business establishments? Do we buy cigarettes or candy every day from certain vending machines? Who owns the parking lot where you park your car? This is totally irrespective of what city you live in, and *it is in these questions that we find out where traditional organized crime can be found. Every person in this room undoubtedly has some money in their pocket or purse. Rest assured that a percentage of that money will end up in the hands of the leadership of traditional organized crime.*[17]   [Emphasis ours]

OC organizations often use legitimate business as fronts for laundered money and work with ruling elites when their fronts become lucrative ventures that help a region's economic development. This allows them to gain respectability. The impact on development can be to slow it down. OC investments are to be found in finance, agriculture, tourism, real estate, and mining; they intersect with government projects and legitimate business operations through complex partnerships and alliances. It is not always the case that OC involvement is economically disadvantageous for a region.[18]

Just like political institutions, economic institutions can be inclusive or extractive. The observable difference between legitimate businesses and OC is that legitimate businesses are inclusive whereas OC enterprises are exclusive and extractive. Legitimate businesses, with the exception of monopolies and duopolies, seek to create and maintain satisfied and loyal customers, recognizing that their customers have the option to go to the competition if they offer better products and services; options that citizens do not have – nor do the "client-victims" – of OC.

Legitimate businesses have to choose whether they believe, like Peter Drucker, that the purpose of business is to create and maintain satisfied customers or whether they endorse Milton Friedman's view that the purpose of business is to maximize shareholder value. Adopting Friedman's view leads a company to value profits more than what is good for the commonwealth.

Setting KPIs and reward/recognition systems, and evaluating reward and punishment for behavior in morally neutral or in the amoral terms on the basis of a pecuniary cost-benefit analysis that has as its fundamental principle the maximization of shareholder value, can lead to tragic mistakes and serious reputational damage for organizations. Consider the infamous Ford Pinto and Boeing 737 MAX cases.

The Pinto was an affordable compact car sold in the US in the 1970s. A deliberate design choice meant that it could leak fuel and burst into flames if the car was hit from behind. More than 500 people died in fires before the car was recalled. An investigation revealed that Ford's response to the competitive pressure from Volkswagen and other small car makers had led the company to rush the introduction of the Pinto, *disregarding the discovery by engineers during pre-production tests* that there was a danger of ruptured fuel tanks when hit from behind.[19]

"Ethical Fading"

"Ethical fading" occurs when we subconsciously avoid or disguise the moral implications of a decision and unethical behavior. In the case of the Pinto, it resulted from framing the decision as purely financial.[20] The cost-benefit analysis added up the costs of a redesign, delayed launch, potential lawsuits, the probability of deaths, and attributed costs to settling any lawsuits. *The rational, amoral, and unempathetic conclusion was that it would cost less for Ford to launch the Pinto unchanged.* The conclusion was the inescapable consequence of the way the decision was framed – that the overriding purpose of a business is to maximize shareholder value.[21]

When decisions are based on numbers, forgetting that these represent people, lives, and physical pain, ethical blindness results. Add to that the fear of being the bearer of bad news, and the likelihood of "being shot as the messenger". Nobody was prepared to recommend redesigning the car because they feared being fired for delaying the launch of Lee Iacocca's baby:

> But Iacocca's speed-up meant Pinto tooling went on at the same time as product development. So, when crash tests revealed a serious defect in the gas tank, it was too late. The tooling was well under way.

> When it was discovered the gas tank was unsafe, did anyone go to Iacocca and tell him? 'Hell no,' replied an engineer who worked on the Pinto, a high company official for many years, who, unlike several others at Ford, maintains a necessarily clandestine concern for safety. 'That person would have been fired. Safety wasn't a popular subject around Ford in those days. With Lee it was taboo. Whenever a problem was raised that meant a delay on the Pinto, Lee would chomp on his cigar, look out the window and say 'Read the product objectives and get back to work.'[22]

Similar behavior caused Boeing's 737 MAX disasters, as evidenced in the case brought against the Boeing board in February 2021. Excerpts from the submission show that Boeing abandoned its safety engineering culture to become a company that was more interested in financial engineering.[23] In the mid-1990s, after its acquisition of McDonnell Douglas, Boeing switched from being a company focused on aircraft safety to one on cost-cutting. As a result, the board had no tools to oversee safety and there were no mechanisms to bring safety issues to the attention of the board. The board failed to evaluate safety until 2019, after the October crash of Lion Air in 2018 and the Ethiopian airlines crash in 2019.[24]

> "Shortly after the Lion Air Crash in 2018, the Board learned that new software on the 737 MAX, the Maneuvering Characteristics Augmentation System ("MCAS"), was a potential cause of the crash, that the FAA had concluded that MCAS posed an unacceptably high risk of catastrophic failure, and that the FAA had issued an emergency directive notifying pilots about the potential danger. The Board did not order an immediate investigation into the safety of the 737 MAX, how Boeing obtained FAA certification of MCAS, or why MCAS was not mentioned in the flight manual for the 737 MAX. *Instead, the Board supported the public relations campaign of then-Chief Executive Officer and Chairman Dennis A. Muilenburg to attack accurate media coverage respecting the 737 MAX.*
>
> The Board compounded its lack of oversight by publicly lying about it. In May 2019, then-Lead Director, now-CEO David Calhoun led a public relations defense of Muilenburg and the Board in order to "*[p]osition* the Boeing Board of Directors as an independent body that has exercised appropriate oversight. The board paid Muilenburg and allowed him to retire – avoiding questions about the Board's culpability in not exercising safety oversight. Calhoun failed upward. The Board named him the new CEO.
>
> The misconduct – no Board-level safety reporting; ignoring red flags including the first 737 MAX crash; defrauding the FAA; frustrating the DOJ investigation; delaying disclosure to the FAA; no internal investigation or assessment of airplane safety; phony public relations campaigns; paying Muilenburg $38 million to which he was not entitled; . . . – reflects the arrogance of Boeing's long-time fiduciaries . . . . In January 2021, the president of . . . Emirates, gave an interview stating that . . . "*there is a top-down culpability and accountability*" and "*[c]learly there were process and practices, attitudes . . . that need[] to be resolved at the top down.*"[25]
>
> [Emphases ours]

Such antisocial and immoral behavior by legitimate businesses is the result of focusing exclusively on shareholder value.

Construction Industry

In 2017, there was a fire at a high-rise tower block (Grenfell Tower) in West London that led to the loss of 72 lives. The rapid "vertical fire spread" of the blaze was caused, among other things, by the flammability of the cladding used on the outside of the building. The tragedy had two roots: first, the industry put profits ahead of safety (like Ford and Boeing); second, the regulatory system and its inspectors were captured by the industry.

During the ongoing inquiry into the causes of the tragedy, the British government's defending counsel, Jason Beer QC, said it was "deeply sorry for its past failures" in overseeing and upholding building safety regulations.

Beer accepted that the department and its predecessors bore at least partial responsibility for a building safety regime that was 'not fit for purpose.' But he said *the construction industry and the suppliers of the cladding and insulation materials, which were found to have been responsible for the rapid spread of the fire at Grenfell, were to blame for abusing the system by putting profit ahead of safety.*

Beer conceded *that had the government had a better grasp of the regulations and a firmer enforcement system, the Grenfell tragedy might have averted.* 'Individually, these errors and missed opportunities from the department and across industry may not have caused the fire at Grenfell tower but cumulatively they created an environment in which such a tragedy was possible,' he said.[26]

The inquiry highlighted a much wider fire safety issue across the UK, affecting 254 tower blocks, with 82 blocks that had been built or upgraded using the same dangerous cladding as Grenfell Tower.[27] The defects make the buildings unsafe to live in or require expensive remediation, for which the residents will have to pay.[28]

Sometimes the reason why construction projects have these kinds of problems, is the pressure that developers put on contractors to be the lowest cost while meeting specifications that do not fully consider if the project is to be "fit for purpose". Sometimes, this problem is exacerbated by rent-seeking elites seeking to skim off so much money in backhanders that there is not enough left to do the work properly.

Oil and Gas

The American Petroleum Institute (the oil and gas industry's trade association) knew about the impact of fossil fuels on climate change as early as 1965:

"*In November 1965*, the president, Lyndon Johnson, released a report authored by the Environmental Pollution Panel of the President's Science Advisory Committee, which set out the likely impact of continued fossil fuel production on global heating.

In the same year, the president of the American Petroleum Institute told its annual gathering: "One of the most important predictions of the [president's report] is that carbon dioxide is being added to the Earth's atmosphere by the burning of coal, oil and natural gas *at such a rate by the year 2000 the heat balance will be so modified as possibly to cause marked changes in climate beyond local or even national efforts.*[29]   [Emphases ours]

Exxon knew the need for a carbon tax as early as 1981:

'There is no doubt that increases in fossil fuel usage and decreases in forest cover are aggravating the potential problem of increased CO_2 in the atmosphere.' Excerpt from a 1980 Imperial Oil internal report. The Exxon subsidiary concluded as far back as 1981 that *curbing global warming would require a high carbon tax.*[30]

The reaction of the industry was to challenge the science, to obfuscate and create doubt in the minds of the public that fossil fuels posed a serious threat to climate stability, and denying that climate change was real. The industry ran a long advertising campaign designed to sow doubt about climate change."[31] Once climate change became an issue, the campaigns systematically worked to undermine the science with ads designed to "Reposition global warming as theory not fact":

> "In 1991, Informed Citizens for the Environment, a front group of coal and utility companies announced that "Doomsday is cancelled" and asked, "Who told you the earth was warming . . . Chicken Little?" They complained about "weak" evidence, "non-existent" proof, inaccurate climate models and asserted that the physics was "open to debate."[32]

The next stage was designed to "emphasize the uncertainty".[33] The headlines used were: "Lies they tell our children," "Apocalypse No," "Science what we know and don't know," and "Unsettled Science."[34] In the final phases, the industry campaign changed to shifting responsibility away from companies and on to consumers. What makes the harm done by funding climate change denial for so long so serious is that *more than half of all the industrial CO_2 ever emitted was emitted in the 26 years between 1988 and 2014.*[35]

The CEOs of ExxonMobil, Chevron, Shell, and BP America continued to deny under oath when testifying to Congress that their companies had known that climate change was real and they had contributed to global warming. The research undertaken by Harvard University told a different story.[36]

Financial Services

Some financial malpractices never change, because the banks settle at the expense of the shareholders, while individuals who broke the laws pay nothing, and put the fines down to "the cost of doing business." Bank remuneration packages effectively incentivize unethical and illegal behavior,[37] so it is unsurprising that (despite major changes in legislation and regulation) behavior has not improved.

Labaton Sucharow LLP, a leading American law firm regularly undertakes surveys of the state of ethics in financial services and banking. The 2012 survey showed that malpractice was rife in US and UK financial institutions, and that a significant proportion of employees were indulging in malpractices, invalidating the "bad apple" defense regularly used by organizations when they have been found to tolerate malfeasance.[38]

Together with the University of Notre Dame, Labaton Sucharow repeated the exercise in 2015, surveying more than 1,223 professionals in financial services and investment banking in the US (925) and the UK (298) from all levels of seniority and accountability.[39] Their findings were a serious cause for concern.[40] The key findings make depressing reading:

1. 47% believed their competition had behaved illegally or unethically (up from 39% in 2012); and among those earning more than $500,000 per year the figure was 51%;
2. 27% believed their industry did not put the needs of clients first, and in the UK, 42% of those with less than 10 years' service disagreed that the industry put the client first;
3. 33% did not believe the industry had changed for the better since the GFC, males (35%), females (28%), and among those earning more than $500,000 - per year (38%);
4. 19% believe that misconduct is a key ingredient in success (up from 12% in 2012);[41]
5. 32% believe that compensation/bonus structures incentivize employees to violate ethical standards or to break the law. Among those earning more than $500,000 per year, 23% had experienced pressure to compromise their values versus 9% earning less than $50,000;
6. 34% of those earning more than $500,000 had witnessed or had first-hand knowledge of wrongdoing in the workplace, compared to 21% who earned less than $50,000. Overall, this represented 22%, (a drop from 26% in 2012); unlike in the US where there was no drop in the percentage of people who had witnessed or had first-hand knowledge of wrongdoing, there was a drop in the UK from 30% in 2012 to 25% in 2015;[42]
7. 23% of all respondents believe it is likely that their colleagues have engaged in illegal or unethical activity in order to get ahead in their company; nearly 25% of employees with less than 10 years of service believe that their colleagues engage in illegal or unethical behavior to get ahead, compared with 20% in employees with more than 21 years;
8. 25% admitted they would engage in insider trading to make a quick $10 million if they thought they could get away with it – 32% of employees with less than 10 years' service, compared with 14% with more than 21 years. Males (27%) were more likely than females (22%) to engage in insider trading.[43]

The following case involved five leading banks and demonstrates the continued misconduct:

> In May 2015, five banks – Citigroup, JP Morgan Chase, Barclays, Royal Bank of Scotland, and UBS – pleaded guilty to criminal charges of manipulating foreign exchange markets, agreeing to pay over $5 billion to the U.S. Justice Department and other regulators. As part of that settlement, UBS pleaded guilty to additional Libor-related fraud, paying $203 million in penalties. However, the Justice Department did not indict any individuals at that time.[44]

The five banks were fined a total of $5 billion, but the perpetrators were not. In December 2021, the EU antitrust regulators fined HSBC, Credit Suisse, Barclays (for the second time), and RBS (also for the second time) a total of €344million, bringing the total settlement (fines) in this long-running investigation to €1.4billion for collusion by their forex traders who had used on-line chat rooms, including one called *Sterling Lads* to share information and to sometimes coordinate their trading strategies.

> Margrethe Vestager, the EU's competition commissioner said *"The collusive behaviour of the banks 'undermined the integrity of the financial sector at the expense of the European economy and consumers.'* The settlement brings the total amount of fines handed down by Brussels over the scandal to €1.4bn since the investigation began. Authorities imposed a collective fine of €261m on Barclays, RBS and HSBC, a figure reduced because the banks co-operated with the investigation. Credit Suisse was fined €83m, missing out on any reduction because the European Commission said it did not co-operate. However, EU regulators said they did shave 4 per cent of the penalty because the bank 'is not held liable for all aspects of the case.' Authorities also settled with UBS, which was spared a €94m fine for first revealing the existence of the cartels."[45]

In response to this settlement by the banks with the EU, a reader of The Financial Times wrote the following, with which we agree:

> Yet again major banks have been fined hundreds of millions, this time by the EU for collusion in the rigging of foreign currency markets . . . *Yet no individuals are named or convicted, and no doubt the banks will simply shrug it off as a business expense (passed on to the customers), and the same misdeeds will be repeated. Companies don't commit crimes, people do. So why aren't there any individuals being convicted, or licences revoked, as would happen for similar misdeeds in other sectors* – one is hesitant to use the word "profession" when referring to banking? UBS says the 'matter is resolved.' I suppose that's all OK then.[46]   [Emphasis ours]

That banking continues to behave in this way validates Stephen Hester's judgment on what has gone wrong in financial services, when he was recruited to resurrect the bankrupted Royal Bank of Scotland in 2012:

> "It is possible to look at the many scandals that have hit banking in recent years and see them as individual episodes of bad judgement or wrong behaviours. In fact, I think it's more accurate to say that most of them are related to one big scandal: *banks have simply not been good enough servants of their customers in the recent past.*

> The banking industry in the decade preceding the crisis was focused on income; it expanded too fast, prioritised sales over service and failed to properly balance the interests of its customers and shareholders with those of its managers. Hubris set in. Too much of the ethos became selfish – personally and institutionally. Of course market economies rely on self-interest as a key mechanism. But it works best where 'enlightened' or 'sustainable' self-interest is what's pursued.

> There is a basic truth about what makes a good company. *Really good companies perform well for their owners, regulators, employees and communities if, above all else, they serve their customers well.* You can have a number of different goals for your company, but at the core *great businesses are driven by their customers' priorities – by their customers' values, goals and needs – and not by their own*

Banking needs to unambiguously recognise that its purpose is to serve customers well. And to serve them in the context of their broader communities and the range of impacts that banks, as a huge industry, have on society – culturally and economically."[47]   [Emphases ours]

Society

There has been a perceived decline in the behavior of political leaders in the past 70 years, ignoring the results of fairly conducted elections, continuing in office after being indicted for corruption, behaving as if they and their cronies are above the law, and putting their citizens at risk by ignoring science during the Covid-19 pandemic, acting as totally inappropriate role models. Totalitarian leaders have violated treaties[i] and murdered citizens who were legally resident in other countries[ii] and have led murderous regimes engaged in killing their own people and appear to have gotten away it.

On June 4, 1963, John Profumo, the British Defence Secretary was forced to resign because he had lied to Parliament about having an affair with a call girl. Investigations by the press uncovered sleaze, leading to the Prime Minister Harold Macmillan's resignation. The consequences of misbehavior were clear for all to see.

In 1997, the Conservatives, under John Major, lost to Labour led by Tony Blair, after Margaret Thatcher had led them to victory in 1979. Once again, the smell of sleaze was in the air, contributing to their defeat. A number of obscure MPs were having affairs which would in previous years have been the end of their careers, and some 30% were "taking cash for questions" to promote business interests in Parliament which prompted Parliament to establish a committee on standards in

---

i Putin's Russian Federation annexed Ukraine's Crimea March 18, 2014, in violation of the December 5, 1994, *Budapest Memorandum on Security Assurances* where Russia was a co-guarantor with the US and UK of the Ukraine's territorial integrity, in return for the Ukraine giving up nuclear weapons the former USSR had installed in the Ukraine. Memorandum on Security Assurances in connection with the Republic of Belarus'/Republic of Kazakhstan's/Ukraine's accession to the Treaty on the Non-Proliferation of Nuclear Weapons, signed on December 5, 2019, Budapest, Hungary, https://en.wikipedia.org/wiki/Treaty_on_the_Non-Proliferation_of_Nuclear_Weapons.

Xi Jinping's People's Republic of China imposed the *"Law of the People's Republic of China on Safeguarding National Security in the Hong Kong Special Administrative Region on Hong Kong"* on June 30, 2020, in violation of provisions agreed in "The Basic Law of the Hong Kong Special Administrative Region of the People's Republic of China" that came into effect on July 1, 1997, that was tabled as an internationally binding treaty at the United Nations.

ii Alexander Litvinenko was poisoned by the KGB using polonium on November 1, 2006, while living in London. There was a failed attempt by GRU officers to poison Sergei Skripal and his daughter using Novichok in Salisbury on March 4, 2018. Only limited sanctions were imposed on Russia, because the UK wanted to preserve London as a haven for Russian oligarchs and their money, and Germany was not prepared to close the Nordstream natural gas pipeline from Russia being built to serve German energy needs.

public life that came out with the Nolan Report on May 1, 1995, with "Seven Principles."[iii],[48] These principles have not been enforced; the current Conservative government and former Prime Minister David Cameron, have behaved in ways that have undermined public faith in the process of government – Cameron by an inappropriately intrusive lobbying effort to get Treasury funding to prevent the Greensill organization from going bankrupt, and where he stood to gain £60 million from his options in the company had he been successful.[49]

A strongly-worded article by Bernard Jenkin, the Conservative MP who is the Chair of the Government Liaison Committee, to whom members of the cabinet are answerable, documents the worrying decline in standards of behavior:

> After the dust settles over the Greensill affair, I suspect we will find that *the lack of judgment over David Cameron's approaches to ministers is less important than the general failure to address what has become a casual approach to conflicts of interest amongst many in government and politics.*
>
> Much of the wrongdoing is exaggerated, but the worst instances of people using public positions to enrich themselves are utterly corrosive of public trust in government . . . This does not just concern "lobbyists" . . . Of much more concern are those in public office who are being lobbied, and whose control over funding of outside organisations, and over contracts and regulation, the outsiders are seeking to influence. *All can now see the general inability of the various codes and systems of oversight, such as the toothless advisory committee on business appointments, to provide sufficient transparency and accountability, . . . what matters most is not whether someone under scrutiny can say, "I have not broken any rules" but whether they are demonstrating integrity, honesty, selflessness and openness in all they do in their life of public service.*[50]   [Emphases ours]

Illustrating further the decline in UK ministerial accountability is the reaction of the Cabinet Office to having lost a case in the High Court brought against Michael Gove, the minister in charge of the Cabinet Office, over the awarding of a contract "showing apparent favouritism." Jolyon Maugham, the lawyer who sued the government and won, explains:

> When you spend public money you have a duty – owed to those whose money it is, to you and me – to spend it properly in service of the public interest. And to be ready to show the public that you have; to justify your decisions. That's the deal. By showing apparent favouritism, the Cabinet Office broke that deal – and *it is very troubling for it to compound the illegality of its actions by pretending it's not a problem.*
>
> So what happens now?

---

iii For details regarding the "Seven Principles," see *The first report of the Committee on Standards in Public Life,* May 1, 1995, pp. 1–2, https://www.gov.uk/government/publications/mps-ministers-and-civil-servants-executive-quangos, accessed on June 7, 2021.

There will be real-world-effects. Government lawyers and civil servants speak to me of a tug-of-war with ministers over spending. Civil servants want a proper decision-making process, and ministers want to bypass it. When ministers lose legal cases, it strengthens the hands of civil servants. *By highlighting the risks of poor decision making, it leads to better quality decisions . . . the question of how to deliver accountability to ministers whose response to court rulings is indifference, even contempt, is one I had hoped never to need to answer.*[51]

[Emphases ours]

In 2008, Benjamin Netanyahu called for the immediate resignation of then Israeli Prime Minister, Ehud Olmert, who had been indicted for corruption:

"A prime minister neck deep in investigations has no moral or public mandate to make fateful decisions for the State of Israel," Netanyahu said of Olmert, he added at the time: "There is a fear, I must say, and it is real and not unfounded, that he will make his decisions based on his personal interest for political survival, not on the national interest."[52]

Yet, when indicted for corruption in 2019, not merely did Netanyahu not resign, but remained in power and fought four elections in the space of two years to try to avoid the consequences of the indictment. Olmert did the honorable thing and resigned. Netanyahu remained the most popular politician in Israel, attacking the freedom of the press[53] and the independence of the judiciary to save his position;[54] for two years before losing the election in March 2021,[55] because not enough of the voters had previously cared about holding him to the standards he himself demanded must be observed eight years earlier.

Lying to Parliament and failing to follow the Ministerial Code used to be considered automatic grounds in the UK for ministerial resignations. Max Hastings, his boss at *The Daily Telegraph,* is on record as saying the following before Johnson was elected leader of the Conservative Party in 2019:

Boris is a gold medal egomaniac . . . his chaotic public persona is not an act – he is indeed manically disorganised about everything except his own image management. He is also a far more ruthless, and frankly nastier, figure than the public appreciates . . . *He is not a man to believe in, to trust or respect, save as a superlative exhibitionist. He is bereft of judgment, loyalty and discretion. Only in the star-crazed Britain of the 21st century could such a man have risen so high, and he is utterly unfit to go higher still.*[56]

[Emphasis ours]

The central propositions of the Brexit campaign were based on promises he knew he not could keep, and has not kept.[57] It does not appear to have hurt his popularity:

Johnson's deceit is "priced in."[58]

When accused of being slippery with the truth, Johnson's defense has been that the narrative – the story he is telling to encourage people to be optimistic and adopt a "can do" mentality – is more important than the facts.[59] This view ignores the damage done to the concept of accountability – an essential component of good governance. It also sets a dangerous example, like Donald Trump's "Big Lie" about the

2020 US Presidential election, which led to three quarters of Republicans believing something that is patently false.[60]

An excellent explanation of the importance of a free press and of independent investigative journalism is found on the Charles Koch Institute's website:

> Freedom of the press is important because it plays a vital role in informing citizens about public affairs and monitoring the actions of government at all levels . . .

> Media-bashing is as old as the nation itself. George Washington once referred testily to the "infamous scribblers" who covered his administration. But our revolutionary forefathers knew that *when the press examines the actions of government, the nation benefits. News organizations expose corruption and cover-ups, deceptions and deceits, illegal actions and unethical behavior – and they hold our leaders and our institutions accountable* . . .

> *'Republics and limited monarchies derive their strength and vigor from a popular examination into the action of the magistrates,'* Benjamin Franklin declared. By sharing knowledge and sparking debate, a free press invigorates and educates the nation's citizens. *Freedom will be 'a short-lived possession' unless the people are informed, Thomas Jefferson once said.* To quote John Adams: *'The liberty of the press is essential to the security of the state.'*

> *Journalists are watchdogs – not cheerleaders. They ignite dialogue on essential issues. They share the truths that powerful people would rather conceal. They are the force that holds our leaders accountable for their actions.*

> When our leaders threaten journalists, they are threatening the First Amendment, along with our most basic rights. *'Our liberty depends on the freedom of the press,'* said Jefferson, *'and that cannot be limited without being lost.'*[61] [Emphases ours]

The article explains the importance of the First Amendment:

> That means the government cannot punish you for your views, thoughts, or words, even if they're unpopular save for very narrow limits . . . the *press can perform its essential role: To agitate, investigate, and scrutinize our leaders and institutions. That freedom is the difference between a democracy and a dictatorship.* [Emphasis ours]

It also points out that nearly half of Americans believed the press was doing "a poor or very poor job" of supporting democracy according to a Knight/Gallup report in 2017. This suggests that in important ways the media are failing to:

1. *Act as watchdogs* and have become cheerleaders instead for particular points of view;
2. *Educate and inform* rather than entertain and mislead, turning politics into a modern-day "bread and circuses,";
3. *Agitate, investigate, and scrutinize thoroughly and persistently* leaders and the institutions of government, rather than jumping on to the next topic in the 24/7 news cycle;
4. *Hold people accountable for their words and actions,* instead of lionizing the egregious behavior of extremists and conspiracy theorists;

5. *Provide platforms for civilized discussion based on balanced advocacy and in-quiry* instead of turning debates into competitions for share of space
6. *To get questions answered* rather than having interviewers allowing interviewees to stick to scripts designed to provide boilerplate non-answers or to change the subject, allowing them to get away with untruths and abusive behavior.

Four factors may explain why the media have behaved in this way.

First, is the concentration of ownership of the mainstream media at national levels, often owned by absentee expatriates who are not interested in the socio-political health of the countries whose media they dominate, but are only interested in maximizing revenue through engaged outrage, regardless of the political consequences, achieved through exaggerating division – a point made by Frances Haugen in her testimony about Facebook to the Senate.

Second, the advent of 24/7 news channels means they have become reality TV events to maintain the interest of viewers, whereas before the launch of CNN, people only watched the news in the morning, at midday, and in the evening. If the news has to be repeated 24 hours a day, it must be spiced up to keep it interesting for both the newscasters and the audiences. Applying reality TV techniques is not expensive, as most people are happy to have their 15 minutes of fame as guest "experts." Discussion becomes debate where the tricks of rhetoric apply, designed to generate heat rather than light. Donald Trump was a master of making news by doing things to grab the limelight; diverting attention from what other people were saying to focus on himself during the Republican primaries. His mastery of communication was responsible for him becoming the only Republican candidate, just as with the rise of Boris Johnson in the UK.

Third, there is another aspect to the way in which the mainstream media contribute to distorted views of what matters with respect to crime. In the US, only certain types of crime are deemed to be newsworthy – opportunistic individual crimes as opposed to systematic business crimes against employees which hardly get a mention, even though the number of people affected are much greater and the sums involved many times more significant.

For example, on June 14, 2021, a reporter from a San Francisco TV station tweeted a cell phone video of a man filling a garbage bag and riding his bicycle out of a Walgreens store. Evidence suggested that the sums involved were between $200 and $950. Not a great deal of money, and yet between June 14 and July 12, this minor incident was reported 309 times, and since July 12 there were dozens more repeats. Mainstream media involved were CNN, the *New York Times*, and *USA Today*. The stories were that the man had gotten away with it. The truth was that he was arrested about a week later, faced 15 charges including "grand theft, second-degree burglary, and shoplifting." He was sent to a county jail and was held without bond.[62]

Compare the extensive coverage of the case above with the single 221-word story only appearing in Bloomberg Law and the absence of any coverage in the *New York Times*, *USA Today*, or CNN of a November 2020 $4.5 million settlement by Walgreens to resolve a class action lawsuit alleging that:

> it stole wages from thousands of its employees in California between 2010 and 2017. The lawsuit alleged that Walgreens *"rounded down employees' hours on their timecards, required employees to pass through security checks before and after their shift without compensating them for time worked, and failed to pay premium wages to employees who were denied legally required meal breaks.* [Emphases ours]

> Walgreens' settlement includes attorney's fees and other penalties, but *$2,830,000 went to Walgreens employees to compensate them for the wages that the company had stolen. And, because it is a settlement, that amount represents a small fraction of the total liability. According to the order approving the settlement, it represents 'approximately 22% of the potential damages.'* [Emphases ours]

> So this is a story of a corporation that stole millions of dollars from its own employees. How much news coverage did it generate? There was a single 221-word story in Bloomberg Law, an industry publication. And that's it. There has been no coverage in the New York Times, USA Today, CNN, or the dozens of other publications that covered the story of a man stealing a few hundred dollars of merchandise."[63] [Emphases ours]

While the man on a bicycle has been behind bars since June 2021, nobody at Walgreens has been held accountable for stealing millions from its employees. Walgreens paid the fine at the shareholders' expense and no one was punished. Instead, the then CEO saw his remuneration rise from $7,133,155 in 2015 to $17,483,187 in 2020 and he became executive Chairman in 2021. Wage theft in the US is common and it is seldom prosecuted or covered in the media. It occurs when companies fail to pay the minimum wage, or do not pay overtime to employees who work more than 40 hours a week, or make workers perform tasks "off the clock" and without pay.[64] A 2017 study of minimum wage violations found that in the ten most populous states:

> '2.4 million workers lose $8bn annually (an average of $3,300 per year for year-round workers) to minimum wage violations – nearly a quarter of their earned wages.' In these states, wage theft affected '17% of low-wage workers, with workers in all demographic categories being cheated out of pay.' *A typical victim of wage theft "is losing, on average, $3,300 per year and receiving only $10,500 in annual wages.*[65] [Emphasis ours]

Scaled up to cover the entire US, the total wages that are stolen from employees as a result of minimum wage violations alone is more than $15 billion a year, which, according to the FBI is more than all property crimes. Moreover, shoplifting is a small percentage of all property crime because more than half arises from car theft and stolen currency. Nevertheless, a search of the Nexis news database in 2021 revealed 11,631 stories on shoplifting, compared with only 2,009 stories mentioning wage theft.[66] Wage theft appears to be of little interest to the media, allowing many companies that do it to get away scot-free because society apparently does not care and their social peers do not regard it as a crime, perhaps instead regarding it as a normal part of focusing on the bottom line.

This lack of media interest in wage theft is, in part, the result of inadequate resources to enforce the laws that do exist. Enforcement at the federal level falls under Wage and Hour Division (WHD) of the US Department of Labor. In 1948, the WHD had 1,000 investigators, responsible for protecting 22.6 million workers (22,600 per investigator). In 2021, it has only 765 investigators, responsible for 143 million workers (186,928 per investigator).[67]

Fourth, has been the rise of social media with its polarizing echo chambers, its promotion of conspiracy theories, its attacks on science and rational argument, and the sense of impunity and lack of accountability it provides for what and how people express themselves, reinforced by disinformation programs of state-sponsored trolls whose agenda is to spread confusion and dissension to advance their geopolitical goals.

Legislation and Regulation

Legitimate businesses need to answer three questions relating to the law and regulations.

First, what is their philosophy regarding adherence to the law? Are they willing to break the law and pay the resulting fines, do they demand adherence to the law as a minimum, or do they set standards that go beyond what is required by the law and regulations?

Second, are they complying with all current laws and regulations that apply to their businesses and are their policies and procedures captured in their codes of conduct and compliance mechanisms?

Third, do they understand the issues and trends that could affect legislation in the future relating to their environment? Do they really understand what is happening to public attitudes to their industry and organization? Do they know where they stand regarding the public's view of the company's social "license to operate"? Are they up-to-date with the legislative agenda of the different political parties they have to deal with? Have they been tracking the malpractices and bad press of their competition, since this may change how they are viewed, even if they themselves have done nothing wrong?[68]

Ensuring organizations satisfy the needs of customers in legal and socially acceptable ways is the responsibility of directors and the role of regulations is to help them do this.

The common complaints about legislation and regulations are that they impose unnecessary costs on doing business, they are wrongly conceived, or lead to a box-ticking mentality destroying thoughtful applications of principled behavior.

It is worth restating why we need regulations.[69] In many emerging markets, regulations are viewed as an opportunity for patronage, bribery, and corruption. In the case of patronage, regulations may be used to channel business opportunities to cronies.[70] In the case of bribery and corruption, every rule provides an opportunity for a negotiated workaround and payoff to the officials responsible for enforcing the rules.

Adam Smith, explained why regulation is necessary:

> markets and trade are, in principle, good things – *provided there is competition and a regulatory framework that prevents ruthless selfishness, greed and rapacity from leading to socially harmful outcomes.*[71]   [Emphasis ours]

Market Failure

Regulation is need to protect society as a whole from the effects of market failure as a result of:

1. Firms ignoring the social costs of their actions because there are no pricing mechanisms to reflect the harmful externalities they create.
2. The tendency of markets to overshoot in the good times, leading to wasted resources; and undershoot in bad times, leading to excessive economic losses.
3. The difference in time horizons and required rates of return for providing "social goods" such as infrastructure, education, and health investments, where private firms cannot participate without government intervention and support.[72]

Social Harm

Regulation is required to protect society as a whole from the harmful effects of unscrupulous, selfish, and rapacious individuals and organizations; the more harmful the effect, the greater the need for regulation.

1. *Rent-seeking:* To protect consumers and clients from the consequences of monopolistic or oligopolistic behavior, seeking to increase economic remuneration by:
   a. Raising prices to unjustified levels;
   b. Restricting access to goods and services through artificial barriers to entry (particularly true of professional services);
   c. Limiting innovation by delaying or eliminating newly competitive ways of doing things;
   d. Mis-selling products and services.
2. *Vested interests:* To distinguish between the interests of vested interests and those of society as a whole.
3. *To define the 'rules of the game' and create level playing fields.*

Rules-based regulations may lead to all the defects attributed to regulations by libertarians: burdensome, over-complicated to implement; easy for clever lawyers to get around by finding loopholes in the wording; and, more seriously, focusing on the legalistic aspects of rules-based regulation allows organizations to find ways of "gaming the system" rather than preventing the problems from arising in the first place:

> The greater the number of laws, rules and regulations, the more people ignore the ethical consequences and focus on compliance only . . . The legalistic culture of the US gives people a strong motive to shuffle off responsibility to others and cover their back.[73]

Principles-based regulations suffer from the fact that they only indicate *what* should be done, but do not give adequate guidance on *how* it should be done.

In a recent set of decisions, Travis Laster, the Vice Chancellor of the Delaware Court of Chancery rebuked the legal profession for a change in values and the way they litigate:

> 'Can-do' lawyering has run amok," said one prominent Delaware attorney referring to professional duty to zealously represent clients' interests. 'Still, you don't want to be the lawyer that just says 'no.' You will never make it.' Laster declined to comment on any specific decision, but offered these thoughts to the Financial Times on the rise of aggressive lawyering: *'Business pressure is part of it. But so is the general polarisation of society. There is an ambient negativity in our discourse that has seeped into professional interactions.'* Laster added: 'The clients that the big firms represent are another piece of the puzzle. They have a goal they want to achieve, and they want a lawyer to help them achieve it. That is how the lawyer adds value. *The role of the lawyer as conscience, as a wise counsellor, has been de-emphasised. The role of the advocate, the enabler, has been accentuated.'*[74]   [Emphases ours]

Regulatory Capture

Regulations can be "captured." The repeal of the Glass-Steagall Act is an example. Passed in 1933, the Act[iv] designed to reduce the excessive financial power of J.D. Rockefeller and J.P. Morgan, and to prevent deposit-taking banks from

---

iv "Senator Carter Glass and Representative Henry Steagall wanted to establish a firewall between banking and securities firms. They were especially concerned with the tremendous financial power of J.P. Morgan and John D. Rockefeller. Under the 1933 Act, institutions were given a year to choose between commercial banking and securities investment. Banks were permitted to receive no more than 10% of their income from the securities markets. Because the limit was so small, most banks just abandoned the securities business and focused on banking." Glass-Steagall Act (P.L. 73–66, 48 STAT. 162), https://www.google.com/search?q=Glass-Steagall+Act+(P.L.+73-66%2C+48+STAT.+162)%2C&oq=-Glass-Steagall+Act+(P.L.+73-66%2C+48+STAT.+162)%2C&aqs=chrome.69i57.1976j0j7&sourceid=chrome&ie=UTF-8 accessed January 12, 2013.

being investment banks and speculating in securities, worked well and the US had very few banking failures as long as Glass-Steagall was in force.

Even with the best qualified staffing and resources, regulatory regimes will not be able prevent malpractice through criminal penalties, and will resort to civil penalties or settlements with no admission of wrongdoing instead as long as four conditions apply:

1. Contract law is based on *caveat emptor* ("buyer beware"), where it is the duty of buyers to protect their interests in the face of asymmetrical information and unscrupulous sellers who are incentivized to *not* put their client's interest first. Changing this can only be achieved by changing the legal basis to "seller beware."

2. Proving malfeasance "beyond a reasonable doubt" in economic and financial crime is difficult and there is the presumption of innocence. Changing this can only be achieved by placing the onus on businesses to prove their products meet the claims made for them.

3. The Silicon Valley culture and mantra of "Fake it until you make it" that is accepted by venture capitalists and would-be investors – tested in the trial of Elisabeth Holmes of Theranos – while it is being exploited by SPAC (special-purpose acquisition company)-led IPOs where the claims being made bear little objective scrutiny.

Credence goods (religion, education, wellness, wealth management) create problems of their own because they depend on the buyer trusting the seller that the long-term promised benefits will materialize and buyers have no way of testing the veracity of claims in the immediate or short-term.

References

1 Georgiadis, P., Strauss, D., Pickard, J., and Kerr, S. (2022), "P&O Chief Admits Breaking Law Over Mass Sackings" *The Financial Times,* March 25, 2022, https://www.ft.com/content/3fbc5918-ad04-4003-8e09-3df12d7dcd40, accessed on March 26' 2022.
2 Acemoglu, D., and Robinson, J. A. (2012), *Why Nations Fail: The Origins of Power, Prosperity, and Poverty* (New York: Currency).
3 Ibid., p. 79.
4 Ibid., p. 80.
5 Ibid., p. 95.
6 Ibid., pp. 123–127.
7 Ibid., p. 153.
8 Ibid.
9 Ibid., p. 156.
10 Ibid.

11 Weinland, D. (2021), "Xi Jinping's Crackdown on Chinese Tech Firms Will Continue," *The Economist*, November 8, 2021, https://www.economist.com/the-world-ahead/2021/11/08/xi-jinpings-crackdown-on-chinese-tech-firms-will-continue, accessed on December 5, 2021.

12 Wheeler, T. (2021), "A Focused Federal Agency is Necessary to Oversee Big Tech," *Brookings*, February 10, 2021, https://www.brookings.edu/research/a-focused-federal-agency-is-necessary-to-oversee-big-tech/, accessed on December 5, 2021.

13 Wheeler, T., and Pita, A. (2021), "Will the Facebook Whistleblower's Testimony Spur New US Digital Regulation?" *Brookings*, October 14, 2021, https://www.brookings.edu/podcast-episode/will-the-facebook-whistleblowers-testimony-spur-new-us-digital-regulation/, accessed on December 5, 2021.

14 Albini, J., and McIllwain, J. (2012), *Deconstructing Organized Crime: A Historical and Theoretical Study* (London, 2012), quoted in ibid., p. 12.

15 Ibrahim, A. (2021), "Lebanon: What Life is Like in a 'Failed State'," *Al-Jazeera*, September 26, 2021, https://www.aljazeera.com/features/2021/9/26/lebanon-what-life-is-like-in-a-failed-state, accessed on December 5, 2021.

16 US Senate, "Organized Crime in Chicago: Hearing Before the Permanent Subcommittee on Investigations of the Committee on Governmental Affairs," March 4, 1983, p. 1, http://catalog.hathitrust.org/Record/002762658, quoted in Dudley, S., "Conceptual Framework: Organized Crime" in "Elites and Organized Crime: Introduction, Methodology, and Conceptual Framework", *Insight Crime*, p. 4, https://idl-bnc-idrc.dspacedirect.org/bitstream/handle/10625/55845/IDL-55845.pdf, accessed on November 17, 2021.

17 Dudley, "Conceptual Framework: Organized Crime," p. 27.

18 Ibid.

19 Dowie, M. (1977), "Pinto Madness," *Mother Jones*, September/October Issue 1977, https://www.motherjones.com/politics/1977/09/pinto-madness/, accessed on June 27, 2021.

20 Bazerman, M. H., and Tenbrunsel, A. E. (2011), "Ethical Breakdowns," *Harvard Business Review*, April 2011, https://hbr.org/2011/04/ethical-breakdowns, accessed on June 26, 2021.

21 Dowie (1997).

22 Ibid.

23 IN RE THE BOEING COMPANY: DERIVATIVE LITIGATION: Consol. C.A. No. 2019–0907-MTZ. In the Court of Chancery of the State of Delaware, EFiled: Feb 05 2021 03:53PM EST, Transaction ID 66314557.

24 Ibid.

25 Ibid.

26 Hammond, G. (2021), "UK Government Apologises for Failures that Led to Grenfell Tragedy," *The Financial Times*, December 7, 2021, https://www.ft.com/content/469b2bb5-0b7e-4205-a7fd-8a6229ac9e52, accessed on December 8, 2021.

27 Kommenda, N., and Torpey, P., (2 (2017), "The English Tower Blocks that Failed the Combustibility Tests – Mapped," *The Guardian*, July 12, 2017, https://www.theguardian.com/uk-news/ng-interactive/2017/jun/27/the-english-tower-blocks-that-have-failed-combustibility-tests-mapped, accessed on December 8, 2021.

28 Ibid.

29 Taylor, M., and Watts, J. (2019), "Revealed: The 20 Firms Behind a Third of All Carbon Emissions," *The Guardian*, October 9, 2019, https://www.theguardian.com/environment/2019/oct/09/revealed-20-firms-third-carbon-emissions, accessed on December 7, 2019.

30 Petri, J. (2019), *Bloomberg Climate Changed*, December 5, 2019, https://mail.google.com/mail/u/0/#inbox/FMfcgxwGCGsXdMglvgmlPgXNJmDSHZDz, accessed December 6, 2019.

31 Supran, G., and Oreskes, N. (2021), "The Forgotten Oil Ads that Told Us that Climate Change Was Nothing," *The Guardian*, November 18, 2021, https://www.theguardian.com/environment/2021/nov/18/the-forgotten-oil-ads-that-told-us-climate-change-was-nothing, accessed on November 25, 2021.

32 Ibid.

33 Ibid.

34 Ibid.

35 Frumhoff, P. (2014), "Global Warming Fact: More than Half of All Industrial CO_2 Pollution Has Been Emitted Since 1988," *Union of Concerned Scientists*, December 15, 2014, https://blog.ucsusa.org/peter-frumhoff/global-warming-fact-co2-emissions-since-1988-764, accessed on December 7, 2019.

36 Lederman, J., (2021), "Big Oil CEOs Deny Lying to the Public about Climate Change," *nbcnews*, October 29, 2021, https://www.nbcnews.com/business/business-news/big-oil-ceos-deny-lying-public-climate-change-rcna4033, accessed on December10, 2021.

37 Labaton Sucharow (2012), *Wall Street, Fleet Street and Main Street: Integrity at a Crossroads*, cited in Zinkin, J. (2014), *Rebuilding Trust in Banks: The Role of Leadership and Governance* (Singapore: John Wiley & Sons), p. 194.

38 Ibid.

39 Tenbrunsel, A., and Thomas, J. (2017), *The Street, The Bull and The Crisis: A Survey of the US & UK Financial Services Industry* (New York: Labaton Sucharow LLP), https://www.secwhistleblower advocate.com/pdf/Labaton-2015-Survey report_12.pdf, accessed on December 11, 2021.

40 Ibid., p. 2.

41 Ibid., p. 6.

42 Ibid., p. 5.

43 Ibid., p. 4.

44 MacBride, J. (2016), "Understanding the LIBOR Scandal," *Council on Foreign Relations*, October 12, 2016, https://www.cfr.org/backgrounder/understanding-libor-scandal, accessed on December 9, 2021.

45 Espinoza, J., and Stafford, P. (2021), "EU Fines Banks €344m in Forex Trading Probe," *The Financial Times*, December 3, 2021, https://www.ft.com/content/dbc8db80-071e-4130-8657-b08bc9845e77, accessed on December 9, 2021.

46 Lenczer, M. (2021), Letter: "The EU Fines the Lenders but Not the Perpetrators," *The Financial Times*, December 8, 2021, https://www.ft.com/content/5df4b16b-9836-4c73-a527-6a28b22d6eb6?emailId=61b0c8b5a40b2200049a9dcd&segmentId=7d033110-c776-45bf-e9f2-7c3a03d2dd26, accessed on December 9, 2021.

47 Hester, S. (2012), *Rebuilding Banking*, Stephen Hester Address to London School of Economics Public Lecture Series, October 1, 2012, pp. 6, 7, quoted in Zinkin, *Rebuilding Trust in Banks*, p. 51.

48 Committee on Standards in Public Life (1995), "Summary of the Nolan Committee's First Report on Standards in Public Life," May 1, 1995, p. 3, https://assets.publishing.service.gov.uk/government/uploads/system/uploads/attachment_data/file/336840/1stInquiry_Summary.pdf, accessed on June 7, 2021.

49 Rawnsley, A. (2021), "David Cameron and the Greensill Scandal is Just the Tip of the Fatberg," *The Guardian*, April 18, 2021, https://www.theguardian.com/commentisfree/2021/apr/18/david-cameron-greensill-scandal-tip-of-fatberg?utm_term=38e92d65c8b6af9906524601d559f20e&utm_campaign=BestOfGuardianOpinionUK&utm_source=esp&utm_medium=Email&CMP=opinionuk_email, accessed on April 20, 2021.

50 Jenkin, B. (2021), "The Line between Public Service and Private Gain is Shamefully Blurred," *The Guardian*, April 17, 2021, https://www.theguardian.com/commentisfree/2021/apr/17/the-line-between-public-service-and-private-gain-is-shamefully-blurred, accessed on April 18, 2021.

51 Maugham, J. (2021), "We Proved in the High Court that Michael Gove Broke the Law. So What Happens Now?" *The Guardian,* June 10, 2021, https://www.theguardian.com/commentisfree/2021/jun/10/high-court-michael-gove-law-cronyism-covid-contracts?utm_term=52799d783f6b7f9666c9045d76b41ea8&utm_campaign=BestOfGuardianOpinionUK&utm_source=esp&utm_medium=Email&CMP=opinionuk_email, accessed on June 11, 2021.

52 TOI Staff (2019), "PM 'Cannot Serve One More Day': Calls for Resignation Multiply Over Indictment," *Times of Israel,* November 21, 2019, https://www.timesofisrael.com/calls-for-pm-to-resign-multiply-after-indictment-announcement/, accessed on June 7, 2021.

53 Heller, A. (2019), "Netanyahu Infuses Campaign with Anti-media Incitement," *Times of Israel,* September 2, 2019, https://www.timesofisrael.com/netanyahu-infuses-campaign-with-anti-media-incitement/, accessed on June 7, 2021.

54 Bachner, M. (2020), "Deputy AG Likens Netanyahu's Attacks on Judiciary to Protocols of Elders of Zion," *Times of Israel,* November 15, 2020, https://www.timesofisrael.com/deputy-ag-likens-netanyahus-attacks-on-judiciary-to-protocols-of-elders-of-zion/, accessed on June 7, 2021.

55 Hendrix, S. (2021), "Netanyahu Has No Clear Path to Remain Prime Minister, Official Israeli Election Results Show," *Washington Post,* March 25, 2021, *St*https://www.washingtonpost.com/world/middle_east/israel-election-netanyahu-final-results/2021/03/25/09dc5758-8d81-11eb-a33e-da28941cb9ac_story.html, accessed on December 6, 2021.

56 Doleman, J. (2019), "Max Hastings on Boris Johnson," James Dolman @jamesdoleman, June 13, 2019 https://twitter.com/jamesdoleman/status/1139109919238623233, accessed on June 8, 2021.

57 Smith, C. (2021), "Video Exposing Boris Johnson's 'Lies' to Parliament Hits 20 million Views," *The Big Issue,* May 27, 2021, https://www.bigissue.com/latest/politics/video-exposing-boris-johnsons-lies-to-parliament-hits-20-million-views/, accessed on June 8, 2021.

58 Harding L, Elgot, J., and Sparrow, A. (2021), "Accusations of Lying Pile up against Johnson. Does it Matter?" *The Guardian,* April 30, 2021, https://www.theguardian.com/politics/2021/apr/30/accusations-of-lying-pile-up-against-boris-johnson-does-it-matter, accessed on June 8, 2021.

59 McTague, T. (2021), "The Minister of Chaos," *The Atlantic*, June 7, 2021, https://www.theatlantic.com/magazine/archive/2021/07/boris-johnson-minister-of-chaos/619010/?utm_source=newsletter&utm_medium=email&utm_campaign=atlantic-daily-newsletter&utm_content=20210607&silverid=%25%25RECIPIENT_ID%25%25&utm_term=The%20Atlantic%20Daily, accessed on June 8, 2021.

60 Montanaro, D. (2021), "Most Americans Trust Elections Are Fair, but Sharp Divide Still Exists," *NPR,* November 1, 2021, https://www.npr.org/2021/11/01/1050291610/most-americans-trust-elections-are-fair-but-sharp-divides-exist-a-new-poll-finds, accessed on December 6, 2021.

61 "Importance of a Free Press," *Charles Koch Institute,* May 3, 2018, https://charleskochinstitute.org/stories/importance-of-a-free-press/, accessed on June 7, 2021.

62 Legum, J. (2021), "Want to be a Criminal in America? Stealing Billions is Your Best Bet to Go Scot-free," *The Guardian,* December 7, 2021, https://www.theguardian.com/commentisfree/2021/dec/07/want-to-be-a-criminal-in-america-stealing-billions-is-your-best-bet-to-go-scot-free?, accessed on December 9, 2021.

63 Ibid.

64 Ibid.

65 Cooper, D., and Kroeger, T. (2017), "Employers Steal Billions from Workers' Paychecks Every Year," *Economic Policy Institute,* May 10, 2021, https://www.epi.org/publication/employers-steal-billions-from-workers-paychecks-each-year/, accessed on December 9, 2021.

66 Legum (2021).

67 Ibid.

68 Zinkin, *Better Governance Across the Board: Creating Value Through Reputation, People and Processes* (Boston/Berlin: Walter Gruyter, Inc), pp. 149–150.

69 For an excellent discussion of the case for and against government regulations, read the *New York Times*, https://www.nytimes.com/2013/06/02/opinion/sunday/sunday-dialogue-more-regulation-or-less.htmlLetters to the Editor, Sunday Dialogue, "More Regulation or Less?," *New York Times*, June 1, 2013, accessed on June 15, 2018.

70 World Bank (2018), *Helping Countries Combat Corruption: The Role of the World Bank*, http://www1.worldbank.org/publicsector/anticorrupt/corruptn/cor02.htm, accessed on June 15, 2018.

71 Kurz, H. D. (2015), Abstract of "Adam Smith on Markets, Competition and Violations of Natural Liberty," *Cambridge Journal of Economics*, 40, No. 2, March 1, 2016, pp. 615–638, https://academic.oup.com/cje/article-abstract/40/2/615/2605099, accessed on June 15, 2018.

72 "15 Astounding Technologies DARPA is Creating Right Now," *Business Insider*, http://www.businessinsider.com/15-current-darpa-innovations-2014-7/?IR=T, accessed on June 15, 2018.

73 Persaud, A., and Plender, J. (2007), *Ethics and Finance: Finding a Moral Compass in Business Today* (London: Longtail Publishing, 2007), pp. 5–8.

74 Indap S. (2021), "Delaware Judge Sends Warning to Zealous Lawyers," *The Financial Times*, December 13, 2021, https://www.ft.com/content/d5a7e86a-a654-4ef0-970c-89788c756a7b, accessed on December 13, 2021.

Chapter 9
Conclusions

> Given the legal definitions of "crime" and "criminal," we are all criminals.

States Define What is Criminal and What is not

States have a critical role in determining where criminality is perceived to sit on the crime continuum. An examination of the behavior of states shows that some of the worst crimes are committed by states but the crimes are then redefined as glorious events by the winners who rewrite the history of the events to justify their actions. The current invasion of Ukraine by Russia is just the last example of criminal behavior claimed to be part of achieving a country's glorious destiny.

People in the top positions in states, organizations, or institutions try to hold onto power for the benefits it brings – benefits that are material, social, and psychological. Just as the state demands exclusive control over its citizens under the guise of benevolence "oriented toward achieving the common good" when it actually reflects the political elite's fears of losing ground, so leaders of economic, bureaucratic, and social elites couch their need for control in the language of promoting the common good. This leads to elites asserting, justifying, and protecting their privileged positions by hook or by crook, especially when they practice extractive economic and social policies.

States and Organized Crime are Natural Competitors

States and OC are mirror images of each other. They provide the same services to their clients, and they seek to control and monopolize the territories they serve in the same way, providing protection of lives and livelihoods in return for payment of taxes (in the case of states) and "protection" (in the case of OC). The extent to which they can flourish at the expense of each other is a function of the amount of violence they control. When the state has a monopoly or near monopoly of violence, OC is weak; when the state does not have an effective monopoly of violence, OC takes its place, establishing local territorial monopolies that form "no-go" areas for servants of the state. States and OC compete or coexist in a permanent see-sawing of power and weakness. Legitimate businesses are caught in the resulting crossfire and have to seek accommodation with whoever is dominant.

https://doi.org/10.1515/9783110712155-009

Differences in Criminality are Ones of Degree

Given that human beings are likely to break rules whenever it pays them to do so; and in particular where the legal and social sanctions have no serious consequences; it should not come as a surprise that the different levels of criminality in the behaviors of state actors, legitimate businesses, and OC are ones of degree and not ones of kind, with states historically committing the worst crimes that they often legitimize in the name of "national security."

The natural tendency of states and businesses to stray into criminal behavior is only constrained by:

1. The existence of clear laws forbidding defined criminal behavior;
2. The severity and effectiveness of the resulting legal penalties in acting as deterrents;
3. The effectiveness with which the laws are enforced fairly and transparently by the authorities – i.e., "nobody is above the law";
4. The extent to which society regards such behavior as unacceptable;
5. The extent to which malefactors are punished for their misbehavior socially as well as by the authorities.

This depends on whether the media (mainstream and social) present the facts accurately or indulge in promoting "alternative facts"; and in the case of social media platforms on how they write the algorithms that drive entertainment and outrage.

Punishment Often does not Fit the Crime

Attitudes to criminality, and crime reflect the harm and damage they are perceived to cause to groups and individuals. Perception of harm is related to the cost of the damage in financial, or social terms. What differentiates the seriousness of crimes is the harms they do, the punishments they incur, and their social acceptability. Criminality is a continuum. Differences between the strategies and behavior of state organized crime (SOC), organized crime (OC), crime that is organized (CTIO), and legitimate businesses are of degree, not of kind. The extent to which communities are prepared to live with criminality depends on (1) the level of harm it causes, and (2) the level to which it is accepted by society. The greater the societal revulsion, the more severe the punishments.

Sadly, often the punishment does not fit the crime. There are five factors that make it difficult to fit the punishment to the crime: (1) impunity of the powerful; (2) regulatory capture; (3) weak regulatory "ecosystems"; (4) social indifference to crimes committed; and (5) mainstream and social media's focus on entertainment and outrage.

Strategic Similarities Greater than Differences

Organized crime organizations are subject to the same external and internal strategic considerations as legitimate businesses, except that the law renders their business illegitimate by definition. The "Five P" performance framework ("Purpose," "Principles," "Power," "People," and "Processes") is a useful way of checking how well both OC and legitimate businesses are aligned to ensure their organizations achieve their agreed missions and visions. It also helps to highlight the differences between OC and legitimate enterprises, given their respective operating conditions.

Legitimate businesses and OC follow strategies with similar needs because the techniques of business strategy are morally neutral and the law does not concern itself with the ethical stances of legitimate businesses. Our conclusions apply to states, legitimate businesses, and OC.

Blurred Ethical Boundaries

As long as activist shareholders (members of the economic elite) claim to have the same rights as investors who are true proprietors, when they are speculators only interested in short-term financial results, they encourage boards and management to behave legally but unethically if it yields better short-term returns. In so doing, they may blur the ethical boundaries between the behavior of OC and legitimate business. They justify their discounting of the ethical implications of the decisions they want management to make, using the Friedmanite argument that the purpose of business is to maximize shareholder value. They then can ignore the ethical implications of the short-term profit maximizing decisions they approve of, regardless of the harms to the environment, communities, and employees that those decisions entail.

The media barons, many of whom do not reside in the countries where they influence the political and economic agendas to advance their interests, often at the expense of the citizens, are a good example of an elite practicing extractive policies at the expense of their reader- or viewership. Their ability to influence the political agenda has increased dramatically in recent times as a result of the decline of local indigenous mainstream media and the rise of "winner take all" social media with their global network effects and their refusal to be accountable for what happens on their platforms. As long as they have so much power, they will continue to be a source of division and outrage because that is what sells, regardless of whether it leads to deaths – as it has in Myanmar.

"Black Letter" Law Matters

Despite the drawbacks of "Black Letter Law," namely that it can be used to "break the law legally" and that it reduces the need to think about the moral implications of a "tick the box" mentality, it does matter. It matters because it lets people know what they can and cannot do. It is an essential part of governance, both political and corporate. It provides a framework to remind powerful elites that there are boundaries to their behavior and that nobody is above the law. It also provides an important system of checks and balances to give the powerful a chance to think twice about the potential harms of decisions they make and maybe change their decisions as a result. And it provides a mechanism for holding elites to account, even if it is not perfect.

Organized Crime's Three Advantages

When comparing OC decision-making with that of legitimate businesses, we conclude that OC has three advantages:

1. *OC has to deal with VUC (volatility, uncertainty, and complexity) only* and does not have to deal with VUCA (volatility, uncertainty, complexity, *and* ambiguity) as legitimate businesses do.

We believe there are three reasons why OC does not have to deal with ambiguity in that same way as legitimate business. The first is that they do not have the same complex set of stakeholders as legitimate business. They therefore do not have to try to reconcile competing stakeholder priorities with all the ambiguities that generates. The second is that because they operate outside the law, they are not constrained by the law in the same way as legitimate business. They can revel in being "free riders" because that is what they are expected to do as law-breakers, whereas legitimate businesses are ambivalent about "free-riding" because they have brand value and market capitalization to protect. The third reason is that because they operate outside the law, they have to focus on immediate generation of ill-gotten gains, as they could be shut down at any moment and they are not in the business of creating socially acceptable sustainable results.

2. *OC has greater clarity about its purpose, principles, and processes.* The fact that OC does not have ambiguity of purpose translates into simple principles, processes, and KPIs. The principles are amoral and the people who join OC have little to no qualms about being asked to do what is necessary to achieve their organizations' objectives. Breaking the law, being cruel, putting loyalty above everything else "is who they are" and they are not hampered by moral injury or cognitive dissonance in carrying out their tasks as commanded. The criteria for meeting or, more seriously, failing to meet KPIs are crystal clear with no doubt regarding the consequences. The punishments

are more extreme and the greater use of violence brooks no discussion, making execution of plans easier to carry out.

3. *OC has greater willingness to embrace risk.* Criminals live with extreme risk on a daily basis; it is part of their lives, myths, and what attracted them to a life of crime in the first place. As a group of people who self-select to live a riskier life than law-abiding citizens, they are comfortable with levels of risk that employees of legitimate businesses are unlikely to accept, allowing OC to embrace levels of risks at both an organizational level and personal level. that only soldiers have to face.

These conclusions make rather depressing reading. However, all is not lost if what matters is building ethical and successful organizations; as we explain in our forthcoming book *The Challenge of Leading Ethical and Successful Organizations.*

List of Figures

https://doi.org/10.1515/9783110712155-010

List of Tables

https://doi.org/10.1515/9783110712155-011

About the Authors

John Zinkin wrote *The Principles and Practice of Effective Leadership* (2021) with Chris Bennett, and has written five books on corporate governance (CG): *The Challenge of Sustainability: Corporate Governance in a Complicated World* (2020), *Better Governance Across the Board: Creating Value Through Reputation, People and Processes* (2019), published by De Gruyter, and *Rebuilding Trust in Banks: The Role of Leadership and Governance* (2014), *Challenges in Implementing Corporate Governance: Whose Business is it Anyway?* (2010), and *Corporate Governance* (2005), published by John Wiley & Sons. He contributed a chapter on "Corporate Governance in Asia Pacific" and another chapter on "Corporate Governance in an Age of Populism" for the *Handbook on Corporate Governance, 2nd edition*, edited by Professor Richard Leblanc, published in 2020 by John Wiley & Sons.

He is a certified training professional. His specialties are "Leading Brand-Based Change," "Reconciling Leadership and Governance" and "Ethics in Business." He has led board effectiveness evaluations in banking, insurance and government entities and has written codes of conduct and board charters for several development banks. Since 2007, he has trained more than 1,700 directors in CG as well as senior managers of public listed companies. He has trained securities regulators from Cambodia, Hong Kong, Laos, Malaysia, Philippines, Singapore, Thailand and Vietnam on behalf of the Australian Government as part of their CG capacity building programs in ASEAN and APEC.

Starting in 1971, John worked in the UK in fast-moving consumer goods (Unilever), insurance broking (Hogg Robinson), management consulting (McKinsey), and office products (Rank Xerox) before moving to Hong Kong in 1985 for Inchcape Pacific. There John ran marketing and distribution companies in a variety of industries across Asia Pacific, before joining Burson-Marsteller in 1997 as the Asia-Pacific Marketing and Change Management Practice Chair. John moved to Malaysia in 2001 and from 2001 to 2006, was Associate Professor of Marketing and Strategy at Nottingham University Business School, Malaysia Campus, responsible for its MBA program. In 2006 he set up the Securities Industry Development Corporation, the training arm of the Securities Commission Malaysia and in 2011 he was appointed Managing Director, Corporate Governance of the Iclif Leadership and Governance Centre under Bank Negara Malaysia, responsible for training directors of banks and insurance companies in CG. Since 2013, he works independently as the Managing Director of Zinkin Ettinger Sendirian Berhad, a boutique consultancy specializing in CG, brand-based change and ethical leadership.

John graduated from Oxford University with a BA in Politics, Philosophy and Economics (1968) and the London Business School with an MSc in Business Administration (1971).

https://doi.org/10.1515/9783110712155-012

Chris Bennett has had a wide ranging career as a director, senior executive, researcher, consultant, and teacher/facilitator. His significant international exposure and working experience includes having lived and worked in six countries and held directorships for major British and American companies in 13. Additionally, he has held senior managerial responsibilities in more than 20 countries across Asia, the Middle East, Europe, Australia, NZ, and the Americas. His employers include Bechtel, Honeywell, Burmah Castrol, BP, Towers Perrin, and Watson Wyatt. He has significant experience of directorship, general management, and Senior HR roles across the engineering construction, electronics, oil and gas, and consulting sectors. Much of his board consulting work was in the banking and finance sectors.

His functional career has three main episodes: first as a human resources executive and director, second as a chief executive and director, third as consultant at board level. His observations and experiences led him to a deep interest in the ways in which individual and group behavior manifest in decision making and approaches to corporate governance of individual directors and boards of directors in different cultures, situations, and in complex company groups.

He was a faculty member of ICLIF (the International Centre for Leadership in Finance – an arm of Bank Negara Malaysia – now part of the Asia School of Business) and is currently an adjunct member of the faculty. He also serves on the faculty of Australian Institute of Company Directors and has facilitated programs for directors in Australia, Shanghai, Hong Kong, Singapore, Jakarta, and Dubai.

He is a doctoral researcher at Aston University where he explores the cultural and behavioral aspects of board and top management team decision making in multicultural, multinational, and complex company groups.

Chris lives in Kuala Lumpur. His publications (with Professor Mak Yuen Teen, National University of Singapore) include *Guardians of the Capital Markets* (BPA 2016), *Insuring the Future* (The Iclif Leadership and Governance Centre 2015); *The Governance of Company Groups* (CPA Australia & Iclif 2014), *Directors Daze* (BPA 2014), *Corporate Governance of 50 Largest Asian Banks* (BPA 2013), and numerous articles and newsletters (http://www.bpa-australasia.com).

Index

https://doi.org/10.1515/9783110712155-013